Do individuals have a positive right of self-defence? And if so, what are the limits of this right? Under what conditions, if any, does this use of force extend to the defence of others? These are some of the issues explored by Dr Uniacke in this comprehensive philosophical discussion of the principles relevant to self-defence as a moral and legal justification of homicide. She establishes a unitary right of self-defence and defence of others, one which grounds the permissibility of the use of necessary and proportionate defensive force against culpable and non-culpable, active and passive unjust threats. Particular topics discussed include: the nature of moral and legal justification and excuse; natural law justifications of homicide in self-defence; the Principle of Double Effect and the claim that homicide in self-defence is justified as unintended killing; and the question of self-preferential killing. This is a lucid and sophisticated account of the complex notion of justification, revolving around a critical discussion of recent trends in the law of self-defence.

Permissible killing

Cambridge Studies in Philosophy and Law

GENERAL EDITOR: JULES COLEMAN (YALE LAW SCHOOL)

David Gauthier (University of Pittsburgh)
David Lyons (Cornell University)
Richard Posner (Judge in the Seventh Circuit Court of Appeals, Chicago)
Martin Shapiro (University of California, Berkeley)

This series reflects and fosters the most original research currently taking place in the study of law and legal theory by publishing the most adventurous monographs in the field as well as rigorously edited collections of essays. It is a specific aim of the series to traverse the boundaries between disciplines and to form bridges between traditional studies of law and many other areas of the human sciences. Books in the series will be of interest not only to philosophers and legal theorists but also to political scientists, sociologists, economists, psychologists, and criminologists.

Other books in the series

Jeffrie G. Murphy and Jean Hampton: *Forgiveness and mercy*
Stephen R. Munzer: *A theory of property*
R. G. Frey and Christopher W. Morris (eds.): *Liability and responsibility: Essays in law and morals*
Robert F. Schopp: *Automatism, insanity, and the psychology of criminal responsibility*
Steven J. Burton: *Judging in good faith*
Jules Coleman: *Risks and wrongs*
Jules Coleman and Allen Buchanan (eds.): *In harm's way*

Permissible killing

The self-defence justification of homicide

SUZANNE UNIACKE

UNIVERSITY OF WOLLONGONG

CAMBRIDGE
UNIVERSITY PRESS

Published by the Press Syndicate of the University of Cambridge
The Pitt Building, Trumpington Street, Cambridge CB2 1RP
40 West 20th Street, New York, NY 10011-4211, USA
10 Stamford Road, Oakleigh, Melbourne 3166, Australia

© Cambridge University Press 1994

First published 1994
Reprinted 1995

Printed in Great Britain by Antony Rowe Ltd, Chippenham, Wiltshire

A catalogue record for this book is available from the British Library

Library of Congress cataloguing in publication data

Uniacke, Suzanne
Permissible killing: the self-defence justification of homicide/Suzanne Uniacke
p. cm.–(Cambridge studies in philosophy and law)
Originally presented as the author's thesis (doctoral – University of Sydney, 1991)
Includes bibliographical references and index.
ISBN 0 521 45408 5 (hardback)
1. Justifiable homicide. 2. Self-defense (Law) 3. Justification (Law)
I. Title.   II. Series.
HV6515.U55   1994
345.73'04 – dc20
[347.3054]   93–31988 CIP

ISBN 0 521 45408 5 hardback

CE

Contents

Acknowledgements

My interest in the principles of justified self-defence stems from David Farrier's stimulating criminal law classes at the University of New South Wales in 1982. This book is a revision of a doctoral dissertation that I submitted in the Department of Traditional and Modern Philosophy at the University of Sydney in 1991. Two debts stand out – one is to Keith Campbell, who was a judicious and reassuring supervisor, the other is to H. J. McCloskey, one of my former teachers at LaTrobe University, who generously wrote very helpful comments on the draft. I have greatly appreciated their suggestions, advice and encouragement. The book has benefited from comments by Jeremy Horder, and from very detailed comments by R. A. Duff for which I am most grateful. A grant from the University of Wollongong during the first half of 1993, and the goodwill of my departmental colleagues, allowed me the time to take these comments into account. I should like to acknowledge the encouragement I received from Tom Campbell, and to thank Geraldine Suter for preparing the index. Thanks are also due to those who discussed some of the ideas and arguments with me at various points along the way. Stephen Buckle deserves special mention for his discussion, from a different but sympathetic perspective, of several troublesome revisions.

The Federation Press has kindly allowed me to draw on material from my article 'What Are Partial Excuses To Murder?', and *The American Journal of Jurisprudence* gave its permission to make extensive use of my article 'Self-Defense and Natural Law'.

My sincere personal thanks go to Udo Thiel and my parents and friends, whose moral support has been invaluable.

Chapter 1

The problem of homicide in self-defence

'If someone attacks me, isn't it obvious that I am allowed to defend myself?' This was the initial reaction of some people, including several philosophers, when told that I was engaged in a philosophical inquiry into the justification of homicide in self-defence. Perhaps this response should have been unsurprising. Self-defence is widely regarded and cited as a paradigm of morally permissible private homicide. Often this view of self-defence has wider application where the permissibility of self-defence is held to ground the justification of defence of others and the justification of defensive warfare.[1]

Compared with controversial issues such as abortion, euthanasia, capital punishment, warfare, nuclear deterrence, animal rights, famine relief, and our obligations to future people, homicide in self-defence has received limited attention as an issue in its own right in the voluminous recent philosophical literature concerned with moral problems of life and death. Undoubtedly this comparative neglect of self-defence is chiefly due to the assumption that the moral justification of homicide in self-defence is straightforward and, hence, philosophically uninteresting. This often uncritical assumption is mistaken, as those relatively few philosophers who have addressed the issue in any depth would, I'm sure, attest.

[1] See, e.g. Cheyney C. Ryan, 'Self-Defense, Pacifism, and the Possibility of Killing', *Ethics*, vol. 93, no. 3, 1983, p. 510.

1.1 THE PHILOSOPHICAL ISSUES

So, what is philosophically problematic and interesting about the justification of homicide in self-defence? Why should the comparative neglect of this issue in practical ethics be remedied? The content of this book answers these two questions in the context of the book's central aim, which is to set out and discuss the principles relevant to justified homicide in self-defence. However, at the outset we can see that even preliminary inquiry indicates why the justification of homicide in self-defence deserves much more careful philosophical attention than it is usually accorded. Consider, for instance, the emphasis placed in much recent writing in practical ethics on the idea that fulfilment of the conditions of personhood grounds a right to life, and also the importance placed on a person's desire for continued existence in accounting for the direct wrongness of killing. At the same time, it is frequently assumed that the justification of homicide in self-defence is unproblematic: that the use of lethal force in self-defence is clearly morally justified since the aggressor has lost or forfeited the right to life. Yet, typically, the victim of homicide in self-defence is an archetypal person who does not want to die: an adult human being who is fully conscious, self-conscious, rational, in good health, with plans for the future. Often a person who is killed in self-defence will have been engaged in human action and responsible for his or her conduct; then again, he or she might have been acted upon (pushed), or acting out of control (deranged), or for some other reason not have been responsible for posing the threat. Can we plausibly claim that all persons killed in self-defence have forfeited the right to life? What is the significance of forfeiture of the right to life to the justification of homicide in self-defence?[2]

The justification of homicide in self-defence must also

---

[2] Problems arising from the theory of forfeiture are brought out in Judith Jarvis Thomson's article 'Self-Defense and Rights', reprinted in her *Rights, Restitution and Risk*, edited by William Parent (Camb. Mass.: Harvard University Press, 1986), pp. 33–48. I discuss these problems in chapter 6.

explicitly recognize and address the fact that the use of lethal force in self-defence involves self-preferential killing: the self-defending agent kills another person in the act of protecting him- or herself. Moreover, in many cases this killing is foreseen by the person acting in self-defence. Foreseen self-preferential killing is not something to be generally morally endorsed. Of course, compassion can be required towards someone who, *in extremis*, protects him- or herself at the foreseen expense of another person's life; but in other circumstances we can regard such conduct as morally inexcusable. Either way, self-preferential killing can inflict a grave injustice on its victim, can be a serious moral wrong. Yet foreseen self-preferential killing *in self-defence* is commonly regarded as a paradigm of morally justified private homicide. Why is homicide in self-defence morally permissible? Our answer to this crucial question will be shaped by what type of justification we take self-defence to be, and also by our background moral theory. A satisfactory account of self-defence as a justification of homicide needs to attend to the complex nature of moral justification and also to the different ways in which conduct can be morally justified. In chapter 2, I set out a sufficiently complex analysis of justification and the relationship between justified and excusable conduct. Subsequent chapters draw on this analysis and take some aspects of it further.

The account of the justification of homicide in self-defence that I develop in this book is implicitly contrary to moral monism, i.e., the view that all morally relevant considerations are reducible to a single value. My reason for deriving the account from a particular, non-monistic moral perspective is partly, but not entirely, a practical one. In adhering to a desirable word-length, I could not discuss the justification of homicide in self-defence against a series of different, competing moral theories without forgoing philosophical depth and much important content. More importantly, in setting out the principles related to justified self-defence from a moral perspective which regards rights as permissions and constraints based on just and unjust treatment of, and interference with, individuals, and which regards benevolence as an independent virtue, my aim is to indicate that moral monism does not do justice to the complexity of this issue. In particular, the more speculative parts of chapter 6, which are concerned with grounding an appropriate specification of the scope of the right to life, should be read with this in mind.

A satisfactory account of the justification of foreseen self-preferential killing in self-defence requires that we characterize homicide *in self-defence*. Under what conditions is force used in self-defence? For instance, must someone against whom force is used in self-defence be an aggressor or an assailant? Or is it possible to use force in self-defence against a passive threat (e.g. someone who has fallen)? Further, as I have suggested above, the account must decide what bearing, if any, the fact that force is used in self-defence has on the justification of self-preferential killing. Is homicide in self-defence morally distinguishable from other types of self-preferential killing in virtue of the fact that lethal force is used *in self-defence*? In this connection, the account needs to answer questions such as the following: Does an aggressor's culpability warrant my using force against him or her in self-defence? Or is it permissible to use force in self-defence against a young child or a deranged person? Is there a single, common principle which justifies the use of force in self-defence against culpable and non-culpable, active and passive threats? Do individuals have a positive right of self-defence; and, if so, what are the limits of this right? Or does the justification of self-defence flow from some wider permission to use force against others in order to protect or preserve oneself? Under what conditions, if any, does the justification of the use of force in self-defence extend to the defence of others?

The relevance of these conceptual and moral questions is broader than the particular bearing they have on the justification of homicide in self-defence. They are also important to the satisfactory resolution of several more fundamental theoretical concerns. These concerns include the conditions under which as individual persons we possess human rights such as the right to life, the appropriate specification of the scope of the right to life (in so far as it is a right not to be killed), and the grounding of an appropriate specification of the scope of this right. The central aim of this book is to set out the principles related to justified homicide in self-defence and to address crucial conceptual and moral questions relating to self-defence, such as those I have outlined above. However, chapters 3, 4, 5 and 6 also bring to the surface the wider significance of these questions, and illustrate the ways in which the justification of homicide in self-defence bears on and illuminates more fundamental issues in moral theory.

My account of the justification of homicide in self-defence does not contain a discussion of metaphysical problems of the self and personal identity and the bearing these issues might have on the justification of self-defence. For the most part I assume that a person acting in self-defence is protecting his or her own person. However, in discussing the moral and legal conditions of necessary and proportionate force, I extend the scope of the self being defended to that of the person engaged in his or her rightful activities. Defence of oneself could also include the protection of goods (e.g. liberty and property) on which one's life depends.

Homicide in self-defence is also frequently said to be legally justified. As I argue in chapter 2, the law in this area reflects the common assumption that use of necessary and proportionate force in self-defence is both morally permissible and a positive moral right. But in several noteworthy respects the law of self-defence appears now to be moving beyond the conditions of morally justified self-defence. Some recent trends in this area complicate or undermine the textbook characterization of the legal plea of Self-Defence as a justification of homicide.[3] This fact raises at least one substantive issue of criminal justice ethics that ought to be of concern.

This book is essentially a work of applied philosophy which

---

[3] Throughout, except in the case of direct quotation, I use 'Self-Defence' for the name of a legal plea as distinguished from self-defence as a more general defence, and so too with the legal pleas of Duress, Necessity and Provocation.

addresses the important moral issue of the justification of homicide in self-defence. Since the question of moral justification is the focus of my interest in self-defence as a legal justification of homicide, I do not engage in detailed legal analysis of the law of self-defence. Rather, where appropriate, and particularly in chapter 2, I apply philosophical analysis to the law pertaining to self-defence and related defences to homicide. (Here my critique is almost exclusively confined to elements of common law, both case law and as codified.) Moral and legal justification are not identical, of course; nor should they be. Nevertheless, morality and the criminal law should be in close alliance in the area of homicide: the law pertaining to self-defence and related defences to homicide should embody morally defensible principles and distinctions.

1.2 HOW THE ACCOUNT PROCEEDS

The use of lethal force in self-defence is commonly regarded as justified, rather than excusable, homicide. More strongly, most of us believe that we obviously have a *right* of self-defence. The use of force in self-defence is widely regarded as an individual, positive moral right, and thus an exception to, rather than a permissible or justified infringement of, the general prohibition of homicide.[4] This characterization of homicide in self-defence is often uncritically assumed in philosophical discussion, rather than carefully enough explained and defended. Nevertheless, it is essentially correct, and I explain and defend it throughout this book.

In chapter 2, I examine the relationship between justification and excuse, and I provide an account of the complex nature of justification which is sufficiently sophisticated to allow us to see what sort of moral and legal justification self-defence is. In this context, I also discuss the pertinent aspects of Self-Defence as a legal plea to homicide. Chapter 3 examines the important contributions of natural law accounts

[4] The distinction between exceptions to, and justified infringements of, general prohibitions is explained in chapter 2.

of self-defence. These accounts do not always address the crucial issues they raise; their importance lies in the fact that they highlight most of the important questions and identify the necessary elements of a satisfactory account of justified homicide in self-defence. The two prominent strands of wider philosophical thinking about the justification of homicide in self-defence can be found in natural law. One of these strands maintains that homicide in self-defence is justified as unintended killing; the other is based on the claim that an unjust aggressor forfeits the right to life. I am not an advocate of natural law, and in chapter 4 I reject the natural law-inspired characterization of homicide in self-defence as always unintended killing. Nevertheless, as I argue in chapters 3 and 4, natural law accounts of self-defence contain and reveal important moral insights concerning the right of self-defence and the limits of justified self-defence. My account in chapter 5 of the essential features of self-defence as a justification of homicide owes a good deal to these insights. Properly understood, the forfeiture strand of natural law thinking is crucial both to the justification of homicide in self-defence as an instance of self-preferential killing (even in cases where such homicide is plausibly characterized as unintended killing), and to the characterization of self-defence as an exception to, rather than a justified infringement of, the general prohibition of homicide.

The book's focus is the justification of *homicide* in self-defence. But the plea of Self-Defence is a potential defence to all crimes, and much of the discussion throughout the book applies to the conditions of justified self-defence more generally. Important aspects of my discussion of homicide in self-defence in chapters 2 and 4 also have more general bearing on the defence of necessity, and on the limits of justified homicidal acts of self-protection and protection of others.

In setting out the principles relevant to justified homicide in self-defence, I develop an account of the right of self-defence as a positive right to use necessary and proportionate force in defence of ourselves and others. My account also

7

characterizes the use of lethal force in self-defence as an exception to the general prohibition of homicide. I try to make as much sense as possible of a unitary right of self-defence, one which grounds the justification of self-defence against culpable and non-culpable, active and passive, unjust threats. In chapter 5, I argue that a unitary justification of homicide in self-defence, one which covers the range of cases in which most of us take self-defence to be justified, requires a particular specification of the scope of the right to life. As to the further, deeper question of why we should accept this specification, I argue in chapter 6 that two currently popular, highly influential kinds of moral theory – a contractualist approach and a sophisticated indirect utilitarianism – do not adequately ground it. This is a strong reason for developing the necessary alternative foundational theory, if I am right that the specification of the scope of the right to life necessary to a unitary justification of homicide in self-defence has strong intuitive plausibility as representing what is morally distinctive about the use of lethal force in self-defence.

Chapter 2

Self-defence as a justification

The claim that homicide in self-defence is justified killing will strike many people as obviously true. Nevertheless, this claim is contestable and the details of its defence are more complex than is often supposed. Hence, the first section of this chapter is concerned with the nature of justification and excuse, the conditions under which the plea of self-defence is a justification of homicide, and the type of justification self-defence is. Homicide in self-defence is also commonly taken to be legally justified homicide; the legal plea of Self-Defence is usually said to be a justification. In the second section of this chapter (2.2) I argue that although the general characterization of homicide in self-defence as justified is essentially correct, it is not entirely straightforward and this is partly due to the complexity of the moral background. Towards the end of the chapter I discuss aspects of the law of self-defence which complicate or to some extent undermine the claim that the conditions of the legal plea of Self-Defence are those of justification.

2.1 SELF-DEFENCE AND THE COMPLEXITY OF JUSTIFICATION AND EXCUSE

In everyday moral evaluation many people use the terminology of justification and excuse loosely without, for instance, differentiating between excusable and justified conduct. Even when we endeavour to be precise there can be legitimate doubt about whether a particular explanation justifies rather

9

than excuses a person's conduct. J. L. Austin, for example, questions whether provocation is an excuse (the agent having been provoked, was not entirely responsible for what he did) or a justification (the agent was entitled to retaliate in the way he did).[1] The legal plea of Provocation seems to me clearly an excuse.[2] In moral evaluation, however, we might cite provocation in maintaining that, for instance, a person's hostile words were justified rather than simply understandable and excusable in the circumstances.[3]

It is also sometimes held that for some purposes and in some contexts a legal distinction between justification and excuse is irrelevant.[4] However, because the distinction between justified and excusable conduct can be important to careful moral evaluation, it can be important to legal evaluation too, especially where a particular plea (e.g. Duress) is being defined or the general appropriateness of allowing a particular plea to a particular offence is being determined.[5] The nature of justification and excuse is more complex than even some very helpful discussions of this matter appear to recognize; and the more general points I make in this chapter in explaining how this is so will outline the conditions under which self-defence is a justification, and also what type of justification it is. As indicated above, the complex nature of justification and excuse also has implications for the law of self-defence. Some of the implications which are brought out in the second section of this chapter will be taken further in subsequent chapters.

[1] J. L. Austin, 'A Plea For Excuses', reprinted in *Philosophy of Action*, edited by Alan White (Oxford University Press, 1968), p. 20.
[2] See this chapter, text accompanying n10 and n11.
[3] In n27 this chapter, I give an example which illustrates the sort of legitimate doubt Austin felt about borderline cases of justification and excuse.
[4] See, e.g. A. P. Bates, T. L. Buddin, and D. J. Meure, *The System of Criminal Law* (Sydney: Butterworths, 1980), p. 500. However, in numerous publications George Fletcher urges the importance of the theory of justification and excuse to the criminal law. See also Stanley Yeo, *Compulsion in the Criminal Law* (Sydney: The Law Book Company, 1990).
[5] As an illustration, see my article 'Killing Under Duress', *Journal of Applied Philosophy*, vol. 6, no. 1, 1989, pp. 53–69.

Justification and excuse

Numerous philosophers and jurisprudents have written on justification and excuse since J. L. Austin's now famous essay, 'A Plea for Excuses'. Much of what I and others have to say in this area is greatly indebted to this work. I agree with Eric D'Arcy that in the case of acts, justifications and excuses both appeal to morally relevant circumstances which are taken as exculpating, and that 'to say that a decision, belief, practice, rule, or act was justified is usually to imply that one's first reaction was to say that there was something wrong with it, though subsequently (on learning the circumstances, or in the light of the consequences) to decide, agree, or admit that it was right: we say that something is justified only when we think, or expect that someone will think, that it needs justification'. 'The effect of a *justifying* circumstance is to *justum facere* an (otherwise wrongful) act, so that it becomes good, or at least permissible: lawful.'[6]

D'Arcy also points out that there are different ways of putting a defence of justification in the case of acts, which reveal different ways in which exculpatory circumstances can justify. One of these ways is when harm is rightly brought about as the lesser evil. D'Arcy does not put this last point in this way, but he points out 'that justification may arise from the urgent personal need of oneself or another. This will often justify, for example, using or damaging another person's property.'[7] Interpreted as the legal recognition of a *permissible or rightful* choice of the lesser evil, the plea of Necessity in this case is a justification.[8]

---

6 Eric D'Arcy, *Human Acts* (Oxford: Clarendon Press, 1963), p. 81 (emphasis original).
7 Ibid., p. 84. My description of this type of justification – as bringing about the lesser evil – does not imply purely consequentialist evaluation of such acts.
8 In *Rethinking Criminal Law* (Boston: Little, Brown, 1978), pp. 856–60, George Fletcher maintains that Necessity, (apparently) so interpreted, is sometimes a justification and sometimes an excuse. Fletcher's reasoning seems perhaps not sufficiently to appreciate that justification involves an overall, all-relevant-things-considered judgment, and also that recognized *exceptions* to rules and permissible *infringements* of rules are both

11

More recently Jenny Teichman has expressed the different view that the defence 'I chose the lesser evil' is not a justification but an excuse, whereas 'I chose the greater good' is a justification. Her reasons for this claim are that the explanation ' "I chose the lesser evil" is of course a confession of having acted wrongly (with or without an excuse)', and that 'in choosing between evils one feels one has to make excuses not only for the wrong decision (i.e., for choosing the greater evil) but also for the right one (i.e., for choosing the lesser evil)'.[9] I am not persuaded by this reasoning. However, Teichman's claim is important because it directs our attention to the question of what 'wrongful' means when it is, rightly, said that excusable conduct is wrongful. This question brings into focus three important features of moral justification that are relevant to distinguishing justification and excuse: justification is an all-relevant-things-considered judgment about the conduct in question; however, there are differing standards, a weaker and a stronger standard of moral justification, and whether some conduct is said to be justified, rather than excusable, can depend on the perspective from which we are evaluating it. I now explain these three features.

Justification: all things considered To describe something as the lesser evil is to evaluate it as *undesirable in itself*. However, conduct which is, or which brings about something which is, undesirable in itself need not be *wrongful*: the overall evaluation of doing or bringing about something undesirable in itself (e.g. causing pain) can include consideration of circumstances and consequences. Of course, we can regard the lesser evil as *morally* undesirable in itself because, e.g. it involves hurting or deceiving someone, or treating a person unfairly. For this reason some philosophers maintain that some acts of this type (e.g. breaking a promise or lying) are usefully char-

justifications. *Permissible* infringements of rules are not excuses, rather than justifications, simply because they are *infringements* of rules. I explain these features of justification more fully below.

[9] Jenny Teichman, *Pacifism and the Just War* (Oxford: Basil Blackwell, 1986), p. 103.

acterized as *prima facie* wrong. But 'I chose the lesser evil' is not a confession of having acted wrongly all things considered when it is intended to explain that I made the right choice in the circumstances.

Although we can speak of different aspects of someone's conduct as justified or otherwise, to evaluate a particular decision or act as justified is to make an overall judgment that it is permissible or right, all aspects taken to be morally relevant having been considered. I emphasize this feature of justification partly because it bears on the disagreement in recent legal literature about whether the plea of Provocation is a partial excuse or a partial justification. Joshua Dressler, for instance, takes issue with Finbarr McAuley's claim that Provocation functions as a partial justification rather than as a partial excuse for homicide.[10] Dressler rightly defends the usual interpretation of Provocation as a partial excuse, but his argument concedes too much to the claim that Provocation functions as a partial justification. A *particular act or offence* cannot be partially justified. Some *elements or aspects* of a person's conduct can be justified while other elements or aspects are unjustified. For example, I may be justified in gleaning certain information from you, but not in passing it on to friends; my reacting angrily towards a colleague might be justified, but not my kicking him; I am entitled to repel your unwanted kiss on the cheek, but not by pushing you under a moving train. However, justification in the area of conduct primarily concerns acts; and to say that a particular act, or some element or aspect of it, is or was justified is to make an overall evaluation of whatever is said to be justified, all relevant things considered. Justification can be a matter of degree: something can be arguably justified, barely justified, amply justified, etc. But conduct described in a particular way is either justified – permissible or right – or it is not. Thus a particular act (e.g. my telling this lie, my killing this person, my kicking him, my breaking this promise, my pushing you under the train) cannot be partially justified. It is either per-

---

10 Joshua Dressler, 'Provocation: Partial Justification or Partial Excuse?', (1988), 51 *Modern Law Review*, pp. 467–80.

missible or right that I do *this* act in the circumstances or it is not.

The fact that a successful plea of Provocation results in conviction of an offence (e.g. manslaughter) means that the accused's conduct was legally wrongful. This is sufficient to identify Provocation as an *excuse*. If Provocation is an excuse because, as some maintain, the victim of the homicide was partly to blame for the accused's loss of self-control, this does not partially justify that particular loss of self-control. Further, even if the accused was justified in the circumstances in taking some action in response to the provocation (e.g. in resorting to hostile words or a degree of force) this does not partially justify *what the accused actually did* if this went beyond what he or she was entitled to do.[11]

So, the first feature of justification to note here is that although justification admits of degrees, justification is a threshold concept which involves an overall judgment about whatever is said to be justified.

Weaker and stronger standards of justification   Secondly, when we ask what relevant considerations are included in a judgment about justification, we can recognize a weaker and a stronger standard of justification. 'What I did was permissible in the circumstances' is a justification, not an excuse; and because many permissible acts are discretionary, 'permissible act' implies a weaker all-things-considered justification than does 'right act'. We should also note that in moral evaluation 'permissible act' is sometimes used in a narrower, somewhat legalistic sense, to indicate the existence of a particular permission (e.g. a right to do *x* or to have *y*); and acts said to be permissible in this narrower sense can be the wrong thing to do all things considered. For instance, in this sense it may be permissible that I insist on my rights in some circumstances

---

[11] Excuses, on the other hand, can be partial because they primarily affect our moral assessment of the agent on account of wrongful conduct. Agents can be more or less to blame, and not all excusing circumstances are wholly exculpating.

when this is not really the right thing for me to do: I ought to be more compassionate, not extract my pound of flesh.[12]

Objective and agent-perspectival justification   Thirdly, it is sometimes necessary to speak of justification from a particular perspective. This is because a justified act need not be permissible or right from a fully informed perspective. We can, and we often do, speak of justification from the perspective of the agent in the circumstances; and justification from this perspective is compatible with mistaken belief on the agent's part.[13] A petrol station attendant who hands over money from the till at the point of a very convincing dummy gun can claim 'I was justified in acting as I did. I did the right thing', even though the threat was a bluff and the attendant need not have sacrificed anything. When evaluated from a more informed perspective such an act is faulty (although the agent is not at fault, not to blame) because based on a mistaken belief.[14]

Although 'justified act' need not imply the act's permissibility or rightness from a fully informed perspective, it may do so. Someone who in the circumstances reasonably believes that his or her act is justified might wonder whether he or she is *really* doing the right thing. We also invoke this more objective sense of justification when from a more informed, a more objective perspective than that of the agent in the circumstances, we say that a particular act is or was the wrong thing to do. Here we mean that the act is or was untoward, or that it is or was not the best act in the circumstances. (In the strongest sense, 'justified act' means objectively the best act.) Think of a case of putative self-defence, one in which I kill

---

12 I return in detail to this general point, and to further remarks about moral permissibility and justification, in 4.3, where further remarks will be more pertinent. To pursue them here would divert us too much from the issues at hand.

13 Kent Greenawalt makes a similar point in 'The Perplexing Borders of Justification and Excuse', *Columbia Law Review*, vol. 84, no. 8, 1984, pp. 1907–9.

14 In conformity with legal literature 'mistaken belief' in this context simply means 'false belief'. No mistake of reasoning on the agent's part is implied.

15

someone in what I reasonably believe to be self-defence against a deadly blow. Sadly, it turns out that the other person's behaviour was entirely harmless. Evaluated from the perspective of the agent in the circumstances, my conduct was justified despite the fact that I killed a harmless person. However, from a later, more informed perspective I can acknowledge that I did the wrong thing, and that a third party, for instance, observing the sequence of events and recognizing my mistake, could justifiably have intervened to stop me. In retrospect we can, and we sometimes do, evaluate untoward acts based on mistaken beliefs in this way. Further, often when this is so we regret not only the outcomes of such acts, but unlike justified choices of lesser evils, we regret these acts – we wish the agent had acted differently – even though we recognize the inappropriateness of remorse or guilt on the agent's part.

When we explain a faulty act as due to the agent's mistaken belief, we do often cite this belief as *excusing* the agent for having caused needless harm, or for not having brought about the best results in the circumstances, rather than maintain that the agent in the circumstances acted permissibly or rightly. Indeed, a *justified* mistaken belief about the circumstances of an act or its likely consequences is probably most commonly regarded as a complete *excuse* of the agent. To excuse an agent implies that his or her conduct was wrongful *by some standard*; and this standard can be derived from a more informed, a more objective perspective than that of the agent in the circumstances. Because this is so, when speaking precisely about a rightful act and justification and a wrongful act and excuse, we need to distinguish between a rightful act from a fully informed perspective, and what was permissible or right from the perspective of the agent in the circumstances. And it seems to me that this precision provides a sufficiently sensitive resolution of the running dispute between those legal theorists who maintain that reasonable mistake in cases of putative self-defence is an excuse and those who argue that it is a justification. There is good reason for insisting on both views (although this is not always reflected in the actual arguments urged on either side).[15] Reasonable mistake can be either an agent-perspectival justification or a complete excuse, depending on the perspective from which the act is evaluated.[16]

So, when speaking precisely about the right act and justification we need to distinguish between the objectively permissible or right act (right[i]) and what is permissible or right from the reasonable perspective of the agent (right[ii]). Objective justification does not ensure agent-perspectival justification; nor does agent-perspectival justification ensure objective justification. (Not handing over the money is objectively the best act in the petrol station example, but from the agent's perspective it is right that she hand it over.) Right[ii] act need not be exclusive – in some circumstances alternative acts could each be right[ii]. In the petrol station example, for instance, it could also be right[ii] for the attendant (say) to scream for help rather than hand over the money, depending on what is reasonably risked in the circumstances. Because right[i] is an objective moral standard it is unusual, although not impossible, that alternative acts would achieve equally satisfactory results and each be right[i]. We also need to keep in mind a similar distinction between objective justification (justification[i]) and what the agent in the circumstances is justified in doing (justification[ii]).[17]

---

15 See Dressler's critique of Fletcher, 'New Thoughts About the Concept of Justification in Criminal Law: A Critique of Fletcher's Thinking and *Rethinking*', 32 *UCLA Law Review*, pp. 61–99. Fletcher holds that reasonable mistake is an excuse because he, wrongly in my view, believes that justification necessarily implies objective rightness. On the other side of the dispute, it sometimes seems, wrongly, to be suggested that lack of moral guilt on the agent's part is sufficient to justify the act rather than excuse the agent (see e.g. Yeo, *Compulsion in the Criminal Law*, p. 32).

16 I have not found a more felicitous name for this type of justification than Robert Young's suggestion: agent-perspectival. 'Subjective justification' comes most naturally to a philosopher; but I avoid 'subjective' here because it could suggest to legal readers that the relevant belief or judgment need not be reasonable in the circumstances.

17 R. A. Duff has pointed out that there are actually two species of *objective* justification within my distinction between objective and agent-perspectival justification. One species of objective justification has to do with what it would in fact (in the light both of the actual circumstances and

These remarks about justification contradict those of George Fletcher, who has maintained in numerous publications that positive rightness (not simply permissibility) and objective rightness are necessary features of justification. Hence, Fletcher regards reasonable putative self-defence as, without qualification, an excuse. But an act's permissibility can be a justification without the act being positively the right thing to do. Further, we can describe one and the same act as objectively the wrong thing to have done but excusable because justified[ii]. Some excuses are agent-perspectival justifications, and this can be true of putative self-defence. (I might also remark in passing that Fletcher's concept of justification does not appear to acknowledge the possibility of agent-relative justifications (he maintains that X cannot be justified in defending himself against Y unless a third party would be justified in defending X against Y). Nor does it appear to accept the possibility of an act that I have a right to do not being, all things considered, the right thing for me to do.)[18]

Fletcher is a leading exponent of the jurisprudential theory that closely aligns criminal defences with the moral evaluation of acts and agents. I, too, accept this theory, and I apply it throughout this book.[19] More specifically, I believe that in the

the actual consequences) be right or best to do in the circumstances; the other species concerns what it would be reasonable to do in the light of whatever predictions it would be reasonable (for the agent or others) to make about the consequences. Consider a case in which surgery to correct a relatively minor problem unexpectedly, against all medical knowledge, causes the patient's death. This death was unforeseeable; hence, the patient's decision for the surgery was not only agent-perspectivally justified but also justified from anyone's perspective, and in *that* sense objectively justified. Contrast this case with one in which normally routine surgery kills a particular patient because of an underlying condition which faulty pre-surgery testing did not reveal. In this latter case, the patient's decision for the surgery was agent-perspectivally justified, but not justified (say) from the perspective of those carelessly conducting the pre-surgery tests: the patient's death was foreseeable given properly conducted tests, but in the circumstances was reasonably not foreseen by the patient.

[18] George Fletcher, 'Rights and Excuses', *Criminal Justice Ethics*, vol. 3, no. 2, 1984, pp. 17–20.

[19] See also my article 'What Are Partial Excuses to Murder?', in *Partial Excuses to Murder*, edited by Stanley Yeo (Sydney: Federation Press,

case of homicide defences, legal justifications and excuses ought to have very close moral analogues, that the legal and non-legal senses of terms like 'provocation', 'duress', and 'self-defence' are generally not very detached from one another, and that legal decision making about defences to homicide invokes moral assumptions and arguments.[20] Nevertheless, closely related moral and legal concepts and categories are not identical in all respects, and the distinction between objective and agent-perspectival justification provides a basis for noting two differences between moral and legal justification.

First, morally justified conduct requires agent-perspectival justification, whereas legal justification does not necessarily require this. For *an agent's act* to be morally justified, from any perspective, the agent in the circumstances must reasonably judge that it is permissible or right. Further, the agent must do it voluntarily and for the right reason. For instance, someone who accidentally brings about the lesser evil while attempting to achieve something else may in fact do what morality permits or requires, but he or she does not thereby act justifiably; and an agent's act is not morally justified if he or she unwittingly does what he or she reasonably judges in the circumstances to be the right thing. However, it can be sufficient for legal justification that an agent's act merely conform with what the law permits or requires.[21] For example, in marrying for a second time one cannot be guilty of bigamy if one is not currently married, even if one remarries believing oneself still to be married to one's first spouse.[22] If I am legally required to register a baby's birth within forty days, and believing the period to be thirty days I register the birth on day thirty-five, legally I do the right thing. In such cases,

1991), pp. 1–18, in which much of the conceptual discussion of the first section of this present chapter is applied to partial legal excuses.
20 See my 'Killing Under Duress'.
21 L. W. Sumner, *The Moral Foundation of Rights* (Oxford: Clarendon Press, 1987), chapter 3, usefully distinguishes between conformance, compliance, and acceptance in the case of legal rules.
22 See George Fletcher, 'The Right Deed for the Wrong Reason', *UCLA Law Review*, vol. 23, 1975, p. 295.

although the agent acts intentionally, believing herself not to be doing what the law permits or requires, her act is legally justified simply because it lacks a definitional element of the relevant offence; her act does not in fact constitute any offence. In contrast, consider lying – speaking a falsehood with the intention to deceive. An agent does not actually lie if, despite her belief to the contrary, in fact she speaks the truth. But when an agent tells what she falsely believes to be a lie, in circumstances where she knows she ought to tell the truth, her act is not morally justified simply because it is not in fact a lie.

Further, consider the type of legal plea (Self-Defence for instance) that is often said to concern a justification distinct from considerations that negate elements of the relevant offence. To the extent that a particular aspect of the *Dadson* principle has been abrogated in some jurisdictions, agent-perspectival justification might not be a necessary condition of legal justification even in some cases of *intentional* homicide. The *Dadson* principle maintains that 'whenever justification or excuse appear in a criminal case, not only must the circumstances of justification or excuse appear but the defendant must have known of, or believed in, those circumstances'.[23] As to the first condition of this principle – that 'the circumstances of justification or excuse appear' – we can note again that putative self-defence *can* be an agent-perspectival justification. However, the aspect of the principle relevant here is the latter condition – 'the defendant must have known of, or believed in, those circumstances'. A necessary element of the fulfilment of this condition is that the defendant *actually* have believed in the existence of circumstances in virtue of which his action is legally justified or excusable. However, the English Law Commission's 1989 *Report and Draft Criminal Code for England and Wales* states that if a person's actions are *in fact* necessary and reasonable to prevent his being (say)

---

[23] *R v Dadson* (1850) 4 Cox. C.C. 358. See B. Hogan's critique of this principle in 'The Dadson Principle', (1989) *Criminal Law Review* 679.

attacked with a knife, this agent commits no offence; it would be immaterial that the agent was unaware that his victim was armed with a knife, or about to attack.[24] Hence, were I to kill someone believing her to be harmless, I would commit no offence provided the objective circumstances were of self-defence: the person I kill is *in fact* on the point of attacking me with a knife and my actions are *in fact* necessary to ward off her attack. Thus, if I interpret the relevant clause correctly, legal justification of my act here would not require that I believe that the existing circumstances provide a legal justification or excuse; nor would it require that I believe in the existence of those circumstances that provide a legal justification or excuse.[25] The objective circumstances would constitute a legal justification. However, these objective facts do not morally justify my killing a person whom I believe to be harmless.

The second difference between moral and legal justification based on the distinction between agent-perspectival and objective justification occurs in cases where the agent mistakenly believes that his or her act is justified. Here, moral justification can be agent-perspectival whereas legal justification cannot. Because we can speak of moral justification from different perspectives, an agent's act can be morally justified because based on the agent's reasonable beliefs and evaluations, although this act is not what morality permits or requires from a more informed, a more objective perspective. But an agent's act is not legally justified (lawful) if the agent in the circumstances reasonably but mistakenly believes that it

24 The Law Commission (Law Com. No. 177), vol. 1: Report and Draft Criminal Code Bill (London HMSO, 1989), Clause 44 (1) (a), Appendix B, 44 (i), p. 165. Henceforth, I refer to this Report and Draft Criminal Code Bill as the *Draft Criminal Code*. References to the *Code* itself are by clause number, references to the commentary are by part and paragraph number.
25 See J. C. Smith's discussion of the theory that the external facts constitute a legal justification irrespective of the defendant's state of mind, *Justification and Excuse in the Criminal Law* (London: Stevens and Co., 1989), pp. 28–44. In Smith's view it is a matter of *policy* whether knowledge of the facts should be required in the case of Self-Defence.

conforms with what the law permits or requires. (This agent's act might be legally excusable, though.)[26]

I have highlighted three important features of moral justification in rejecting Teichman's reasoning that the *right* decision is sometimes excusable, rather than justified, because 'I chose the lesser evil' is a confession of having acted wrongly. These three features are: justification involves an all-things-considered evaluation of whatever is said to be justified; there is a weaker (permissible act) and a stronger (right act) standard of justification; and justification can be agent-perspectival or objective. As to Teichman's second reason for claiming that 'I chose the lesser evil' is an excuse rather than a justification, I think that when we apologise and make excuses to someone who is wronged or even simply inconvenienced by what we do, we sometimes appeal to considerations which really justify our conduct, for example, 'I'm sorry, I cannot come; my child is ill and needs me.' This particular explanation of my non-attendance provides a different morally extenuating consideration from, for example, both of the following: 'When I accepted your invitation, I'd forgotten a prior engagement', and 'My car has broken down and I have no other transport.' These latter considerations, if (at least partly) exculpating, are excuses: they do not make my not keeping the engagement with you right, but instead relieve me from (a degree of) blame for not turning up. Even so, the former of these excuses is like the justification 'my child is ill and needs me', in that I urge as the explanation of my non-attendance a conflicting obligation which is more stringent in the circumstances and which I rightly choose to fulfil. But it is unlike the justification in that the conflict of obligations is due to faulty behaviour on my part, viz. my forgetting the prior engagement. It might be argued that whereas 'I had forgotten the prior engagement' explains, and is meant to excuse, my predicament of conflicting engagements, my decision to keep the other engagement is *then* permissible or right in the circumstances. However, the

[26] Putative self-defence is *not* an exception to this. See my discussion of putative self-defence and legal justification and excuse in 2.2.

fact that the circumstances in which I fail to keep the later engagement are due to my forgetfulness is, I think, a sufficient reason for regarding the whole explanation of my breaking the later engagement as an excuse. Faulty behaviour or inability which may excuse our wrongful conduct need not, of course, be something for which we are culpable (my car's breaking down need not be my fault), and is typically not culpable when we accept the morally extenuating consideration as a complete excuse (e.g. 'I am too ill to attend').[27]

Justification, excuse and responsibility D'Arcy distinguishes justification and excuse as follows: 'If an act is justified, the agent is responsible for it, but the act is, in the circumstances, not wrong. If it is excused, the act is a wrongful one, but the agent is, because of some special circumstances, not responsible for it, and hence not guilty.' 'An excusing condition, therefore primarily affects the agent; a justifying circumstance primarily affects the act: its species description, or its moral appraisal.'[28] Both parts of the last of these claims seem right to me. However, whereas agent-perspectival justification (justification[ii]) implies the agent's full responsibility for the act as described from within that perspective, it need not imply the agent's full responsibility for what he or she *actually* did. And this is the reason why an agent-perspectival justification can completely excuse an agent whose conduct is judged wrongful from a more objective perspective. Although the agent in the circumstances was justified, for example, in shooting someone who seemed to be an unjust attacker, or in handing over the money from the till at the

---

27 'I am too ill to attend' does seem a case in which excuse and justification meet. Am I saying that I am unable to attend because too ill (excuse), or that because I am ill I do the right thing in staying at home (justification)?

28 *Human Acts*, p. 85. Justification and excuse might usefully be distinguished in various ways which underscore D'Arcy's distinction. For instance, there is the suggestion that justifications are action-guiding, whereas excuses are not. To say that a certain action is justified serves, partly, to tell agents what they may do – what is permissible or right. To hold that conduct is excusable – that the agent is not to blame, or not fully so, on this count – is not to offer any such guidance. R. A. Duff drew my attention to this line of thought.

point of a convincing-looking gun, and she is responsible for *this* conduct so described and can account for it as permissible or right in the circumstances, the agent is *not responsible for*, and hence is *excused of*, what she *actually* did (needlessly killed someone, handed over the money unnecessarily).

'Responsible' is used in moral evaluation in a number of senses. And as D'Arcy's characterization of justification implies, where we deliberately choose the lesser evil, we are responsible for bringing about this evil in the sense that we are morally accountable for what we do. Our having a particular type of acceptable explanation, namely that we acted rightly in the circumstances, means that we are not culpable, not to blame, for having brought about something in itself undesirable. In legal literature 'criminal liability' and 'criminal responsibility' are often used interchangeably, in much the same way that 'responsible' sometimes means 'to blame' in moral appraisal. But in a case of necessity, for instance, we can regard the agent as responsible (answerable) for, e.g. exceeding the speed limit in order to rush a gravely ill person to hospital, and yet consistently say that because this conduct was permissible or right in the circumstances the agent is not criminally responsible on this count.

D'Arcy distinguishes responsibility and culpability in the case of justification. However, his characterization of excuse follows J. L. Austin in suggesting a conceptual link between all excuses and lack of responsibility, and hence lack of guilt. In my view, this characterization of excuse is misleading in two respects. First, it does not allow for partial excuse; but circumstances can be partly exculpating, and excuse need not be all-or-nothing. In the light of certain considerations we speak of persons as bearing less than full responsibility and of their being guilty of lesser moral or legal offences. For the sake of clarity, some people might reserve 'excuse' for a consideration which is entirely exculpating, and refer to 'mitigating circumstances' when an agent's responsibility or culpability is merely lessened. But this is not required by the concept of moral excuse or by its legal counterpart.

Secondly, while all successful excuses relieve the agent of

24

some degree of culpability, not all excuses deny the agent's full responsibility for the conduct in question. I have in mind here a particular sort of (what we might call) failed justification; a failed justification being an explanation offered by the agent which we, as moral evaluators, do not accept as a justification. We may, for example, disagree with some of the agent's beliefs or moral priorities, or with what he or she regards as proportionate harm or an acceptable risk. Even so, if we accept that there are morally difficult cases about which reasonable people can disagree, and that in the particular case the agent's own belief or evaluation is both honest and reasonable (although, we believe, wrong), we may believe that he or she is not culpable, or not fully so, for acting (in our view) wrongly. However, in this case the agent is fully responsible for his or her conduct: this agent's acts are fully voluntary and intentional. Here, the fact that considerations such as the agent's own beliefs and evaluations primarily affect our *moral evaluation of the agent*, and not our assessment of the act, is a good reason for regarding these considerations as (from our point of view) *excuses*. (Although to refer to an action based on the agent's conscientious, reasonable beliefs as excusable may seem to demean the agent. This is probably due to the fact that paradigm excuses for particular conduct, e.g. non-culpable incapacity and ignorance, relieve the agent of responsibility for it.)

Summary and application to self-defence   The common assumption that homicide in self-defence is justified usually expresses the view that *actual* self-defence is justified, i.e., that actual self-defence is permissible or rightful conduct as distinct from wrongful conduct for which the agent is excused of responsibility or blame. Once we take into account the distinction between agent-perspectival and objective justification, we can say that *putative* self-defence, where based on the agent's reasonable beliefs, is agent-perspectivally justified. From a more objective perspective we can also say that putative self-defence, where based on the agent's reasonable beliefs, is excusable conduct.

'Permissible act' invokes a weaker standard of justification than does 'right act'. Discretionary acts which are permissible all things considered are justified without being positively the right thing to do. The claim that homicide in self-defence is justified can, indeed commonly does, express the view that homicide in self-defence is both permissible all things considered and discretionary. *Pace* Fletcher, the claim that homicide in self-defence is justified need not express the view that it is positively the right thing to do.

'Permissible' can also be used in a narrower sense, to identify the existence of a particular permission the exercise of which can be wrong in some circumstances all things considered. In chapters 4 and 5, I argue that the *right* of self-defence is such a permission: the positive *right* to use force in self-defence against an unjust threat *grounds* the justification of homicide in self-defence, it does not guarantee that homicide in self-defence is justified all things considered.

Weaker and stronger justifications

Having outlined some important features of justification which are highlighted by the distinction between justification and excuse, I now draw attention to the fact that conduct can be justified in different ways,[29] with corresponding differences in the source and strength of the permission involved. The contrast between two *types* of objective justification is necessary in order to explain the claim that self-defence is an exception to, rather than a justified or excusable infringement of, the general prohibition of homicide.

Justification arises when an act which is normally wrong, because (say) it infringes someone else's rights, is chosen as the lesser evil. Because this act is the right thing to do in *these* circumstances, it is *thereby* something the agent is entitled to do even though this act *wrongs* its victim as well as injures him or her.[30] D'Arcy's examples of justification arising from

[29] D'Arcy, *Human Acts*, pp. 81–5.
[30] I would prefer to use 'harms' rather than 'injures' here, because 'injures' often (narrowly) suggests physical injury. But I avoid using 'harms'

the urgent personal need of myself or another are justifications of this type. For example, I may be justified in destroying your car in an emergency, and even be justified in wounding you by steering a runaway vehicle towards you rather than into a crowd. Nevertheless, I wrong you – I infringe your rights – in doing either of these things. This type of justification is distinguishable from a justification which invokes *a positive right* on the part of the agent to act as he or she does, so that someone whose interests are damaged by the act is *not thereby wronged*. An example of this second type of justification is where I require you to return something that you need, which I have lent you on the understanding that you will return it when I need it. Another example is where I withdraw a gratuitous service to you because I can no longer spare the time. In acting in these ways I cause you hardship and I thwart your interests, but I do not thereby wrong you. Paradigm cases of permissible self-defence, too, are not justified infringements of the unjust aggressor's rights, even when both the conflict and the injury inflicted on the aggressor are regrettable. Individual persons have a positive right to *defend* themselves against unjust aggression, and the injured victim of legitimate self-defensive action is not thereby wronged. (Some writers distinguish between culpable aggressors and morally innocent unjust aggressors (e.g. insane attackers), to the effect that only culpable aggressors are not wronged by the use of self-defensive force. In chapter 5, I argue that this distinction is mistaken.)

D'Arcy maintains that justified acts of both types fulfil the following description: It is true that this act is an instance of X (something which is normally an offence); but given C (a

whenever I need to distinguish between damaging a person's interests and wronging him or her. Joel Feinberg and others have pointed out that alongside the sense in which to harm someone is to thwart, set back, or defeat his or her interests, there is a sense of 'harming' which means 'wronging'. Feinberg argues that the Harm Principle implies this moral sense, *Harm To Others* (New York: Oxford University Press, 1984), chapter 1. Hobbes used 'injury' to mean 'injustice'. But there are limits to the concessions one can make in deference to the possible moral loading of words which have a perfectly straightforward wider sense.

27

justifying circumstance), this is one of the recognized exceptions to the rule 'X is wrong', and this act is good or at least permissible.[31] In my view, whereas killing an unjust aggressor in self-defence *is* a recognized exception to the rule 'Killing is wrong', this is not because self-defensive force permissibly wrongs an unjust aggressor. Use of legitimate force in self-defence is not within the scope of the rule 'Killing is wrong', because an unjust aggressor is not wronged by the use of such force even if he or she is killed by it. On the other hand, breaking a promise and destroying someone else's property without permission in an emergency – both of which infringe the injured person's rights – are *not* recognized *exceptions* (respectively) to the rules, 'Do not break promises', and 'Do not destroy another's property without permission.' They are, rather, recognized *justified infringements* of these rules and the other person's rights.

Of course, if the relevant rights or rules were held to be absolute (never permissibly infringed) then it would be necessary to exclude all justified acts from the scope of the relevant right or rule by appropriate specification. (Thus exponents of the Principle of Double Effect often argue that self-defence is permissible because the absolute moral prohibition is of *intended* killing and homicide in self-defence is not intended killing.) But we seem to denude the claim that, for example, I have a right that my car not be destroyed without my permission, if I have the relevant right only in so far as no one is justified in destroying my car without my permission. This is because what makes it (normally) wrong to destroy my car without my permission is (mostly) that I have a right that this not be done. And an important consideration in determining whether your destroying my car without my permission would be justified in certain circumstances is that I have a right that this not be done. Further, if in an emergency you justifiably destroy my car without my permission, I am nevertheless owed an apology and (probably) compensation for the wrong to me and not just for the

[31] *Human Acts*, p. 85.

injury.[32] This seems to me the element of truth in Teichman's claim that we act wrongly in choosing the lesser evil, even when this is the right decision.[33]

Homicide in self-defence as justified killing

An important qualification and an important assumption lie behind the common view that the use of force in *actual* self-defence is justified. The qualification is that the use of force in self-defence against *unjust* aggression is justified.[34] The assumption is that self-defence is a positive right: that is to say, the use of lethal force in genuine self-defence against

32 See Thomson, 'Rights and Compensation', reprinted in *Rights, Restitution, and Risk*, pp. 66–77. In general, Thomson distinguishes between infringing a right (overriding it justifiably) and violating it (overriding it unjustifiably). The substance of her distinction is important. But the distinction between infringing and violating a right is apt to be read as a distinction without a difference unless 'infringed' is re-defined. (See Teichman, *Pacifism and the Just War*, pp. 73–4.) I use 'infringe' and 'violate' interchangeably in respect of rights, and speak about justified and unjustified infringement/violation.

33 Feinberg argues about the relationship between the invasion of rights and moral indefensibility as follows: 'If Abel invades *any* nonmoribund, nonwicked interest of Baker's *indefensibly*, he has thereby wronged Baker. But suppose the circumstances are such that if Abel does not harm Baker's interest in X, his own interest in Y will itself be harmed. If interests of this type are more important than interests of type X, then Abel may understandably feel morally justified in invading Baker's interest in X, and if he is in fact justified, then he has not acted indefensibly, and Baker has been harmed but not wronged by him. The result is the same if Abel violates Baker's interest in Y in order to protect Charley's more important interest in Z', *Harm to Others*, p. 113 (emphases original). Here Feinberg is using 'wrongs' to refer to those harms which people have a *legal right* not to have inflicted upon them, pp. 111–13. Even so, I think it is a mistake to conflate wronging someone with *indefensibly* invading his or her interests where this involves invasion of rights, be the invaded rights moral or legal. One can injure/harm someone (damage her interests) indefensibly without harming/wronging her (invading her rights), and one can wrong someone (invade her rights) justifiably. I return to these issues, and to the problems of the specification of rights, in chapters 4 and 5.

34 Some people may think that this qualification needs to be stated more broadly, viz., that the use of force in self-defence is justified against aggression that is *not just*. See my remarks on my use of 'unjust threat' in chapter 3, n28 and accompanying text.

29

unjust aggression is not a justified infringement of the rule
'Killing is wrong'; rather, it is a recognized exception to that
rule. In chapter 5, I defend this view of homicide in self-
defence in conjunction with the claim that there is no such
positive right to use lethal force on an unoffending person
(someone who poses no unjust threat) for some good end.
There may be circumstances in which I would be morally
justified in killing an unoffending person, e.g. where this is
unavoidable in acting to avert some greater evil, and *hence* be
entitled so to act. But in so acting I infringe a general rule and
the unoffending person's rights. Putative self-defence, where
this conduct is reasonable in the circumstances, is justified[ii].
For this reason, from a more objective perspective *putative*
self-defence is an excusable *infringement* of its victim's rights.

2.2 SELF-DEFENCE AND LEGAL JUSTIFICATION

Homicide in self-defence is also held to be legally permissible,
and the plea of Self-Defence is usually said to be a justification. The plea of Self-Defence has been invoked as a
justification of homicide in judicial decision making, particularly in the course of distinguishing Self-Defence as an
admissible, complete defence to murder, from the related
pleas of Necessity and Duress.[35] In *Compulsion in the Criminal
Law*, Stanley Yeo argues that these three related common law
defences should continue to be kept separate because they
'do not all share the same underlying rationale be it of justification or excuse'.[36] Yeo quotes the Canadian Law Reform
Commission as putting the matter succinctly as follows:

Despite their common fundamental nature, duress, self-defence
and necessity are kept separate in [the Commission's draft legisla-
tion because] ... the distinction is based on moral differences
between the three defences. In self-defence the accused seeks protection against aggression and in so doing promotes a value supported by the law. In duress, he avoids harm wrongfully threatened

[35] See in particular *R v Dudley and Stephens* (1884)14 Q.B.D. 273, and *R v Howe* (1987) A.C. 417.
[36] *Compulsion in the Criminal Law*, p. 28.

to him but does so at the expense of an innocent third party or by controvention of the law and therefore does not promote a value supported by the law. In necessity he may sometimes promote a value supported by the law and contravene the letter of the law to secure some greater good (for example an unlicensed motorist drives an emergency case to hospital to save life); at other times he may fail to promote such a value but may avoid harm to himself at the expense of an innocent person or of controvention of the law (for example a shipwrecked sailor saves himself by repelling another from a plank sufficient only to carry one).[37]

Western legal systems *permit* private individuals to use force in self-defence against unjust aggression.[38] Where attack is sudden, there is usually no possibility of legal protection, and if we are not legally entitled to defend ourselves then we must either be potential criminals or else at the mercy of those who would unjustly overpower us. Most people would regard this dilemma as morally intolerable, and would urge the individual's *right* to act in self-defence. However, this presumed moral right of self-defence is not unlimited, permitting use of any means of warding off unjust harm: it is confined to use of necessary force. I am not entitled to aim at an attacker's heart if I can shoot him in the leg and this is sufficient for self-defence in the circumstances. Further, there is not a general right to use necessary force in self-defence irrespective of other morally relevant considerations: sometimes the seriousness of the consequences of self-defence can make the use of force in self-defence impermissible. For example, it is not morally permissible that I use lethal force on

[37] Canadian Law Reform Commission, Working Paper No. 29, *Criminal Law The General Part: Liability and Defences* (1982), pp. 90–1. (This quotation is from Yeo, *Compulsion in the Criminal Law*, p. 28.) The Canadian Commission might have chosen a clearer example of so-called excusatory necessity. The sailor's act of *repelling* another might arguably be self-defence, depending on the particular facts of the case. (See my discussion of these sorts of examples in 3.2.) A better example is where a driver swerves into someone on the footpath in order to avoid hitting a boulder on the road.

[38] Although they diverge in their rationale for limiting the scope of the plea of Self-Defence and defence of others. See George Fletcher, 'Proportionality and the Psychotic Aggressor: A Vignette in Comparative Criminal Theory', (1973) 8 *Israel Law Review*, pp. 367–90.

someone as the only available means of preventing her stepping on my toe.

Necessity and proportionality

These moral limits of the right of self-defence are reflected in two essential elements of the common law plea of Self-Defence: necessity and proportionality. These two requirements are sometimes described as different aspects of one general principle: the accused must have acted within the necessity of the occasion.[39] This is a useful general characterization, provided we remember that when speaking of justification in the case of self-defence we are making evaluative judgments about reasonableness and proportionality. The sense of 'necessity' relevant to Self-Defence, and also to the related plea of (justificatory) Necessity, is indispensability or unavoidability, not inevitability or compulsion. The former sense, unlike the latter, is in this context hypothetical: in explaining why a particular degree of force is necessary we refer to some aim, purpose, or end for which, or in the achievement of which, this force is indispensable or unavoidable.[40] (For this reason I am uncomfortable with use of 'excusatory necessity' in excusing an agent for wrongfully succumbing to the pressures of the occasion.)[41]

When the amount of force used has not been excessive, an acquittal is appropriate if the foreseeable injury the agent has inflicted on the aggressor in self-defence was proportionate to the harm the force was intended to prevent. The Criminal Code Bill Commission of 1879 made an exemplary statement of these two conditions of Self-Defence; it also very clearly characterized the common law plea as a justification: 'We take

[39] See Norval Morris and Colin Howard, *Studies in Criminal Law* (Oxford: Clarendon Press, 1964), ch. 4, p. 120; *Russell on Crime*, 12th ed. (1964), vol. 1, p. 680: 'The use of force is lawful; for the necessary defence of self or others or of property; but the justification is limited to the necessity of the occasion'; and A. P. Bates, et al., *The System of Criminal Law*, pp. 500–2.

[40] I discuss this more fully in 3.2 and 4.2.

[41] Yeo, *Compulsion in the Criminal Law*, p. 46, refers to justificatory and excusatory necessity.

one great principle of the common law to be, that though it *sanctions* the defence of a man's person, liberty, and property against illegal violence, and *permits* the use of force to prevent crimes, to preserve the public peace, and to bring offenders to justice, yet all this is subject to the restriction that the force used is necessary; that is, that *the mischief sought to be prevented could not be prevented by less violent means; and that the mischief done by, or which might reasonably be anticipated from, the force used is not disproportioned to the injury or mischief which it is inflicted to prevent'.*[42]

Traditionally, the standard in judging these matters has been the legal objective test, that is, the standard of what was reasonable in the circumstances. The accused must reasonably have judged that the degree of force was necessary in the circumstances to avoid the threatened harm; the circumstances must have been such that a reasonable person in the position of the accused would not have considered that the injury foreseeably inflicted in avoiding the threatened harm was disproportionate.[43]

These two limits of permissible self-defence – necessity and proportionality – are conceptually and morally distinct, and they can raise separate problems. Unfortunately, these two requirements are not always distinguished carefully enough. Conceptual imprecision which can lead to their confusion

---

[42] Quoted by Smith J., in *R v McKay* (1957) V.R. 560 (emphases added). (I owe this reference to A. P. Bates, et al., *The System of Criminal Law*, p. 506.) A. J. Ashworth also clearly distinguishes necessity and proportionality in 'Self-Defence and the Right to Life', *Cambridge Law Journal*, 34 (2), 1975, pp. 296–7. Ashworth quotes the Royal Commission of 1879 as observing that a law whose only requirement was necessity 'would justify every weak lad whose hair was about to be pulled by a stronger one, in shooting the bully if he could not otherwise prevent the assault'. See also George P. Fletcher, 'Passion and Reason in Self-Defense', in *Philosophy of Law*, edited by Conrad Johnson (New York: Macmillan Publishing Co., 1993), pp. 651–2.

[43] The objective test can be stated with varying degrees of objectivity, and jurisdictions differ on this matter. There is an arguable difference between the standard of what the accused reasonably believed in the circumstances, and what a reasonable person in the position of the accused could or would have believed. However, this is not important here.

33

mars some legal judgments about excessive defence (e.g. where a farmer shoots and kills an escaping chicken thief), some recommended codification of the law in this area, and also some philosophical discussions of self-defence.[44] An example of the latter occurs in *Fundamentals of Ethics*, where John Finnis isolates what he regards as a genuine principle of proportionality in Aquinas' claim that an act done with a good intention can be rendered morally bad by being disproportionate to its end. Thus Finnis claims, 'if stunning one's assailant will suffice for self-defence, one must not shoot him through the heart; that would not be proportionate'. We can speak of use of disproportionate force here, provided we recognize that killing is impermissible in this case because it is *unnecessary*: as Finnis says, it inflicts needless harm.[45] Whether killing one's assailant would also inflict disproportionate harm depends on the nature of the harm against which one is defending oneself. For instance, if I really do need to push someone off a cliff in order to prevent her stepping on my toe, use of this force in self-defence would be impermissible because disproportionate to the interest being protected.

Homicide in self-defence: legal justification or excuse?

In his *Commentaries on the Laws of England*, William Blackstone classified homicide *se defendendo* as excusable rather than justified: a private individual has no duty to kill in self-defence, but acts out of necessity or compulsion.[46] To our

---

44 The chicken thief example alludes to *R v McKay* (1957) V.R. 560. However, the conceptual imprecision on which I remark here is not a feature of the leading judgment in that case (in which the distinction between the conditions of necessity and proportionality is clearly drawn by Smith J.), but of *R v Howe* (1958) 100 C.L.R. 448. The *Draft Criminal Code* refers to 'such force as, in the circumstances which exist or which (the accused) believes to exist, is immediately necessary and reasonable', Clause 44 (1).

45 John Finnis, *Fundamentals of Ethics* (Oxford: Clarendon Press, 1983), p. 85. Kent Greenawalt also conflates the distinguishable conditions of necessity and proportionality in his discussion of the justification of Necessity, *Conflicts of Law and Morality* (Oxford University Press, 1989), p. 292.

46 I owe this reference to Hugo Bedau, 'The Right to Life', *The Monist*, vol. 52, 1968, p. 559.

minds there are a number of confusions in this early thinking. First, justified acts can be both morally and legally optional: they can be permissible acts without being acts we are morally or legally obliged to perform. Secondly, Blackstone regarded self-defence as a special case of necessity, and we now recognize necessity as a type of justification. Thirdly, to explain that a person acted *under* compulsion is to offer an excuse for his or her (wrongful) conduct: an act done under compulsion is done without, or against, the person's will. However, there is a sense in which 'compulsion' might express a justification rather than an excuse. In cases of necessary choice of evils, agents sometimes say that in choosing the lesser evil they were compelled to an alternative. Such acts are justified: they are permissible or the right thing to do in the circumstances. Further, even if Blackstone meant that some agents who act in self-defence act *under* compulsion, this would not necessarily preclude the use of force in self-defence being objectively justified conduct. Someone acting under compulsion is not directly responsible for what he or she does. Nevertheless, this agent can do what is objectively permissible or right in the circumstances. If the use of force in self-defence is permissible conduct, the *excuse* of compulsion is inappropriate even if an agent did in fact act under compulsion.

Although our concepts of justification and excuse are more refined than were Blackstone's, the current law of self-defence does not necessarily represent a finely tuned set of moral requirements and distinctions. All the same, Self-Defence is now very widely regarded as a justification. Some legal theorists, Kent Greenawalt for instance, also explicitly recognize 'the right to use otherwise illegal force in self-defense' as a specific exception to the relevant rule, rather than a justified infringement of that rule.[47] This characterization of actual self-defence is essentially correct in my view. Nevertheless, in legal discussions the plea of Self-Defence is occasionally described as an excuse. This description might simply reveal a lack of appreciation of the difference between

[47] *Conflicts of Law and Morality*, p. 286.

justification and excuse; alternatively, it might flow from a denial of the practical importance of a legal distinction between justification and excuse since the plea of Self-Defence is a complete defence. But where it is seriously maintained that the law does not regard the use of force in self-defence as justified, two closely related objections might be urged against the contrary view. The first objection claims that because the criminal law must be realistic, must recognize the limitations of ordinary persons, in accepting self-defence as entirely exculpating the law assumes nothing about justification but simply recognizes the futility of trying to deter people from defending themselves. The second objection claims that the law of self-defence simply rests on a view about how a person under attack can reasonably be expected to behave.

These related objections to the claim that the law regards the use of force in self-defence as justified are unpersuasive. And they are unpersuasive even if we concede that agents often act in self-defence out of fear, and also that a person's desire to defend his or her life against direct attack is a very basic desire which would not be much influenced in practice by the unavailability of a complete legal defence. A very important reason why these objections are unpersuasive is that a successful plea of Self-Defence requires the accused to have been, or (where the plea also covers putative self-defence) to have believed that he or she was, the victim of an *unjust* threat.[48] For instance, a hijacker holding hostages at gunpoint as human shields, who picks off a police sharp-shooter about to fire at him, may act out of fear, may have a very strong, even an irresistible, desire to defend his life, but he cannot plead Self-Defence. In *Leviathan*, Hobbes held that individuals always retain the (liberty) *right* of nature to defend their own lives, even against just punishment.[49] Most

[48] This does not mean that the original aggressor could never plead Self-Defence. The rights and wrongs of a conflict can change. See Yeo's discussion of the law on this matter, *Compulsion in the Criminal Law*, pp. 167–73.

[49] Thomas Hobbes, *Leviathan* (Harmondsworth: Penguin Books, 1974), p. 199. (All further references are to this edition.)

people now do not accept that there is an unqualified right of self-defence; nor, I believe, would most people accept Jenny Teichman's view that an individual retains the right of self-defence irrespective of the rights and wrongs of the original quarrel.[50] And the law accepts neither view.[51]

The law regards actual self-defence against unjust threat as justified, and as a specific exception to the general prohibition of homicide. However, before arguing further for this claim, it is important that I discuss two developments of the law of self-defence, the first of which complicates, and the second of which undermines, the claim that the conditions of the plea of Self-Defence to murder are those of justified homicide. The first development concerns the extension of the plea of Self-Defence to putative self-defence against lawful conduct; the second is a move away from an objective test of one of the elements of Self-Defence as a complete defence.

Lawful conduct and putative self-defence In response to a problem which can arise with putative self-defence against lawful conduct, the Law Reform Commission of Victoria has recommended that the common law condition that the victim's conduct be *unlawful* no longer be a requirement of the plea of Self-Defence.[52] This recommendation, and similar suggested law reform elsewhere, is motivated by examples such as the following: '... a woman is told to stop by an undercover police officer holding a gun. He does not identify himself as a police officer. The police officer has reasonable grounds for believing she is involved in drug-dealing. The woman believes she is about to be killed. She draws a gun and shoots him.'

---

50 *Pacifism and the Just War*, pp. 80–2. The example of the police sharpshooter comes from Teichman.
51 Self-defence is not legally permissible against the necessary and proportionate self-defence of the victim of one's culpable attack. See, e.g. Peter W. Low, *Criminal Law*, St Paul, Minn.: West Publishing Co., 1990, p. 166, and W. LaFave and A. Scott, *Criminal Law*, St Paul, Minn.: West Publishing Co., 1986, pp. 455–9.
52 Law Reform Commission of Victoria, Report No. 40, *Homicide* (1991), p. 99.

The Commission's Report comments: 'There is some doubt under existing law about whether she would be entitled to acquittal on the basis of self-defence because the victim's act was lawful. Such a person should be able to plead self-defence ... Only if the defendant knew that the victim's use of force was lawful or justifiable or was reckless as to whether it was lawful or justifiable should she or he lose the right of self-defence.' It goes on to recommend: 'A person should be entitled to an aquittal on the basis of self-defence even if the victim's conduct was lawful, but only if the person did not know that it was lawful or was (sic) reckless with regard to its lawfulness.'[53]

In the particular example described, the victim's conduct is positively lawful (not simply harmless) although it is believed by the defendant to be an unlawful attack.[54] In this example, the defendant believed that the victim's actions (telling her to stop at gunpoint) were unlawful, and on the basis of this the defendant believed that she was about to be shot in cold blood. This example collapses two issues: one is the problem that Self-Defence is unavailable to the defendant if that plea requires the victim's conduct to have been unlawful; the other is the more general issue of putative self-defence, because although the defendant was treated in an alarming manner, she was not actually about to be killed.[55]

---

[53] Presumably this should be: '... did not know that it was lawful and was not reckless with regard to its lawfulness'.

[54] J. C. Smith discusses similar issues arising from a case of mistaken identity, *Justification and Excuse in the Criminal Law*, pp. 20–7.

[55] As to the former issue, 'unlawful' is commonly defined as not criminal or tortious. So it is worth noting that in cases of self-defence against, e.g. a child or a deranged person (where the victim is not guilty of any offence) Self-Defence does not require the victim's conduct to have been unlawful. Here the victim's conduct is wrongful without being (strictly speaking) unlawful. The *Draft Criminal Code*, Clause 44 (3), deals with this by specifying that for the purposes of the relevant section (44) 'an act is "unlawful" although a person charged with an offence in respect of it would be aquitted on the ground only that – (a) he was under ten years of age; or (b) he lacked the fault required for the offence or believed that an exempting circumstance existed; or (c) he acted in persuance of a reasonable suspicion; or (d) he acted under duress, whether by threats or

One consequence of allowing the victim's conduct to have been lawful is that the plea of Self-Defence could be available to an accused in the following case: an accused, X, kills another person, Y, in circumstances in which Y is engaged in self-defence against X and in which Y could later have pleaded Self-Defence had he or she killed X. Say, as in the Victorian Commission's example, the undercover police officer, Ferret, lawfully holds a gun at (the defendant) D's back, etc. D, believing that she is about to be killed, uses force on Ferret. Under the Commission's recommendation, D could plead Self-Defence. But *then*, Ferret defends himself against D's violent response, killing D. Ferret could plead Self-Defence. Now, if the plea of Self-Defence always implies use of lawful force, both Ferret and D are acting lawfully. However, if D *is* acting lawfully, it would seem that Ferret is not entitled to an aquittal on the basis of Self-Defence if Ferret realizes, but is unable to rectify in time, that D is acting on the mistaken belief that she is about to be killed, and Ferret knows that D can plead Self-Defence. ('An accused is entitled to an aquittal on the basis of self-defence even if the victim's conduct was lawful, but only if the person did not know that it was lawful ...') This particular (presumably unwanted) implication of extending the plea of Self-Defence to putative self-defence can arise because *self-defence* is usually regarded as positively lawful, something the law *permits*: an *exception* to the legal prohibition of private homicide, rather than a justified infringement of that prohibition.

It seems generally undesirable that the law allow one and the same act (e.g. D's violent response) to be both lawful private homicide and at the same time objectively wrongful, an unjust threat to someone who may (presumably) lawfully defend him- or herself. (Because of the special status of police it is, of course, possible for the action of a police officer to be both lawful and, because based on a mistaken belief, objectively a wrongful threat to someone.) In the extended

of circumstances; or (e) he was in a state of automatism or suffering from severe mental illness or severe mental handicap'.

example of Ferret and D, surely only Ferret's response to D (provided it is necessary and proportionate) is lawful self-defence. D's conduct in fact threatens Ferret with imminent, irreparable unjust harm; Ferret's conduct is not in fact an unjust threat to D, even though D reasonably believes otherwise. Even were Ferret to realize that D's threat is agent-perspectivally justified, Ferret should be entitled to an aquittal on the basis of Self-Defence because he knows that D's threat is in fact wrongful.

The law can, if it so wishes, explicitly *permit* putative self-defence even though putative self-defence is objectively unjustified. In that case, homicide in putative self-defence would be lawful homicide, and the above implications would arise. Alternatively, in extending the plea of Self-Defence to putative self-defence, the law might regard homicide in putative self-defence as excusable. In that case, the plea of Self-Defence would cover both justified (lawful) and excusable homicide. In either case, where the plea of Self-Defence covers both actual and putative self-defence, the scope of this plea extends beyond that of the moral *right* of self-defence and the *exception* to the moral prohibition of homicide. This is because only *actual* self-defence is an exception to the moral prohibition of homicide. The *right* of self-defence against unjust aggression does not *itself* include the right to engage in what one wrongly, even if reasonably, believes to be self-defence. In this respect the moral right of self-defence is unlike, e.g. the right to liberty, which *itself* permits one to act in ways which one reasonably believes will enhance one's freedom, even if they in fact thwart or destroy it. The dissimilarity between these two rights stems from the fact that in the case of self-defence, the permissibility of *self-preference* requires *the positive right to use force on someone else in protecting one's own proportionate interest*. This positive right, in turn, depends on the abrogation of the moral status of an unjust aggressor in comparison with that of an unoffending person. (I explain and defend these claims in chapters 4 and 5.) Putative self-defence, however reasonable this conduct might be from the perspective of the agent in the circumstances, is not part of the exercise of the positive right of self-defence.[56]

Self-defence against an actual unjust threat is positively lawful: a specific exception to the prohibition of homicide, not a justified or an excusable infringement of that prohibition. Putative self-defence can be agent-perspectivally justified; nevertheless, putative self-defence both wrongs its victim (violates his or her rights) and is objectively unjustified. Because this is so, it would seem better that the law regard homicide in putative self-defence as excusable rather than lawful where, in recognition of the fact that putative self-defence can be agent-perspectivally justified, the plea of Self-Defence is available to putative self-defenders. The plea of Self-Defence, so extended, would be either a justification (in the case of actual self-defence) or a complete excuse (in the case of justified[ii] putative self-defence). However, because 'self-defence' very strongly suggests *lawful* homicide, where one and the same plea covers both actual and putative self-defence, in principle it would seem preferable that some more general term or description be used, rather than the common law term 'self-defence'.[57]

Justification and reasonable beliefs   The second development of the law of self-defence, which undermines the characterization of the conditions of the plea of Self-Defence to murder as those of justified homicide, involves a move away from an objective test of one of the elements of Self-Defence as a complete defence.

[56] In commenting that the defendant should lose 'the right of self-defence' only if she knew that the victim's conduct was lawful, or was reckless as to whether it was, the Law Reform Commission of Victoria appears to equate the extension of the *plea* of Self-Defence (in order to allow acquittal in some cases of putative self-defence against lawful conduct), with possession of a *right* of self-defence against lawful conduct.

[57] In covering both actual and putative self-defence, the *Draft Criminal Code* does not use 'self-defence' in the relevant recommendation, Clause 44. But with codification, use of the name of the common law defence is bound to continue in the absence of a broader term to cover both actual and putative self-defence. Fletcher claims that under American law there

In the case of *actual* self-defence the accused need not believe that he or she is under *unlawful* attack: the accused may defend him- or herself against a wrongful attack which he or she knows is not an offence because, for example, the attacker is obviously a young child or insane. However, for actual or putative self-defence to be justified[ii], the agent must believe on reasonable grounds that he or she is the victim of an *objectively wrongful* threat. (Ferret might realize that D's response is justified[ii]; but for Ferret's self-defence then to be justified[ii], Ferret must justifiably[ii] believe that D's response is not justified[i].) There are clear examples, perhaps the clearest being where a culpable unjust aggressor defends him- or herself against the victim's legitimate self-defence, in which an agent will know that the threat to him or her is not wrongful.

If the plea of Self-Defence is to represent an *agent-perspectival justification* in the case of *putative* self-defence, then in my view the standard required of the accused on each of three counts cannot be more subjective than that of belief which is justified[ii]. These three counts are: the agent's belief about the existing circumstances (that he or she is under a particular threat, e.g. about to be knifed); the agent's belief that the degree of force used is necessary to ward off the threat (necessity); and the agent's belief that what is necessary for self-defence is not disproportionate to the threat (proportionality). Another way of expressing this standard is to say that the particular agent in the circumstances must have held these three beliefs on good or reasonable grounds. This accords with the present law of self-defence in Australia which invokes a standard of reasonableness on all three counts, whilst allowing for the exigency of the situation.[58]

is no distinction between putative and actual self-defence, 'Passion and Reason in Self-Defense', p. 654.

[58] *Zedevic v DPP* (1987) 162 C.L.R. 645; *Dziduch*, C.C.A., NSW, (1990) 47 A. Crim. R. 378. See also Yeo's discussion, *Compulsion in the Criminal Law*, pp. 208–10. Nevertheless, Australian courts tend to collapse the second and third counts (necessity and proportionality) by referring to a single test of whether the force used by the accused was reasonably proportionate to the danger which the accused believed he or she faced. Further, while

However, Australian and English law differ on this matter, the latter having now adopted the requirement of honest belief as sufficient in respect of the accused's belief about the nature of the existing circumstances. (Some American commentators claim that honest belief on this count is sufficient for the defence; others say that this belief must be reasonable in the circumstances.)[59] A highly influential element in the English adoption of this subjective standard in the case of self-defence has been the view that an accused's honest belief that he or she is not acting unlawfully is sufficient to negate the mental element of crimes of violence including murder.[60] This mental element is said to be the intent to apply unlawful force to the victim; it is then argued that the defendant's belief that the force was not unlawful cancels this mental element. It seems to me that an unlawful intent is not necessarily an intent to act unlawfully: an unlawful intent is simply the necessary *mens rea* of the offence; and in the case of any crime of violence it is a substantive question as to whether or not the *mens rea* requires the intention to inflict unlawful force. However, it is not part of my concern to buy into a debate about the development of English common law on

it is very important to allow for the exigency of the situation in determining whether in the circumstances the defendant had reasonable grounds for a belief, to over-emphasize factors such as duress, or the defendant's confusion or fear as the grounds of exculpation, is to make self-defence more like an excuse than a justification. Paul H. Robinson comments on the inappropriate, not uncommon 'commixture of justification and excuse' in self-defence provisions of American law, *Criminal Law Defenses* (St Paul, Minn.: West Publishing Co., 1984), vol. 1, p. 110. For a philosophical instance of this commixture, see Nancy Davis, 'Abortion and Self-Defense', *Philosophy and Public Affairs*, vol. 13, no. 3, 1984, p. 186.

59 See, e.g. F. Lee Bailey and Henry B. Rothblatt, *Crimes of Violence* (vol. 1): *Homicide and Assault* (New York: The Lawyers Cooperative Publishing Co., 1973), p. 485; Low, *Criminal Law*, p. 168; and LaFave and Scott, *Criminal Law*, pp. 457–8.

60 *Draft Criminal Code*, Part 7, Paragraph 7. 3 (i), p. 185. *R v Williams* (1987) 3 All E.R. 411 held that the mental element necessary to constitute guilt is intent to apply unlawful force to the victim. Hence, the defendant's belief, however unreasonable, that the force was not unlawful cancels the necessary mental element; conviction is not appropriate on the basis of recklessness.

this matter.[61] One Canadian commentator argues that if the circumstances of self-defence negate the offence elements of murder – either the *mens rea* or the *actus reus* – then the defence is not Self-Defence but lack of *mens rea* or *actus reus*, as the case may be; and in this case the accused is not advancing the justification of self-defence and need not comply with the requirements of the defence.[62] Australian cases have taken the view that the direction of self-defence assumes that the ingredients of the offence charged have been made out, even where those elements are denied.[63]

On the surface, by not giving a name to the proposed codified defence, the *Draft Criminal Code* avoids the question of whether the plea of Self-Defence is always a justification, or sometimes an excuse. The *Draft Criminal Code*, Clause 44 (1), simply states that: 'A person does not commit an offence by using such force as, in the circumstances which exist or which he believes to exist, is immediately necessary and reasonable ... (c) to protect himself or another from unlawful force or unlawful personal harm ...' However, alongside its apparent abrogation of the *Dadson* principle, this provision also represents the prevailing trend in English common law in undermining Self-Defence as a justificatory defence. In so doing it raises a substantive issue of criminal justice ethics that ought to be of concern. Whatever the merits of the argument that because the accused's actual belief in the lawful nature of his or her conduct defeats a definitional element of crimes of violence, a mistaken belief need not be reasonable in order to afford a defence; it is one thing to maintain that a person, X, is not guilty of murder if X kills Y because X foolishly believes Y is attacking him, and another thing to hold that in these circumstances X is not guilty of any offence provided his use of lethal force would have been immediately necessary and reasonable in the circumstances which he believed to exist.

[61] See Yeo's careful critique, *Compulsion in the Criminal Law*, pp. 198–208.
[62] A. W. Mewett, 'Murder and Intent: Self-Defence and Provocation', (1984) 27 *Criminal Law Quarterly* 433. (I owe this reference to Yeo, *Compulsion in the Criminal Law*, p. 205, n22.)
[63] See *Dziduch*, C.C.A., NSW, (1990) 47 A. Crim. R. at 379.

The *Draft Criminal Code* does regard the reasonableness of the accused's belief in the nature of the existing circumstances as relevant to the defence in an evidentiary way: it requires courts and juries to consider whether the accused had reasonable grounds for this belief in coming to a view about whether the accused in fact held this belief.[64] But honest, unreasonable beliefs about circumstances are possible; further, we know that some people (e.g. the paranoid and those who jump to conclusions) do hold such beliefs. Of course, an honest, unreasonable belief can sometimes *excuse* a person's conduct, either partly or entirely. But whether or not, and to what extent, an unreasonable belief in the existing circumstances constitutes an excuse for wrongful conduct depends on the degree to which the agent is responsible and culpable for holding this belief and for acting on it. The fact that a homicide would have been justified had the circumstances been as the accused believed them to be, is not itself a justification of the act; nor do these conditions unquestionably completely excuse the agent of culpability.[65]

Further, given the circumstances which existed or which the accused believed to exist, the *Draft Criminal Code* requires the degree of force used to have been 'immediately necessary and reasonable' (necessity and proportionality), this being a matter of judgment by the jury. The *Draft Criminal Code* recommends that an accused be guilty of manslaughter where the force used was excessive, where it went beyond what was 'immediately necessary and reasonable' in the circumstances which existed or which the accused believed to exist (Clauses 55 and 59). If, for argument's sake, we accept the claim that in respect of the accused's belief in the existing

---

64 *Draft Criminal Code*, Clause 14, p. 50. See also *R v Williams* (1987) at 415.
65 The Law Reform Commission of Victoria's Report recommends (contra *Zedevic v DPP* (1987)) that the objective test for the defence of self-defence to murder be abolished, p. 98. This recommendation is made with the provision that someone whose beliefs are very unreasonable may be convicted of manslaughter by gross negligence or culpable homicide.

circumstances, an honest belief that he or she was acting lawfully defeats a definitional element of murder, this does not itself justify the adoption of different standards for a complete defence: a wholly subjective standard in the case of the accused's belief in the existing circumstances, and (against that background) an objective standard as to the necessity and reasonableness of the force used. In response, it has been suggested that different standards are appropriate in matters of fact and matters of value. But even if this is so (and it needs to be argued), the different standards as applied to the ingredients of a complete defence (of private defence) in the *Draft Criminal Code* do not straightforwardly correspond to a distinction between matters of fact and matters of value. Certainly a value judgment is involved in requiring an objective standard as to the necessity and reasonableness of the force used. But the accused's belief in the existing circumstances is a belief about a matter of fact; the judgment that the force used was proportionate is a value judgment; and the judgment that a particular degree of force was necessary to resist or repel a particular (believed) threat is a judgment pertaining to a matter of fact.[66] The conditions of the plea of Self-Defence, or its codified counterpart, do not seem to express clear principles and differences of culpability in allowing that an accused's unreasonable belief about the existing circumstances is a complete defence to murder where the degree of force used would have been necessary and reasonable were the circumstances to have been as the accused believed them to be, whereas 'use of excessive force' is a partial excuse where the circumstances were actually as the accused believed them to be. Someone who makes a grossly negligent mistake about the circumstances can be aquitted; whereas someone who is actually being attacked will be convicted of manslaughter if he or she uses force beyond

[66] In 3.2, I argue that evaluative considerations, such as that an alternative means of defence would involve an unacceptable risk or cost, must sometimes form part of the normative background against which necessity is judged. But they do not always do so.

what is judged to have been necessary and reasonable in the circumstances.[67]

Defence of others and pleas related to Self-Defence

The extension of Self-Defence to putative self-defence complicates, and the adoption of a subjective test of one of the elements of the defence undermines, the claim that the conditions of the plea of Self-Defence to murder are always those of justified homicide. However, other aspects of Self-Defence as a defence to murder, together with a comparison between Self-Defence and the related pleas of Necessity, Duress, and also Provocation, strongly reinforce the claim that the law regards the use of necessary and proportionate force in actual self-defence against an unjust threat as justified. First, although we usually speak of self-defence in a strict sense in which self-defence is distinguishable from defence of another person, in legal contexts 'Self-Defence' is sometimes used more widely and extends to defence of others.[68] Self-defence and defence of others have also been regarded as *morally* on a par, for instance by George Fletcher, who claims that the moral right to repel an attack lends itself to universalization, and this being so, any third person should be able to intervene on behalf of the victim. Fletcher also asserts that western legal systems now recognize the right of third-party intervention as a matter of course.[69]

Fletcher's particular equation of self-defence and third-party intervention (defence of others) characterizes self-defence as a justification according to the stronger standard of justification (right act). Even against this standard, Fletcher's equation of self-defence and third-party intervention oversimplifies both the moral and legal positions. In some respects

[67] See Yeo's detailed critique of the differences between English and Australian law on this and related issues, *Compulsion in the Criminal Law*, pp. 198–226. I am grateful to David Farrier, David Neal, and Stanley Yeo for discussing the issues in the last three paragraphs with me.

[68] Sometimes 'private defence' is used to cover both.

[69] George Fletcher, 'The Right to Life', *The Monist*, vol. 63, 1980, p. 140.

the justification of defence of others can be morally more complicated than that of self-defence. Most people will disagree with Hobbes, and will believe that individuals have a right but not an absolute duty to preserve themselves. A *discretionary* right of self-defence might not extend to third-party intervention where the victim decides against exercising this right.[70] Further, those directly involved in a conflict are often in a better position to judge the facts – including the rights and wrongs of the conflict itself – than are third parties: what to an outsider might seem obvious unjust aggression by one party towards another may not be such. (Greenawalt mentions the case of *People v Young*, in which a man came upon two middle-aged men beating and struggling with a youth.[71] Reasonably believing the youth was being unlawfully assaulted, Young intervened violently. The two men turned out to be plain clothes policemen trying to arrest the youth.) A third, more fundamental concern with Fletcher's equation of self-defence and third-party intervention is the possibility that there is not a general right of self-defence which is universalizable in the way that Fletcher claims it is. Some writers argue, for instance, that self-defence against a morally innocent aggressor, and the use of lethal force against an aggressor in defence of an interest other than life, are both agent-relative permissions confined to the person who is being attacked.[72] Phillip Montague argues, in the opposite direction to that pursued by Fletcher, that the right of self-defence against a culpable unjust aggressor is unproblematic because it follows from the obligation of third-party interven-

[70] I owe this point to Hugh LaFollette. (The point is refined in chapter 5.) Further, the alter ego rule (see Low, *Criminal Law*, p. 169, and LaFave and Scott, *Criminal Law*, p. 462) – that a third party is privileged to defend another only when this other person is privileged to make a defence – does not entail that a third party is privileged to defend another whenever the other person is privileged to make a defence. LaFave and Scott, p. 464, wrongly say that this rule holds that the right to defend another is 'coextensive' with the right of the other to defend himself.

[71] 'The Perplexing Borders of Justification and Excuse', p. 1919, n65.

[72] In 'Innumerate Ethics', *Philosophy and Public Affairs*, vol. 7, no. 4, 1978, Derek Parfit describes one person's killing another in order to save *his own* arm as an agent-relative permission.

tion on behalf of the innocent victim.[73] Montague's argument also leaves open the question of whether in some cases of self-defence the permission is agent-relative. (At various points in chapters 3, 4, and 5, I discuss the possibility that the right of self-defence is sometimes an agent-relative permission.)

The *Draft Criminal Code* groups self-defence, in the strict sense, and defence of others.[74] However, English case law has tended to avoid explicit recognition of a private right to intervene in defence of others, instead sanctioning intervention which would receive the whole-hearted moral approval of most people in terms of the very general private right to act in prevention of a felony.[75] This rationale could be either useless or fictional in a situation in which a third person intervenes against an aggressor who does not even seem to be committing any offence (e.g. a very young child or someone suffering from automatism). Nevertheless, the law does permit third-party intervention, and with the exception of defence of someone very close to the accused, the explanation is clearly not that the defendant's intervention is excusable because it is an inevitable natural response.[76] The *right* of private defence extends to the defence of third persons generally and is not confined to defence of close relatives;[77] the use of necessary and proportionate force by a third party who intervenes in defence of the victim of unjust aggression is legally *permissible*, not legally excusable.

The fact that the scope of the plea of Self-Defence can also extend to defence of interests other than life also supports the claim that the law regards the use of force in self-defence as justified. This particular extension of the *moral* right of self-defence is also frequently assumed. George Fletcher, for example, claims that threatened rape is a relatively non-

---

[73] Phillip Montague, 'Self Defense and Choosing Between Lives', *Philosophical Studies*, vol. 40, 1981, p. 216.

[74] The *Draft Criminal Code*, Clause 44, (1) (c), p. 61.

[75] See, e.g. *R v Duffy* (1967) 1 Q.B. 63, *R v Williams* (1987) 3 All E.R. 411.

[76] The often cited case of Kitty Genovese shows that defence of others is not an inevitable response.

[77] See J. C. Smith, *Justification and Excuse in the Criminal Law*, p. 123.

controversial case of aggression generating a right of self-defence which includes use of deadly force.[78] There is, of course, often the grave risk that a victim of rape will be killed or seriously injured; and this can also be true of the victims of assault, kidnap, and even some property offences. However, the legal permissibility of using lethal force against 'the most extreme intrusions on freedom of the person (e.g., kidnapping and rape)', which do not immediately threaten life, need not depend on this risk.[79] People are likely to disagree about proportionality in the case of defensive homicide against, e.g. rape, in some circumstances in which the victim is clearly not at risk of being killed or physically injured. This being so, it is very difficult to maintain that the law simply condones the use of lethal force in the protection of some interests other than life because, the use of such force being inevitable, any attempt legally to deter it would be pointless.

Further, lack of a complete defence to murder is unlikely to deter killing in some circumstances of provocation, necessity and duress. So another important consideration in characterizing the use of force in self-defence as legally permissible is a comparison of the plea of Self-Defence with the related pleas of Necessity, Duress and Provocation. Until recently the plea of Provocation reduced murder to manslaughter only if it was accepted that a reasonable person in the circumstances of the accused would have lost self-control sufficiently to form an intention to kill. Arguably this standard – that a *reasonable* person in the circumstances *would* have lost self-control in this way – is sufficiently strong to warrant Provocation so defined being a complete defence. This is

[78] 'The Right to Life', p. 139.
[79] LaFave and Scott, *Criminal Law*, p. 456. It is doubtful that Self-Defence is admissible where the accused has used lethal force to prevent interference with property (say to prevent invasion of a dwelling house) unless the particular circumstances of the property offence made it reasonable for the accused to believe that the invader intended to commit a felony. (See again LaFave and Scott, p. 465.) George P. Fletcher states as a 'peculiarity of New York law' that it allows a plea of Self-Defence to be based on a robbery about to be committed, where there might be minimal threat of assault, 'Passion and Reason in Self-Defense', p. 652.

because, where this standard is met, it seems unreasonable to expect the accused not to have lost self-control sufficiently to form an intention to kill. If it is unreasonable to expect someone not to have lost self-control sufficiently to form an *intention* to kill, can it be reasonable to expect this person to have maintained sufficient self-control not to have acted on this intention? Those who maintain that this strong standard of Provocation does not warrant a complete defence need to provide a plausible argument for the answer 'yes'.

Suitably defined, Provocation is a paradigm mitigating circumstance. Provocation is a *partial excuse* for murder: an excuse which recognizes that although the accused's conduct fell below a standard with which it is reasonable to expect people to comply, and was wrongful and culpable, this was due to a loss of self-control on the part of the accused which in the circumstances was sufficiently humanly understandable to make it appropriate to convict him or her of a lesser offence than murder. (In jurisdictions where 'murder' is reserved for the most serious homicide offence, Provocation is appropriate as a partial excuse which reduces murder to manslaughter. In jurisdictions which recognize degrees of murder, Provocation could excuse murder to a degree.) The rationale of the plea of Provocation, *as a partial excuse*, is better captured by the weaker standard increasingly emphasized in case law. According to this standard, Provocation requires there to have been conduct which could have caused an ordinary person of reasonable firmness and with the characteristics of the accused to lose self-control sufficiently to form an intention to kill.[80] Yet even on this weaker standard of loss of self-control, lack of a complete legal defence could be at least as feeble a deterrent to someone *really* so affected as to someone who is being attacked.[81] Even so, Provocation is a

[80] See *R v Stingel* (1990) 65 A.L.J.R. 141, at 147.
[81] This weaker standard has been criticized on a number of counts – one being that its threshold of self-control (that an ordinary person *could* have lost self-control) is too low. Both the *Draft Criminal Code* and the Law Reform Commission of Victoria's Report No. 40, *Homicide* (1991), favour a much more straightforward test of Provocation which requires a sufficiently substantial reason for loss of self-control and which allows

partial excuse for murder; Self-Defence is a complete defence. The Law Reform Commission of Victoria states this difference as follows: in the case of provocation 'a person is not *entitled* to kill or *justified* in killing, as in the case of self-defence ... Rather the partial defence recognises that, in extreme cases, a person is culpable but cannot be treated as fully responsible for his or her actions.'[82]

The law clearly *permits* self-help and 'an individual's right to life to override the social duty not to use force' only in cases of sudden attack or (where putative defence is deemed permissible) believed sudden attack. But the orthodox legal rationale for this stand does not sharply distinguish the plea of Self-Defence from the related pleas of Necessity and Duress. For it may also be arguable on the facts in cases where (were they admissible) Necessity and Duress would apply, that 'the protection of society and its laws is no longer effective', the individual alone being 'left to protect his right to life and physical security'.[83] The conditions under which homicide in self-defence is lawful – necessity and proportionality – might sometimes be arguable in cases of claimed necessity, for instance in the famous leading case of *Dudley and Stephens*, where after twenty days adrift in an open dinghy two shipwrecked sailors killed and ate the cabin boy so that they and a third man might survive.[84] Dudley and Stephens were convicted of murder, even though the jury accepted that 'if the three men had not fed upon the body of the boy they would probably not have survived to be so

the jury to address the defendant's liability for murder directly. The Law Reform Commission of Victoria's Report recommends that '(w)here a person suffers a loss of self-control as a result of provocation ... and intentionally kills or is a party to a killing of another, he or she is not guilty of murder but guilty of manslaughter if, in all the circumstances, including any of the defendant's personal characteristics, there is a sufficient reason to reduce the offence from murder to manslaughter', p. 84. This is a modified version of the *Draft Criminal Code* provision, Clause 58, p. 68.

[82] *Homicide*, p. 72 (emphases original).

[83] The above three quoted phrases are from A. J. Ashworth, 'Self-Defence and the Right to Life', pp. 282–3.

[84] *R v Dudley and Stephens* (1884) 14 Q.B.D. 273.

picked up and rescued', and further 'that the boy being in a much weaker condition was likely to have died before them'. (Later, such considerations served to mitigate the sentence.) In cases of duress there is the additional, important argument for leniency: that the will of the accused was overborne. Yet in these other circumstances we are faced with either breaking the criminal law or else being at the mercy of those forces which would overpower us. We are legally expected to forgo even vital interests rather than protect them by intentionally killing unoffending persons.

The status of both Necessity and Duress as admissible defences to murder is dubious. Where Duress has been admitted by the courts as a defence to murder it has been restricted to aiders and abetters (those who have not participated in the actual killing) and has been only a partial excuse, reducing murder to manslaughter.[85] The present direction of English common law seems to be away from admitting Duress as any defence to murder. *R v Howe* (1987) affirmed that Duress is not a defence to murder.[86] In that landmark case, some of the Lords expressed the view that if Duress were to be recognized as a defence to murder the proper means to effect such a reform is parliamentary. But others rejected Duress outright as a defence to murder on the basis of authority and by appealing to the necessary connection of law and morality in the matter of protecting the lives of innocent persons. The recognition of both Necessity and Duress as defences to murder has been raised more openly – albeit somewhat tremulously – in Australian and English reports which aim at codification of the law of homicide. For example, the Law Reform Commission of Victoria's Report No. 40, *Homicide* (1991), recommends that Duress and Neces-

---

[85] *DPP for Northern Ireland v Lynch* (1975) A.C. 653, and *Abbott v The Queen* (1977) A.C. 755; *R v McConnell, McFarland and Holland* (1977) 1 N.S.W.L.R. 714; *R v Harding* (1976) V.R. 129; *R v Evans and Gardiner* (no. 1) (1976) V.R. 517. See also Stanley Yeo, *Compulsion in the Criminal Law*, pp. 144, n165, for details of Australian and Canadian common law on this matter.

[86] *R v Howe* (1987) A.C. 417. *R v Gotts* (1992) 1 All E.R. 832 held that Duress is not available as a defence to a charge of attempted murder, since Duress is not a defence to murder.

sity be available as defences to murder, but notes that three (out of seven) of the Commissioners, including the Chairman and Deputy Chairperson, disagreed.[87] Despite considerable academic criticism of *Howe* (1987), and the fact that the English Law Commission had in its Report prior to *Howe* recommended that Duress should be a defence to all crimes, the *Draft Criminal Code* explicitly excludes both duress by threats (Duress) and duress of circumstances (Necessity) as defences to murder or attempted murder.[88] However, these exclusions are contained in square brackets, with the comment that this is in order to indicate that the earlier recommendation has not been abandoned![89]

It might be claimed that the legal permissibility of homicide in self-defence does not reflect the judgment that, whereas the intentional killing of unoffending persons in circumstances of necessity and duress is morally wrong, the use of force in self-defence is morally justified. Rather, it might be argued, the law permits private individuals to use lethal force against unjust aggressors simply in order to deter unjust aggression. In contrast, Duress and Necessity are unavailable as defences to murder because the law seeks to deter people from killing unoffending persons under duress and in circumstances of necessity. Some judicial decisions and some legal commentaries certainly suggest this alternative, more utilitarian explanation of the law in this area. For instance, the predicted dire social consequences of allowing Duress and

---

[87] *Homicide*, p. 106.

[88] *Draft Criminal Code*, Clause 43 (3) (a), p. 61, and Part 12, Paragraph 12.13, p. 229.

[89] I think there are good reasons for admitting Necessity and Duress as defences to murder. (See my 'Killing Under Duress'.) However, the Law Reform Commission of Victoria characterizes Duress and Necessity as complete defences. In my view, the sympathetic examples cited in the Commission's Report in favour of admitting Necessity as a complete defence to murder – cases of justified risk taking – need to be distinguished somehow from cases in which Necessity and Duress ought to be admissible defences to murder but not wholly exculpating. Some cases of killing in circumstances of necessity and duress, whilst distinguishable from 'cold blooded killing', are nevertheless *culpable* homicide. (See also chapter 4, n18.)

Necessity as defences to murder were clearly never far from the minds of some of the judges in *Howe* (1987). But at the same time they, together with others who have urged this consideration, also emphasized what they took to be an obvious, very weighty moral justification for the legal distinction between homicide in self-defence and killing in cases of necessity and duress.[90] Although alternative explanations are possible, the reasoning behind the distinction between these related defences most often appeals to the different moral status of the person killed in self-defence. A person killed in self-defence is an unjust aggressor, whereas someone killed under duress or in circumstances of necessity is not him- or herself an unjust threat to the accused. To kill an unoffending person intentionally in order to protect one's own interests violates a principle widely accepted as morally fundamental, and accepted by some as a moral absolute or near-absolute. The fundamental principle of the 'inviolability of innocent human life' is explicitly invoked in judicial rejections of both Necessity and Duress as defences to murder. The plea of Necessity was not admitted as a defence to murder in the case of *Dudley and Stephens* because Necessity was interpreted as a justification, and it was held that the deliberate killing of an 'innocent and unoffending' boy was wrongful homicide.[91] Whereas homicide in self-defence is regarded as justified self-preferential killing, the killing of the cabin boy was held to have been unjustified self-preference on the part of Dudley and Stephens in the circumstances. In rejecting Duress as a defence to murder, judicial concern has been about Duress as an *excuse for deliberate wrongdoing* of this type, and about the wider social consequences of allowing Duress, as an *excuse for deliberate wrongful homicide*, as a defence to murder.

A number of prominent philosophers and jurisprudents

---

90 Echoing Lord Coleridge's judgment in *Dudley and Stephens* about Necessity as a defence to murder, Lord Hailsham argued in *Howe* (1987) that to allow Duress as a defence to murder would be to divorce law and morality on this matter. See also, e.g. Anthony Kenny, 'Duress *Per Minas* as a Defence to Crime II', (1982) *Law and Philosophy* 1, pp. 197–205.

91 The ruling in this case, far from now being anachronistic, was reaffirmed by the House of Lords in *Howe* (1987).

who invoke the principle of the inviolability of innocent human life seek to distinguish homicide in self-defence from impermissible self-preferential killing in terms of one or other of two general lines of argument. These two general lines of argument are probably the most commonly exploited in philosophical thinking about the justification of homicide in self-defence. The first is based on the idea that homicide in self-defence can be justified as unintended killing; the second claims that the victim of homicide in self-defence has lost or forfeited the right to life. I examine these lines of argument in detail in chapters 4 and 5, and I argue in 4.3 that there is a very important, sometimes suppressed, connection between them. In this present chapter, I have maintained that homicide in (actual) self-defence is widely regarded as morally justified and a positive right, and that the law in this area reflects this view. However the claim that self-defence is morally justified and a positive right describes not one, but a range of views with possible variations at points within that range. I identify and discuss these variations in the next chapter, in the context of an examination of probably the most explicit and influential philosophical approach to the justification of self-defence, that of natural law.

Chapter 3

Self-defence and natural law[1]

The moral permissibility of homicide in self-defence has been widely held to be derivable from natural law. Natural law has directly and indirectly shaped much western philosophical thinking about the principles of justified self-defence. Indeed the two major lines of thought about justified self-defence are to be found in natural law accounts. The first of these two lines emphasizes the claimed moral importance of the self-defending agent's intention to the permissibility of homicide in self-defence; the second maintains that the permissibility of self-preference in the case of self-defence derives from the abrogated moral status of an unjust aggressor compared with that of the unoffending victim. I discuss these two general lines of argument in detail in chapters 4 and 5. In this present chapter, I examine a number of influential natural law accounts of self-defence, drawing from these accounts the important details of two strands which correspond to the two lines of argument that I have just mentioned.[2]

[1] This chapter and part of chapter 5 draw on material from my article 'Self-Defense and Natural Law', *The American Journal of Jurisprudence*, vol. 36, 1991, pp. 73–101.

[2] The concern of my discussion of natural law accounts of self-defence is their contribution to elucidating the principles relevant to self-defence as a justification of homicide. I do not compare the development of the common law of self-defence with the development of philosophical thinking about the relevant principles. However, my reading of accounts of the development of English law, e.g. William Blackstone, *Commentaries on the Laws of England*, vol. iv, 9th ed. (reprint of the 1783 ed.) (New York: Garland Publishing, Inc., 1978), ch. 14, and T. A. Green, *Verdict According to Conscience* (Chicago: University of Chicago Press, 1985), ch. 3, suggests that such a comparison might make a complex and interesting study.

Philosophers who argue from natural law emphasize various grounds and conditions of justified self-defence, and they leave open possible, and sometimes reveal actual, differences in the scope and strength of the permission involved. These differences expose important issues which are not, and should not be, confined to natural law justifications of self-defence. These issues must be addressed by any full account of justified self-defence. Not all natural law accounts address all or even most of the issues that I am about to list, nor where they discuss or allude to some do they necessarily do so in the terms which I use. The more important possibilities which these accounts expose can overlap in scope, and even within the groupings listed immediately below are not always mutually exclusive.

3.1 POSSIBLE DIFFERENCES IN SCOPE AND STRENGTH

The strength of the moral permission (i)

(a) Self-defence might be an agent-relative permission, its permissibility deriving from the legitimate desire for self-preservation and a view about the type and amount of self-sacrifice that is unreasonably required of people. This permission to defend oneself in certain ways against particular threats would not itself imply that one may similarly defend other people (except perhaps one's close relatives) in circumstances where these others may defend themselves; (b) Individuals might be thought to have a more full-bodied right of self-defence, which itself implies the legitimacy of assistance by others (even strangers), as well as the legitimacy of assisting others, in the exercise of this right; (c) Individuals might be thought to have no moral obligation to refrain from self-defence; however it might be held that it is sometimes, even mostly, morally better that they not defend themselves; (d) Self-defence might be thought not only permissible or a right in the full-bodied sense, but also mostly, even always, a duty. (This right of self-defence is not discretionary.) This duty the individual has to him- or herself (or even to God) independently of any duty (say) to dependants or to society; this duty

58

might, although need not, be absolute. One might, for instance, have a duty to defend oneself except at very great cost to others or at the expense of something which one rightly values more than one's own life or limb.

Some natural law theorists discuss self-defence in terms of rights, duties and justification, whereas others (including Aquinas) maintain that self-defence is morally permissible.

The relevance of fault and guilt (ii)

(a) Self-defence might be thought permissible only against culpable unjust aggressors or those (reasonably) believed so; (b) Self-defence might be thought permissible against non-culpable unjust aggressors (e.g. young children, the psychotic, unwitting threats, etc.); (c) Non-aggressors (e.g. innocent bystanders, hostages) might or might not be thought permissibly harmed in the course of self-defence; (d) Self-defence might or might not be thought sometimes permissible against just violence, or against force which from the perspective of the aggressor appears not to be unjust, or to be permissible at some stage irrespective of the rights and wrongs of the original conflict.[3]

The relevance of proportionality (iii)

(a) Proportionality might or might not be thought a necessary condition of permissible self-defence. As explained in chapter 2, proportionality is distinguishable from the requirement that the degree of force used in self-defence not exceed what is necessary in the circumstances to avoid the infliction of a particular harm. Necessary force can inflict disproportionate harm (my warding off a slap on the arm might push the offender off a tall building); (b) Considerations such as an aggressor's culpability and the victim's innocence, the number of aggressors foreseeably injured in self-defence, and also the interests of third parties who are either threatened by

---

[3] See Teichman on Hobbes, *Pacifism and the Just War*, pp. 82–3.

the aggression or foreseeably directly or indirectly harmed by defensive action, might or might not be thought relevant to the permissibility of self-defence. (These possibilities, together with those in (ii) (a)–(c), suggest mixed views on two of the issues grouped under (i); for instance, the view that killing a non-culpable unjust aggressor is only an agent-relative permission, whereas the right (or duty) to kill a culpable unjust aggressor implies the legitimacy of assistance from others.)

What proportionality requires (iv)

Self-defence which foreseeably kills or grievously injures the aggressor might or might not be thought permissible only against a threat of the same type of harm. The requirement of proportionality can leave open whether prevention of a particular harm (e.g. rape, assault, theft) could itself warrant killing someone. Where one's life is threatened it might be thought permissible to kill if necessary; but if one kills in order to avoid, e.g. loss of a limb, this might be thought permissible or, alternatively, wrong but excusable. (This suggests possible mixed views on some of the issues grouped under (i) and (ii); for instance, the view that individuals have a right to defend their own lives by killing if necessary, and that this implies the legitimacy of assistance from others, but that killing in defence of (say) a limb is an agent-relative permission; or the view that the aggressor's culpability affects proportionality, making killing in self-defence a right in the more full-bodied sense, rather than, as in the case of a non-culpable unjust aggressor, an agent-relative permission.)

The relevance of intention (v)

Homicide in self-defence might or might not be thought permissible only where the death of the aggressor (and possibly others who will be killed) is unintended.

3.2 A RANGE OF VIEWS

The nature and strength of the permission

From the above possibilities we can describe an extreme view, one which few would accept, and one which might seem the antithesis of any possible position derivable from natural law. This is the view that we have an absolute natural right and duty to defend ourselves by any means necessary, at whatever cost to others, irrespective of the nature of the threat to us.

This is not an unfair description of what Hobbes says in *Leviathan* about natural law and self-preservation in the State of Nature. Hobbes maintains that natural rights are liberties, the essence of a right being that its exercise is discretionary. Yet it follows from what Hobbes says about self-preservation (namely, that self-preservation is a Law of Nature, and that we cannot act other than for this end) that self-defence can be a dictate of natural law, and will be what natural law mostly requires. To use terminology which Hobbes explicitly rejects as conceptually and morally confused, self-preservation, which can imply self-defence, would seem to be for Hobbes both a natural right and a natural obligation.[4]

---

[4] At the start of chapter 14, Hobbes defines 'The Right of Nature', 'Liberty', and 'A Law of Nature' as follows: 'The Right of Nature *Jus Naturale*, is the Liberty each man hath, to use his power, as he will himselfe, for the preservation of his own Nature; that is to say, of his own life; and consequently, of doing any thing, which in his own Judgement, and reason, hee shall conceive to be the aptest means thereunto. By Liberty, is understood, according to the proper signification of the word, the absence of externall Impediments: which Impediments, may oft take away part of a mans power to do what he would; but cannot hinder him from using the power left him, according to his own judgement, and reason shall dictate to him. A Law of Nature, (*Lex Naturalis,*) is a Precept, or generall Rule, found out by Reason, by which a man is forbidden to do, that, which is destructive of his life, or taketh away the means of preserving the same; and to omit, that, by which he thinketh it may be best preserved.' Hobbes' definition of 'Liberty' above – as an actual power to do as one will, in the absence of external impediments – is consistent with the Right of Nature (defined as a Liberty) also being a Law of Nature. But Hobbes' use of 'Liberty' in defining 'Right' suggests not an actual power, but another sense familiar to us: a permission to do or to refrain. This

An important reason for the differences between Hobbes and others who derive the conditions of permissible self-defence from claims about natural law, is that natural law is typically said to include non-instrumental moral obligations towards other people which make it necessary to justify the use of force in self-defence. The onus is reversed in Hobbes. He maintains a powerful, pivotal natural right of self-preservation, limited only by necessity. This means that if I must kill others to preserve myself, I act within my rights. (Self-preservation is obviously wider than self-defence.[5] Further, self-preservation need not always require defence of one's physical life, and could even be consistent with sacrificing one's life in the achievement of some goal with which one identifies and which one values more than one's own physical life.[6] Nevertheless, self-defence against a threat to one's life will mostly be required for self-preservation.)

Further, individuals retain this right of self-preservation in civil society. Not only would it be self-defeating for them to give up this right, but they cannot agree to give it up. Such a covenant would be void since, according to Hobbes, individuals are psychologically incapable of performance.[7] And whereas there is no right of group resistance in civil society, nor a right to resist in defence of others (guilty or innocent),[8] individuals can exercise their natural right of self-preservation in extreme circumstances. Capital punishment at the judgment of the Sovereign is not unjust according to Hobbes;[9] nevertheless, even guilty individuals have the right to resist it if they can.[10] Hobbes' view also implies that an

latter sense is inconsistent with a Right's also being a Law. And it is this latter sense which Hobbes emphasizes in distinguishing a Right and a Law: 'Right, consisteth in liberty to do or to forbeare; Whereas Law, determineth, and bindeth to one of them: so that Law and Right, differ as much, as Obligation, and Liberty; which in one and the same matter are inconsistent'. (See also David Gauthier's discussion, *The Logic of the Leviathan* (Oxford: Clarendon Press, 1969), pp. 29–47.)

5 See Teichman's discussion, *Pacifism and the Just War*, p. 86.
6 Helen Pringle and Robert Lawton argue this, in 'A Life Well Lost? Hobbes and Self Preservation' (unpublished paper).
7 *Leviathan*, pp. 198–9.   8 Ibid., pp. 270–1.   9 Ibid., pp. 264–5.
10 Ibid., pp. 264–5 and pp. 270–1.

aggressor has the right to resist the victim's self-defence. If we are psychologically constituted so as always to be motivated by self-preservation, when we realize what is necessary for this end we cannot reasonably be expected to act otherwise.

For Hobbes, all obligations properly so called are created by voluntary acts. Some argue that this, taken with the fact that for Hobbes even the individual's most basic 'right of nature' does not itself imply a moral presumption of non-interference by others, means that Hobbes is a moral contractarian rather than someone presenting an unusual version of natural law. Nevertheless, Hobbes' account of the right of self-preservation is an instructive comparison, because he shares with those who, unlike him, hold that natural laws are moral laws in terms of which we can wrong others, the view that the permissibility of self-defence stems from the legitimate natural desire for, and natural right of, self-preservation. Despite this common ground between Hobbes and others, the emphasis in most natural law discussions is not the positive individual right of self-preservation, but rather the presumption (sometimes prohibition) against private homicide and the specification of the conditions under which homicide in self-defence is exempt. A sharp contrast with Hobbes is Aquinas' much earlier discussion of self-defence, although the accounts of some others who are more centrally within the natural law tradition than is Hobbes (e.g. Grotius, Pufendorf, Locke) more closely resemble Hobbes' emphasis.

Aquinas concentrates on distinguishing homicide in self-defence from intentional killing.[11] This distinction is usually taken to be the source of the subsequent Principle of Double Effect, which says that although private persons are prohibited from engaging in intentional killing, under specified conditions they can permissibly act for some good end foreseeing that someone's death will result, provided this effect is unintended. Homicide in self-defence is said to have two foreseen effects – one good (saving myself) and the other bad (the aggressor is killed). Where I intend to do only what is

11 *Summa Theologiæ*, 2a 2ae 64, especially article 7. All references are to the Blackfriars edition (London: Eyre and Spottiswoode Ltd, 1966).

necessary to save myself (itself a legitimate intention), the foreseen bad effect is said to be unintended. Some natural law theorists maintain that this distinction grounds the permissibility of homicide in self-defence (as do some others who believe that private intentional killing is impermissible). The twentieth-century natural law philosophers, G. E. M. Anscombe, Germain Grisez, and John Finnis, invoke the Principle of Double Effect in justifying homicide in self-defence; they characterize the aggressor's death as a side-effect, reflecting Aquinas' classification of it as incidental to the act of self-defence.[12] However, in deriving the permissibility of self-defence from natural law, some prominent seventeenth-century philosophers (e.g. Pufendorf and Locke) do not mention the agent's intention. This strongly suggests that they regard lack of intention to kill as unnecessary to the permissibility of homicide in self-defence. Grotius endorses the Thomistic claim that a person killed in self-defence is not killed by intention, but he does not say that in his view lack of intention is necessary to permissible homicide in self-defence.[13]

Like Hobbes, Grotius grounds the permissibility of self-defence in the natural right of self-preservation, the basic natural right which he says gives rise to all the rest. Self-preservation can be more than merely sustaining life and avoiding serious injury. But Grotius does not really set the

[12] G. E. M. Anscombe, 'War and Murder' and 'Modern Moral Philosophy', both reprinted in Anscombe, *Collected Philosophical Papers*, vol. III (Oxford: Basil Blackwell, 1981); Germain Grisez, 'Toward a Consistent Natural Law Ethics of Killing', *The American Journal of Jurisprudence*, vol.15, 1970, pp. 64–96; John Finnis, *Fundamentals of Ethics* and 'Intention and Side-Effects', the latter in *Liability and Responsibility*, edited by R. G. Frey and C. W. Morris (Cambridge: Cambridge University Press, 1991). Philip Devine, *The Ethics of Homicide* (London: Cornell University Press, 1978), is sympathetic to natural law but rejects the Double Effect justification of homicide in self-defence. Garrett Barden, 'Defending Self-Defence', *Irish Philosophical Journal*, vol. 1, no. 2, 1984, pp. 25–35, distinguishes Aquinas' classification of homicide in self-defence from the central distinction of the Principle of Double Effect.

[13] Hugo Grotius, *The Rights of War and Peace*, an abridged translation by William Whewell (Cambridge University Press, 1853), pp. 61–8. All references to Grotius are to these pages.

limit of legitimate defence at what is necessary for self-preser-vation, unless his notion of self-preservation is extremely and implausibly wide. Instead he makes the extraordinary claim that 'although a buffet and death are very unequal, he who is about to do me an injury, thereby gives me a Right, that is a moral claim against him, *in infinitum*, so far as I cannot other-wise repel the evil. And even benevolence *per se* does not appear to bind us to the advantage of him who does us wrong.' A morally innocent person (e.g. a sleepwalker) can do us a wrong, and for Grotius this makes no moral difference to the legitimacy of self-defence. Grotius characterizes self-defence as an extremely strong natural law permission, which is overridden by the natural obligation of benevolence only where non-aggressors (e.g. bystanders) will be killed by self-defensive action, and overridden by Gospel law in the case of killing to avoid minor harms. However, Grotius also com-ments that although it is lawful to defend one's life by killing, it is more laudable *to be killed* rather than to kill. So, self-defence is permissible, self-sacrifice is a higher, non-obliga-tory moral goal, and we have no general moral duty to defend ourselves. In this last respect, Grotius does not even except 'those whose lives concern other persons' (presumably those with family, special obligations to others, positions of responsibility, etc.), but only those who have a special duty to protect others from force (e.g. 'companies on the road' engaged in protecting others, and rulers).

Grotius holds that where I am threatened with bodily harm, self-sacrifice is mostly (what we call) supererogatory: that which 'benevolence often counsels'. However, he also says that the interests of unoffending third parties who will be harmed *indirectly* by self-defence are relevant to the per-missibility of my killing an aggressor whose life is 'useful to many'. Here (surprisingly) self-sacrifice is obligatory: bene-volence *commands* that I not prefer my own sole good. The required benevolence, said here to 'bind us' not to defend ourselves, is held to be *part of* natural law. (Grotius does not comment that, although foreseen and wrong in his view, my indirectly harming these other people would be neither homicide nor intended.) Where others will be harmed because the aggressor's life is useful to them, large numbers must make the difference for Grotius; but he does not say how large.

Pufendorf discusses killing and maiming in self-defence as a moral problem arising out of the apparent conflict of two requirements of natural law: self-preservation – a most sensitive instinct which reason commends to man – and the precept of sociability.[14] Homicide in self-defence appears to violate sociability because I must 'destroy an image of myself, with whom I am bound to maintain the social life'; further, 'a violent defence seems to cause a greater disturbance than if I either take to flight, or yield my body submissively to my assailant'. Pufendorf suggests that sociability may seem inevitably undermined simply by the occasion of having to choose either self-defence or self-sacrifice, because 'the human race seems to suffer an equal loss, whether my assailant is killed, or I myself perish'. Nevertheless, he maintains that sociability is not really violated by self-defence, and so self-defence is permissible in accordance with the natural right of self-preservation.

Pufendorf seeks 'to explain how far self-defence is to be tempered by restraint'. One restraint is necessity: killing is an extreme last resort when my safety cannot otherwise be secured. He qualifies this, though, saying that I am not required to flee imminent danger where this would expose me to attack from behind; nor am I required to retreat rather than stand and fight, because to do so might weaken the position from which I can defend myself. Further, the condition of necessary force does not require that I never expose myself to danger by simply going about my business. But it does mean that if I *impermissibly* court risk to my life, e.g. by accepting the challenge of a duel, I cannot plead self-defence when it comes to the point where I must kill to save myself.

14 Samuel von Pufendorf, *De Officio Hominis et Civis Juxta Legem Naturalem Libri Duo*, vol. 2, chapter v, the translation by Frank Gardner Moore (New York: Oxford University Press, 1927), pp. 3–36. All references to Pufendorf are to these pages.

Pufendorf says one should 'practice patience in the case of a slight injury'. His reason – that retaliation might cause one greater harm – might suggest that this prescription arises from the condition of necessity. Retaliation for a slight injury could escalate the force necessary for self-defence, 'especially where the thing attacked is one which can easily be repaired or made good'. However, unlike Grotius who believes that benevolence requires non-retaliation for minor harms which do not really risk one's safety, Pufendorf regards non-retaliation here as a matter of waiving one's rights in the interests of one's own safety: it is 'the part of prudence'.

The bounds of what Pufendorf regards as blameless defence all appear to be requirements of natural law. Nevertheless, he distinguishes permissible acts of defence in the state of natural freedom (where I am 'not subject to any mortal') from what natural law permits where I am responsible to civil authority. In the state of natural liberty the primary concern is security, and I am allowed to take any necessary measures against an aggressor to secure my own life. These extend, for reasons similar to those Locke gives, to my killing to prevent myself being wounded, and even to prevent theft. I may also pursue an assailant who shows no signs of genuine repentance 'until I have secured myself against him for the future'. But in civil society the circumstances in which it is permissible to use force in self-defence are far more restricted. This is because security can often be sought from the common ruler, both when attack is anticipated and when the attacker is repelled or has withdrawn.

Pufendorf claims that, if necessary, it is permissible to expose an unoffending person (e.g. someone who happens to be in the way of my escape) 'indirectly to the danger of death or serious injury ... it being no purpose of ours to harm him'. Part of the obvious disagreement with Grotius here might concern the issue of whether such a person is harmed intentionally. But harm to another is not permissible provided only that it is unintended; and Pufendorf recognizes that proportionality is also relevant here. Pufendorf also remarks that although the right of self-defence belongs to the non-aggressor, an aggressor can rightly defend himself if after he has desisted and offered reparation and future security, 'the injured man in a harsh spirit rejects his offer and endeavours to avenge himself with his own hand'.

The relevance of fault and guilt

With the obvious exception of Hobbes, most natural law accounts share Pufendorf's view that the right of self-defence belongs to the non-aggressor. They also agree that the right of self-defence is a right against an aggressor whose conduct is at fault – in the wrong – in a sense that need not imply responsibility or guilt on the aggressor's part. One has a right of self-defence against a morally innocent unjust aggressor, such as a deranged person or an attacking sleepwalker. The assumptions which underpin this view raise two basic issues which must be addressed by a satisfactory account of the right of self-defence as a right against unjust aggression. The first concerns the conditions under which force is used *in self-defence*; the second concerns the conditions under which someone is an *unjust aggressor*.

Self-defence and unjust aggression Pufendorf discusses an overloaded lifeboat example as a case of necessity. This highlights the basic, general point that someone against whom I use force *in self-defence* must be identifiable as a *threat* to me. Those who *overload* a lifeboat pose a threat to others; and if those already on board know that the lifeboat is full, they can be acting in self-defence in preventing those who would overload the boat from getting in. But in Pufendorf's example no *particular* people overload the lifeboat. Say I am among twenty people who have already clambered aboard a lifeboat which can carry only ten. Which, if any, of the others pose a threat to me? We should say, with Pufendorf, that in these circumstances all are endangered. This is also the appropriate response to some other examples in which *particular* individuals more clearly compete with me for resources, for instance, where another trapped person is competing with me for a limited air or food supply. In this case, I am not a threat to her, nor is she a threat to me; in these circumstances we are both endangered. In stopping another trapped person from breathing normally in order to conserve the limited air supply for myself, or in tipping another person out of a lifeboat into which too many have clambered, I am not defending myself against these persons. On the contrary, I am attacking them in the cause of self-preservation.

Someone who poses a threat to me will, if unchecked, cause me to be worse-off than I would otherwise be. But someone is not a threat to me provided only that his or her existence, presence, or conduct thwarts my interests. Normative considerations can be relevant to determining the *status quo* against which another person's existence, presence, or conduct is a threat. For instance, I have a legitimate claim to parts of my living body, my property, my position in a queue, etc.; so someone competing with me for these things is a threat to me, and not I to him. But the considerations which determine the *status quo* are not necessarily strongly normative (the police sharp-shooter is a threat to the hijacker holding hostages); and they can be a matter of luck (those who get to the lifeboat first are threatened by those arriving later, and not vice versa). Pufendorf maintains that in the case of shipwreck where more persons are in a lifeboat than the boat will carry, it is right to draw lots to see who 'shall be thrown overboard. And if anyone shall refuse the hazard of the lot, he can be thrown into the water, without casting his lot, as one who seeks the destruction of all.'[15] Presumably, Pufendorf characterizes those who refuse the lot as *aggressors* (as seeking the destruction of all) in order to justify casting them off against their wills for the good of the others.

The use of force *in self-defence* is often described as the use of self-protective force against an *aggressor*. However, natural law accounts bring out that 'self-protective force used against

[15] Pufendorf does not say whether he regards the deaths of those thrown overboard in these lifeboat cases as unintended. But those who invoke Double Effect in allowing homicide in self-defence may well maintain that in these cases, too, death is not intended.

an aggressor' is in some respects too wide, and in other respects too narrow, a description of the use of force in self-defence. Where 'aggression' and 'aggressor' are appropriately used in the context of self-defence, they require qualification and can be somewhat imprecise. First, we can say that someone spoke aggressively; but the use of force in self-defence requires an actual threat beyond the mere verbal expression of an intention to harm. A person who intends to launch an unprovoked attack may be only a potential aggressor; he is not an actual aggressor until the point at which he acts on the intention (e.g. by taking up arms). However, having acted on the intention, he is an attacker before actually striking a blow. (This marks the distinction between (say) someone's taking up a gun with the clear intention of firing it and his actually firing it.) Grotius says that the threatened injury which we repel must be a 'present danger', 'imminent in point of time'. But this condition may be fulfilled where there is manifest intention to kill on the part of someone who takes up weapons. We might add that it could also be fulfilled where the victim of an ongoing or intermittent attack uses force against an aggressor who has paused to reload a weapon or prepare himself for the next onslaught, or has stumbled or temporarily lost consciousness. Sometimes we can act in self-defence in anticipating the deed. (Nevertheless, Grotius warns that although a certain latitude of judgment is inevitable, mere fear does not give a right of killing for prevention. This is because where the danger is uncertain, or can be otherwise averted, there can be recourse to other means of avoidance (e.g. leaving the scene) or legal remedies. Grotius and Locke share the general condition that homicide in self-defence is legitimate only where necessary to avoid a threatened injury which will be an irretrievable loss.) A further, related point is that an actual threat need not be unconditional: one can use force in self-defence against a conditional threat, such as one posed by duress. For example, if I use force against someone who threatens to kill me then and there unless I participate in a killing or betray an innocent person's whereabouts, then I act in self-defence, and not simply in order to protect someone or something else.

Secondly, force can be used in self-defence against someone who is not an aggressor in the sense of being the instigator of the conflict. 'Aggressor' typically refers to the instigator of a conflict, but aggression on the part of one party towards another is not invariably unprovoked by the other. As Pufendorf's discussion suggests, someone can become an aggressor by unreasonably escalating a conflict instigated by the other party, e.g. by moving from a verbal hostility to physical violence. Further, the designation 'aggressor' can shift during the course of a conflict from the instigator to the other party, e.g. when the instigator publicly and sincerely attempts to withdraw, or to introduce peaceful negotiations aimed at settlement, and the victim then unreasonably continues the hostility.

Thirdly, one can use self-protective force against an aggressor and not be acting in self-defence. In allowing that the use of force in self-defence can anticipate a blow, Grotius also recognizes the essential point that an act of self-defence directly repels present force. Force used in self-defence *resists, repels, or wards off* conduct which is itself an *immediate* threat. The scope of 'the use of self-protective force against an aggressor' is wider than that of 'the use of force in self-defence': the former can include, for instance, killing for prevention, and also killing in the course of self-defence. The instigator of a contract killing is an aggressor for whom the immediate threat (the hit man) acts as an agent. I act in self-defence if I use force against the hit man about to shoot. But I might use force against the instigator instead: I might kill him so that the contract is off, or I might use his body as a means of eliminating or resisting the hit man (e.g. I shoot the instigator so that he falls on the hit man, or I use the instigator's body as a shield). The first of these options – killing the instigator so that the contract is off – is a case of killing for prevention. In taking the second option – in using force on the instigator as a means of self-defence – I kill the instigator in the course of self-defence against the hit man.

Natural law accounts also bring out that force can be used

in self-defence against persons who are not aggressors. Hobbes' strong right *of self-defence* makes clear that an aggressor can act in self-defence. The hijacker holding hostages remains the aggressor in the ensuing conflict with police; yet the hijacker fires at the police sharp-shooter in self-defence. The sharp-shooter is an immediate threat to the hijacker, but he is not an aggressor. Further, in explaining the right of self-defence as a right against unjust aggression, other natural law accounts allow a right of self-defence against some threats (e.g. attacking sleepwalkers) who are aggressors only in a rather stretched sense. Grotius describes the notion of aggression relevant to self-defence as 'present force'. He holds that someone who has no culpable design on my life can be an aggressor. But is a design (even such as a sleepwalker might have) to do me an injury necessary for aggression on Grotius' view? Or is someone who unwittingly acts in a way which endangers me (e.g. someone about to fire a weapon) an aggressor in the relevant sense? Does 'making the danger', in the sense which makes an act of self-protection an act of self-defence, require an act at all (even such as a sleepwalker might perform)? Or can it also include someone who has been thrown at me, or someone who falls on me, or someone with a highly contagious disease? Or are those in this last group on a par with the man in Pufendorf's example who happens to be in the way of my escape?

The following points should be emphasized as part of a general response to questions such as those I have raised above. Grotius' and Pufendorf's discussions of the permissibility of inflicting harm on unoffending persons (e.g. innocent bystanders, innocent shields of threats)[16] allow us to see that

[16] Robert Nozick speaks of 'innocent shields of threats', *Anarchy, State and Utopia* (Oxford: Basil Blackwell, 1974), p. 35. These include innocent persons strapped to the front of the tanks of aggressors so that the tanks cannot be hit without also hitting them. Nozick defines 'innocent shields of threats' as 'those innocent persons who are so situated that they will be damaged by the only means available for stopping the aggressor'. The term 'innocent shield' as used by Nozick seems too narrow, as his definition includes those who are not *shields* of threats but who are merely bystanders or otherwise (not by the aggressor's design) unfortu-

non-threats who are harmed as a means, or as an incidental effect, of warding off a threat, are not harmed in self-defence; rather, they are harmed in the course of self-defence. Force used *in self-defence* resists, repels, or wards off an *immediate threat*. Some persons who can pose such threats (e.g. someone unwittingly about to fire a weapon at you, someone thrown down a well at you) can be called aggressors only in a rather stretched sense.[17] And some persons who are clearly non-aggressors (e.g. the police sharp-shooter, someone defending himself against an unjust attack) can pose threats against which force might be used in self-defence. Having recognized that 'immediate threat' is more precise than 'aggressor' in the context of self-defence, we must then specify the *conditions* of immediate threat relevant to acting in self-defence. For instance, under what conditions is force used in self-defence against passive and involuntary threats?

An account of the right of self-defence needs to explain the conditions under which force is used *in self-defence* against an immediate threat: it needs to distinguish persons who pose threats in the relevant sense from those who do not, and to distinguish the use of force in self-defence from the use of force in the course of self-defence and (more generally) in the cause of self-protection and self-preservation. For the reasons given above, 'the use of self-protective force against an aggressor' can be an inaccurate description of the use of force in self-defence. Nevertheless, the common use of 'aggressor' to refer to a person against whom force is used in self-defence is mostly accurate in the particular circumstances under discussion; and in this book I shall continue to use 'aggressor' in this loose sense where it is not misleading to do so. In my

nately situated so that they will be killed by defensive action against the aggressor.

[17] Nozick, ibid., pp. 34–5, points out that a person can be a threat, and innocent, without being an aggressor: 'If someone picks up a third party and throws him at you down at the bottom of a deep well, the third party is innocent and a threat.' (Further, the third party can be an unjust threat.) Nozick thinks that this third party would be an aggressor, however, had he chosen to launch himself at you in that trajectory. This is certainly right, although (for the reasons given above) aggression need not be a voluntary act.

account of the right of self-defence in chapter 5, I argue that there is an important conceptual link between aggression and the conditions of immediate threat relevant to acting in self-defence.

Natural law discussions of homicide in self-defence are mostly confined to the justification of self-defence against imminent and actual unjust assailants, attackers, and those reasonably believed to be such. These accounts typically hold that the fact that the other person is offending – an unjust threat – is the basic, necessary condition of permissible self-defence. However, justifications of homicide in self-defence which posit a morally important distinction between killing an unjust threat on the one hand, and killing an unoffending person on the other, need to address the moral grounding of self-defence against passive threats. We need to know what counts as an *unjust* threat, and why there is a morally crucial distinction between offending and unoffending persons. Those who maintain that the unoffending are the causally innocent (those doing no unjust harm) usually do not say whether an *act* is necessary, or whether it is sufficient for non-innocence simply that one pose an unjust immediate threat (e.g. the man thrown down the well). If passive threats are held to be unoffending because they are *doing* no harm, then we need to know the moral significance of *act* here, since posing an active threat can be involuntary and some active threats are certainly as blameless as non-threats. If, on the other hand, passive threats can be offending, then we need to know on what basis someone is reasonably classified as an unjust threat. We also need to know why the fact that someone poses an unjust immediate threat is the morally significant factor in grounding a right *of self-defence*, since some unjust immediate threats (e.g. the man thrown down the well) are certainly as blameless as some non-threats (e.g. innocent bystanders, innocent shields), and some indirect and contingent threats are culpable (e.g. the instigator of a contract killing, someone who deliberately blocks my escape).

I tackle these issues in chapter 5 as part of my positive account of the right of self-defence.

The significance of innocence   The natural law prohibition of intentional killing can be stated narrowly or more broadly. This seems the likely source of one apparent difference in the claimed conditions of permissible self-defence. Locke, for instance, in maintaining that it is 'reasonable and just that I should have a Right to destroy that which threatens me with destruction', stresses the natural right of self-preservation and urges the individual's duty to preserve *innocent* life. (This strongly suggests that for Locke self-defence is not simply a permission.) He adds that a person's 'Power' to kill another in defence of his own life extends to 'any one who joyns ... in his Defence, and espouses his Quarrel: it being reasonable and just I should have a Right to destroy that which threatens me with destruction'. Here Locke assumes that the threatened person is innocent. He also seems to take the right of self-defence to include assistance from others – but perhaps not, if he is simply pointing out that the quarrel can extend beyond the initial protagonists. Even so, if there has been no design on their own lives and they are not themselves endangered by the attack on me, others need a justification for joining my cause, and this must be something more than *my* right to defend *myself*. Where I am the innocent victim, liable to be killed, and the aggressor is culpable, this justification may be the duty Locke says we all have to preserve innocent life. Arguably Locke also allows a right to assist others as part of the natural right he says we have to punish an attacker. But if this is so we would need to be confident in the circumstances that a particular party to a conflict is culpable as well as in the wrong.

My remarks on Locke's views on self-defence are derived from chapter III of the second of his *Two Treatises of Government* in which he discusses the State of War.[18] The State of War is a relationship which can exist between people who are fellow subjects under a Superior on Earth, and it is introduced there when one person declares 'by Word or Action, not a

---

[18] John Locke, *The Second Treatise of Government*, revised edition by Peter Laslett (Mentor Books, 1963), pp. 308–34. All further references to Locke are to these pages.

passionate and hasty, but a sedate and settled Design, upon another man's life'.[19] Locke distinguishes the State of Nature from the State of War. The State of Nature (properly so called) is one in which men 'live together according to reason, without a common Superior on Earth, with Authority to judge between them'; the State of War is created by 'force, or a declared design of force upon the Person of another, where there is no common Superior on earth to appeal to for relief'. Locke says that it is the want of an appeal to a common Superior which can give me the Right of War even against an aggressor who is a fellow subject: 'the Law, which was made for my Preservation, where it cannot interpose to secure my Life from present force, which if lost, is capable of no reparation, permits me my own Defence'. This is not a general right to act against another in preserving myself whenever there is obvious, imminent, and irreparable danger, but a right of *self-defence*. So in addition to the lack of legal protection, Locke must say why I have a Right of War against an aggressor. His most basic (insufficient) reason is the 'Fundamental Law of Nature, Man being to be preserved'. Locke then focuses, rightly, on the need for a justification of self-preference 'when all cannot be preserved', and he claims not only that the 'safety of the Innocent is to be preferred', but that by his own actions the aggressor has 'exposed his life to the others Power to be taken away from him' to the extent that he may be treated as are dangerous 'Beasts of Prey'.

[19] Presumably this requirement emphasizes that a State of War exists only where there is a serious declaration and intention to act. A hasty expression of extreme anger and frustration, 'I'll kill you for this', which is not literally meant, does not introduce the State of War. However, we may want to reply to Locke that some passionate and hasty designs can be very serious, and also that sometimes where there is room for doubt about the intention behind another's hasty words or actions it may nevertheless be reasonable to act on the assumption that one is in immediate danger. If Locke's requirement that the design be sedate and settled really excludes the case where someone suddenly rushes at me in a fit of anger wielding a knife, then many cases of homicide in self-defence cannot plausibly be defended by what is permissible in the State of War. This seems a very unlikely intended implication of Locke's requirement, even though the examples which he goes on to discuss all suggest premeditation as well as intention.

Dangerous beasts are blameless, and Locke does not seem to think that a human aggressor's design on another's life must be culpable as well as apparent and fixed for self-defence to be legitimate. But perhaps, in addition to establishing a real intention to kill, Locke's requirement that the design be 'sedate and settled' also implies that this is something for which the aggressor is responsible and culpable. At first this position might seem morally implied by Locke's claim that the aggressor by his own actions confers on the victim the 'Power' to take his life away, and hence that the victim's self-preference is not only reasonable but just. But Aquinas, for instance, does not say that the permissibility of self-defence derives partly from the aggressor's culpability, Grotius explicitly denies that it does, and Locke might not believe that it must. However, given his own views, Locke should regard killing a human aggressor as morally more complex than killing a dangerous beast.

Locke's comparison of an assailant and a wild beast is reminiscent of Aquinas' justification of capital punishment. In this discussion Aquinas explicitly relies on the claimed inferior moral status of the person who transgresses natural law.[20] Aquinas holds that capital punishment by public authority is justified for the good of all, because by deviating from the rational order and so losing 'his human dignity in so far as man is naturally free and an end unto himself', the sinner 'lapses into the subjection of the beasts and their exploitation by others'. For Aquinas, the judgment that warrants intentional killing belongs only to public authorities, so he must defend private self-defence as unintended homicide. Locke, on the other hand, maintains that a private individual has authority to judge another in the State of Nature (and the right to punish), and that a private individual also has authority to judge who is innocent and who may be treated like a beast of prey in the State of War. In Locke's State of War those with a design on the lives of others may be killed intentionally. For Locke, it is intentional killing of innocent persons in the State of Nature that is impermissible.

[20] *Summa Theologiæ*, 2a 2ae. 64, article 2.

77

So, it might be held (narrowly) that a private individual is not permitted to kill an innocent person intentionally. (Grotius says this.) Self-defence against the non-innocent is then outside the scope of the prohibition, and could be permissible intentional killing. Aquinas accepts that it is always impermissible for a private individual intentionally to kill an innocent person, because he maintains a wider, more restrictive prohibition which includes the narrower one: it is never permissible for a private person to kill anyone intentionally. Aquinas does not say that the permissibility of homicide in self-defence derives (even partly) from the culpability of the unjust aggressor. Thus, provided the aggressor's death is not intended, there is no immediate reason to think that Aquinas considers the use of lethal force against a non-culpable unjust aggressor to be morally more difficult than the use of lethal force against a culpable one. However, within this view, the characterization of homicide in self-defence as unintended killing would provide only a necessary condition of its permissibility: it would establish that homicide in self-defence is not *absolutely* prohibited. In addition, the force used must be necessary for self-defence, and self-preference must be legitimate. Thus, for homicide in self-defence *per se* to be clearly justified as a case of 'double effect', the self-defending agent must legitimately weigh the protection of his or her own life more heavily than the comparable interest of the aggressor.[21] This is explicitly maintained by Grotius and Pufendorf, where it is arguably part of a view that Aquinas rejects: namely, that intentional killing in self-defence is permissible.

The innocent and the unoffending   Whether all cases of private homicide in self-defence against unjust aggressors escape the narrower prohibition – that the innocent must not be killed

[21] Some writers deny that the Principle of Double Effect can require that the good effect outweigh the bad. For instance, Robert Campbell and Diané Collinson, *Ending Lives* (Oxford: Basil Blackwell, 1988), p. 156, maintain that the proportionality condition of Double Effect *only ever* requires that the good and bad effects be comparable in order of magnitude. But, given fulfilment of the Principle's other conditions, this interpretation of proportionality is insufficient to justify my deflecting a

intentionally – depends partly on what 'innocent' means. It could mean 'morally innocent'; if it does, then the prohibition forbids the intentional killing of non-culpable unjust aggressors such as young children and the insane. Alternatively, 'innocent' might, as Grotius maintains, mean 'unoffending', and refer only to those who do not threaten or cause unjust injury. The genuinely innocent for Grotius are those who do not themselves 'make the danger'. If 'innocent' means 'unoffending', then the use of force in self-defence could be permissible intended killing.

Grotius explicitly denies that the legitimacy of self-defence depends in any way upon 'the injustice or fault of another who makes the danger': I have a right to kill blameless unjust aggressors in self-defence. But his characterization of *unjust* aggression is not detailed enough to allow us to say, for instance, whether someone using force against me under a reasonable, mistaken belief that I am attacking him is an unjust aggressor. While I do not deserve the injury this person will inflict, if the use of force is justified on the basis of the agent's reasonable beliefs, then this person may be acting within his rights. Grotius does consider whether those who are simply in the way of my 'defence or flight without which death cannot be avoided' may be cut down or trampled down. He concedes that some authorities (even Divines) think it lawful that the genuinely innocent be killed in these circumstances. He agrees that this view is reasonable if we confine ourselves to the dictates of natural law which (where there is a conflict) 'cares much less for ties of society, than for the defence of the individual'. Nevertheless, he urges that the 'law of love which commands us to regard another as ourselves, plainly does not permit this'. Thus Grotius believes, as noted above, that where the only available means of self-defence will kill an unoffending person, the right of self-defence is overridden by an obligation of benevolence. (We

threat to my life in the direction of some *unoffending* person who will then certainly be killed. I discuss legitimate self-preference and the interpretation of proportionality in 4.3.

may well ask why the law of love does not also bind us not to kill the unfortunate sleepwalker about to buffet us.)

Pufendorf maintains that homicide in self-defence is consistent with sociability. His reasons appeal to *fault* on the part of the unjust aggressor, in terms which imply culpability.[22] However, Pufendorf echoes Grotius' denial that permissible self-defence depends on the aggressor's culpability. He says that it is permissible to kill an insane person in self-defence, and also to kill one who mistakes me for another with whom he has a quarrel: 'it is enough that the other have no right to attack or kill me, and there be on my side no obligation to die in vain'. Although Pufendorf describes the aggressor as the one 'who first conceived the will to injure', and he confines permissible self-defence to those 'who are assaulted by others without provocation', he says that allowances must be made for the excitement and urgency of the situation in determining how careful our judgment about the immediacy of the danger must be in order for anticipation to be permissible. Again, this seems to leave in doubt the permissibility of self-defence against someone acting under a reasonable, mistaken belief that I am attacking him or her.

Those who equate the innocent with the unoffending in justifying self-defence should, I think, explain the difference they see between offending and unoffending persons in terms of a distinction between unjust aggressors (unjust threats) and others, rather than conflate 'unoffending' and 'innocent'. 'Innocent' should not refer only to those who are unoffending, who pose no unjust threat. It is possible, for instance, for unprovoked attacks to be perpetrated by non-culpable agents (e.g. the insane), and we need to refer to such agents as (morally) innocent unjust aggressors. (Further, despite the fact that aggression is usually an unprovoked attack, the act of beginning a quarrel or war, 'unjust

---

[22] E.g. '... there is no law which commands me to betray my own safety, that another's malice may attack me with impunity. And whoever in such a case is hurt or killed, has reason to blame his own perversity, which put upon me that necessity', and 'the good would be exposed as a ready prey to the bad, if they must never offer them violence'.

aggressor' and 'unjust assailant' are not pleonasms. It is possible for an aggressive act or attack, one (say) by A on B in
defence of C who is helpless and being persecuted by B, to be
just.)[23]

The relevance of intention

If 'innocent person' in the natural law prohibition of intentional homicide refers to someone who is unoffending (not an
unjust threat), then appeal to something like the Principle of
Double Effect may not be essential to the permissibility of
homicide in self-defence.[24] This is because, under the prohibition so interpreted, it is not absolutely impermissible
intentionally to kill an unjust aggressor; the prohibition probably also excepts killing an unjust threat who is not, strictly
speaking, an aggressor. However, there needs to be an
independent reason for limiting the prohibition of intentional
killing to unoffending persons – a reason other than the
assumption that because unjust aggressors are permissibly
killed in self-defence they are outside the scope of the prohibition. This is necessary if we are to *explain* why it is permissible to use lethal force in self-defence against an unjust
threat.[25]

I have said that we should not use 'innocent' to mean
'unoffending', and that homicide *in self-defence* requires the
person killed to have been an immediate threat. Those who
maintain that it is always impermissible intentionally to kill
unoffending persons, and those who believe that the fact that
someone is offending (an unjust threat) is relevant to the
moral permissibility of killing him or her intentionally, will
need to appeal to something like Double Effect in deciding
whether innocent bystanders and shields of threats are permissibly killed in the course of self-defence. However, if
'innocent' in the prohibition means morally innocent (non-
culpable) then two separate justifications of homicide in self-

[23] See also Teichman, *Pacifism and the Just War*, p. 80.
[24] I take this issue further in chapter 4.
[25] I take this point from Thomson, 'Self-Defense and Rights', p. 39.

defence could arise: one appealing to Double Effect and the other not, depending on whether or not the unjust aggressor is morally innocent. Indeed, some writers suggest that killing a non-culpable unjust aggressor in self-defence is morally more complex than killing a culpable one, the former being an act for which we need a separate, or at least an additional, justification.

But this last claim will strike others as plainly wrong. They will think that what justifies the use of force in self-defence is my danger and the fact that the other person poses an unjust immediate threat, and that it does not matter whether or not this person is culpable. The attraction of the Double Effect approach on *this* view might be the prospect of a unitary justification of all permissible homicide in self-defence, one that will seem to many people to make precisely the required point: namely, that what I am doing in using force in self-defence is simply resisting, repelling, or warding off an unjust threat, something which, if the defence is not dispropor-tionate, I am morally entitled to do. In chapter 5, I defend a unitary right of self-defence along these lines, independently of the Principle of Double Effect.

Necessity and proportionality

Aquinas explicitly maintains that 'somebody who uses more violence than is necessary to defend himself will be doing something wrong'. This is described as a condition of propor-tionality: an 'act that is properly motivated may, nevertheless, become vitiated if it is not proportionate to the end intended'. As I remarked in chapter 2, Finnis accepts this as a genuine principle of proportionality, although what Aquinas had in mind was the condition of necessary force.

Necessary force is a general moral and legal condition of permissible self-defence. Nevertheless, this condition cannot be interpreted absolutely literally: it must sometimes involve an evaluation of relative costs and the reasonableness of alternative courses of action. It may be, for example, that instead of using lethal force against an aggressor I could avoid being killed myself by complying with the aggressor's demands, (say) by participating in a murder or by revealing the whereabouts of someone who will then be endangered. Here the use of lethal force is not unnecessary simply because there is another way of achieving the specific aim of saving myself, one which would cause less immediate or less certain injury. Although necessity and proportionality are distinguishable conditions of permissible self-defence, considerations of proportionality (such as that an alternative means would involve an unacceptable risk or cost) must sometimes form part of the normative background against which necessity is judged. The agent must believe that the force used is necessary for self-defence in the circumstances. But necessary force can allow that an agent may regard a degree of force as indispensable even though there are apparent alternative means of self-defence. There are values, and interests of our own and of others, which we are entitled, and sometimes obliged to protect, and these too can form part of the normative background against which judgments about necessary force are made. These values and interests include, for instance, our not giving in to some forms of duress and, as Pufendorf points out, our engaging in our rightful activities. If I am attacked while going for a walk, the use of force in self-defence on this occasion is not unnecessary simply because I could have avoided muggers by staying at home. Nevertheless, our judgment about the permissibility of self-defence in this and similar cases can be influenced by, for example, my recklessly exposing myself to danger, or by my taking unnecessary risks when the incidence of mugging in the area is high. Although the mugger is entirely in the wrong, it can make a difference to the normative background that I do things such as court the risk which I then act to ward off, or go looking for trouble. Here Pufendorf is right, Hobbes is wrong: in the case of a hijacker holding hostages who kills in self-defence in a shoot-out with police, it very clearly makes a difference to the normative background that the hijacker has foreseeably and *wrongfully* created the circum-stances in which he is endangered.[26]

What counts as genuinely proportionate harm – that is, injury inflicted in self-defence that is proportionate to the harm prevented – can be problematic. Aquinas' discussion of homicide in self-defence seems to assume that the agent is defending his or her own life. However, seventeenth-century natural law accounts are not silent on the question of propor-tionality where killing is necessary in order to prevent harms such as rape, assault, and theft. Although Grotius and Pufen-dorf wrote prior to, and influenced Locke, Locke is in some respects less forthcoming on proportionality than are they.

Locke discusses whether the Right of War extends to my killing someone who threatens to enslave me or to steal from me. He concludes that it does, where the threat is to my *liberty*, which Locke says is vital to my *security*. I may kill where there is a close connection between the attempt to inflict other harms on me and a threat to my *preservation*. Locke does not claim that killing is permissible because harms such as slavery and theft are themselves equivalent to death. For Locke, the connection between slavery and a threat to my life is a very close one; but this is not necessarily so with theft. Once enslaved I have no 'security of my Preservation', and it 'must necessarily be supposed' that someone who attempts to take away my freedom has a design to take away everything else. Locke thinks much the same reason makes it lawful for me to kill a thief who tries *to get me into his power* in order to steal from me, even in the absence of any declared design on my life. Whatever the thief's pretence, 'I have no reason to suppose that he, who would take away my Liberty, would not when he had me in his Power, take away everything else.' The Right of War, whereby I may kill an attacker in civil society, extends only to defence of my life where the law is powerless to protect it, the reason being that I am innocent and the harm done me will be irreparable. I may not kill a thief because he is in the process of stealing 'all I am worth',

[26] Teichman takes a different view of self-defence against the police sharp-shooter, *Pacifism and the Just War*, p. 80.

because I have recourse to the law to recover my goods. However, I may kill the thief who sets on me to rob me of no more than my horse and coat, not because the threatened loss of these goods warrants killing someone, but because my life is at risk.

Grotius says that as far as killing an aggressor is concerned, natural law requires *only* necessity where one is in physical ,danger: 'If the body be menaced by present force with danger of life not otherwise evitable, war is lawful, even to the slaying of the aggressor.' Later he appeals to what at first looks like a condition of proportionality in discussing whether killing is permissible where necessary to avoid injuries, even bodily ones, which cannot seriously be regarded as themselves on a par with death, which will not lead to death, and by which 'our true estimation is not damaged'. However, the command which Grotius says makes it unlawful to kill the aggressor in these cases is not a dictate of natural law, but a Gospel improvement on natural law in the direction of reinforcing benevolence.

Grotius regards as straightforward the legitimacy of killing to avoid the loss or mutilation of a limb, or in defence of chastity. In both cases, Grotius claims, the threatened injury is *itself* as bad as death. Moreover, in the case of mutilation, he says that 'it can hardly be known whether it do not bring in its train loss of life'. Presumably death is a likely consequence of mutilation not only because, as Locke would argue, one's power to defend one's life is abrogated and one might reasonably surmise that there is also a design on one's life, but also because as a result of serious injury one might bleed to death. Grotius regards this last consideration – that death might flow from the injury – as sufficient to warrant slaying the aggressor if loss of limb cannot be otherwise avoided. And those who accept this view might also urge Locke's reason – that one's life is also endangered – in cases of killing to avoid rape, whether or not they are impressed by Grotius' claim that loss of chastity is itself on a par with death. (Later Grotius mentions that chastity, like life and unlike most property, once lost cannot be recovered. This is true of virginity; but a blameless victim of rape, whether or not previously a virgin, is not unchaste in the sense of morally impure.)

Grotius at first concedes that natural law alone permits killing if necessary to preserve our goods. Life and goods are unequal, but he says that the difference is 'compensated by the preference to be given to the innocent and the condemnation incurred by the robber'. So in the case of property, unlike attack on the person, the permissibility of defence in natural law depends partly on culpability (if it is to incur condemnation) on the side of the thief. Here it is insufficient that I am not bound to suffer what the thief attempts to inflict. (Grotius does not comment on this difference.) Again, the benevolence required by natural law seems concerned only with the interests of unoffending persons, and does not oppose defence against the aggressor unless the 'thing stolen be a trifle'.

Nevertheless, Grotius himself is clearly of the view that it is impermissible to slay a thief for the sake of recovering property, and he says that slaying a thief can be permissible only when there is a threat to life. The circumstances of danger to life which he thinks permit killing are far less restricted than those Locke describes (where a thief tries to overpower me so as to steal from me), and include my coming into danger in trying to defend or to recover my goods, because I have a *right* to act in these ways. (As noted above, Pufendorf too extends the sense of self I may defend from the person to the person engaged in his or her rightful activities.)[27] If I kill a thief when there is no danger to my life, Grotius says that I am guilty of homicide. (Grotius not only takes 'innocent' to mean 'unoffending' when he says that homicide is the intentional killing of innocent persons, but further, he implies that to be offending one must be a direct or indirect threat *to the person*.) Killing in order to protect property is also permissible on Grotius' view when the theft will deprive us of something on which our life depends, which cannot be recovered at law (or

[27] Keith Campbell drew my attention to this and to its significance.

if it can, presumably not before it is too late for our life to be satisfactorily protected). Grotius assures his readers that even if civil law allows us to kill a thief with impunity for the sake of mere goods, this only removes the punishment; it does not give us the (presumably moral) right. Thus, the impermissibility of killing a thief for the sake of property is not like the impermissibility of killing an aggressor in order to avoid a buffet. The latter we have a natural right to do, although a higher obligation overrules it; the former, apparently, we have no right to do. (Grotius does not go into the question of how to reconcile this with his earlier claim about what natural law permits in defence of property.)

Pufendorf's comments on the permissibility of killing in defence of limbs, and in defence of chastity, are similar to those of Grotius; although Pufendorf takes them further, remarking that in addition to the wrong of very great insult and loss of esteem, violation of chastity may reduce a woman to the necessity of 'rearing her offspring for a public enemy'. In the state of natural liberty it can be permissible to kill in defence of property if need be. But Pufendorf's reasons are confined to the connection between some attempted thefts and a threat to life. There is no suggestion that defence of property itself warrants killing. In civil society, killing in defence of property is not regularly permitted, the exception being where the thief cannot be brought to court.

The claim that natural law permits killing an unjust aggressor to avoid a slap on the face or the loss of property requires the assumption that the unjust aggressor's moral standing is very considerably abrogated in comparison with that of the victim. This seems very harsh, and harsher still without any reference to the aggressor's culpability. Not surprisingly, reasons (where given) for so drastically discounting the interests or rights of the aggressor mostly suggest culpability on the aggressor's part, unless the context is homicide in self-defence against the threat of death or serious injury.

3.3 IMPORTANT SIMILARITIES AND DIFFERENCES, AND TWO LINES OF JUSTIFICATION

A universal feature of natural law justifications of self-defence is the condition that the force used be necessary in the circumstances. Some accounts may assume that the aggressor's culpability is necessary for justified self-defence. However, where the threat is to my life or to something on which my life depends, unjust aggression is usually taken to justify homicide in self-defence. Here 'aggression' is used loosely enough to allow that aggression need not be a voluntary act. But it is uncertain what some accounts would say about the permissibility of using lethal force in self-defence against some passive threats (e.g. the man thrown down the well).

Some natural law accounts explicitly hold that I have a *right* to use force in self-defence when I have the reasonable belief that there is imminent unjust aggression. But *unjust* aggression – more precisely, unjust threat – is not carefully enough explained to allow us to say, first, whether or not, on this view, a putative self-defender acting on a reasonable mistaken belief is an unjust aggressor. Either answer seems to have awkward implications if homicide in self-defence is justified against a putative self-defender who is acting on the basis of reasonable beliefs. If this putative self-defender *is* held to pose an unjust threat, then one and the same act is permissible (putative) self-defence and at the same time an unjust threat to someone. If this putative self-defender does *not* pose an unjust threat, and I can justifiably defend myself, then unjust threat is not necessary for justified self-defence after all.

Despite the apparent contradiction it suggests, the former alternative is preferable. It can be accepted, provided we distinguish the issue of just and unjust threat from that of justification, and we speak of justification from different perspectives. Objectively, the force used by the putative self-defender is unjust in that, although not malicious, it is directed at an unoffending person: it is unprovoked and objectively undeserved by the intended recipient. It is not unwarranted, however, and in the circumstances the putative self-defender is justified[ii] in acting as he or she does.

Both alternatives yield the conclusion that there can be cases in which both parties can justifiably act in self-defence or putative self-defence. In my view, we can, and we should, qualify this conclusion by again invoking the distinction between objective and agent-perspectival justification: the force used by the putative self-defender is not justified[i], although in the circumstances putative self-defence is justified[ii]. (This qualification implicitly rejects the view that a person's justified[ii] belief that she is unjustly threatened is sufficient to establish a positive *right* of (putative) self-defence. As I argued in chapter 2, although putative self-defence can be justified[ii], the positive right of self-defence does not itself include a positive right of putative self-defence. From a more objective perspective, putative self-defence is excusable conduct.)

Secondly, unjust aggression is not carefully enough explained in these natural law accounts to allow us to say whether, for example, an attacking sleepwalker and someone having a fit pose unjust threats in endangering me. These people certainly do not pose just threats. My own inclination is to say that they do pose unjust threats: rights violation need not be voluntary, and as an unoffending person I have a right against these people that they do not strike me in these ways. However, some people will consider that 'unjust threat' should not include threats which do not constitute intentional action which is, under some description, an injustice.[28] On this latter view, a unitary account of justified self-defence would need to invoke a broader category of *non-just* threat against which self-defence is permissible. (I return to the issue of unjust threat in chapter 5.)

The natural law accounts I have discussed in this present chapter are not sufficiently detailed or carefully enough defended to answer the crucial questions they raise. Their interest lies in the fact that they raise questions which must be

[28] R.A. Duff has expressed this concern about my wider use of 'unjust threat'.

addressed in setting out the principles relevant to justified self-defence, and also in the important lines of argument they suggest.

The two major lines of argument about justified homicide in self-defence both arise from a moral principle which is both commonly and legally taken to distinguish homicide in self-defence from impermissible private homicide. This is the principle that a private person must not intentionally kill an innocent person.[29] The Thomistic strand of natural law thinking on self-defence emphasizes the importance of the self-defending agent's intention: it distinguishes and grounds permissible self-defence in something like the Principle of Double Effect. The Double Effect justification of self-defence now extends beyond natural law, and I discuss it in detail in chapter 4. The other strand, pursued by writers like Grotius, Pufendorf, and Locke, emphasizes the relevance of innocence in the prohibition against taking human life. Here 'innocent' mostly means 'unoffending'; and an unoffending person is someone who is not him- or herself an unjust threat. To be offending one need not be culpable, nor need one intend to harm, nor (possibly) need one even be acting. Those who justify homicide in self-defence along these lines need to say what the conditions of being an unjust threat are, and also how, if this concept can be satisfactorily explained, it legitimizes self-preference. Whichever strand is pursued, the legitimacy of self-preferential killing needs to be defended; and this requirement has given rise, more widely, to the view that self-preference is legitimate in the case of homicide in self-defence because an unjust aggressor forfeits certain rights.

In chapter 5, I maintain that the important insight of natural law discussions is that the justification of the use of force in self-defence is grounded in the fact that it resists, repels, or wards off an unjust immediate threat. However, it is not an easy task to define the conditions under which someone is offending, an unjust threat to another. At this

---

[29] Some who accept this principle as distinguishing homicide in self-defence from (say) killing under duress, would qualify it in order to permit voluntary euthanasia.

stage we can at least say that culpability is not a necessary condition: someone can innocently pose an unjust threat to another person. Further, in my view, intentional action is not a necessary condition: the attacking sleepwalker poses an unjust threat. A precise account of the conditions under which someone is an unjust threat would need to be derived from an appropriate derivation and specification of rights such as the right to life. Although a comprehensive account of the nature and limits of such rights is beyond the scope of this book, in chapter 6 I outline what I consider to be essential features of an appropriate specification of the right to life as part of the justification of homicide in self-defence.

Chapter 4

The Double Effect justification

Homicide in self-defence has been characterized as unintended killing, and said to be justified under the conditions of the Principle of Double Effect. Those who appeal to this Principle distinguish an effect of an act which the agent intends from an effect which the agent merely foresees. Traditionally, those who have sought to justify homicide in self-defence in terms of Double Effect have maintained that, while as a private person I must not engage in intentional killing, it can be permissible for me to act foreseeing that my act will kill someone, provided I do not intend this effect. On the Double Effect view, because intentional killing is prohibited, the agent's intention is crucial to the permissibility of self-defence when the aggressor's death is foreseen as a certain or highly probable effect. Foreseen homicide in self-defence poses both the most difficult case of self-defence for the Double Effect justification, and the case of self-defence for which, on this view, the Double Effect justification is crucial. Here it is held that, provided the agent intends only to use necessary force to defend him- or herself, the aggressor's death is unintended.[1] As explained so far, the Principle of Double Effect could also permit homicide in defence of others.[2]

[1] The foreseen bad effect is sometimes said not to be directly intended.
[2] Anscombe, for instance, says that the 'plea of self-defence (or defence of someone else) made by a private man who has killed someone else must in conscience – even if not in law – be a plea that the death of the other was not intended, but was a side-effect of the measures taken to ward off the attack', 'War and Murder', p. 54. However, in n75 this chapter and accompanying text, I question the extension of the Double Effect justification of homicide in self-defence to defence of others.

4.1 THE RELEVANCE OF DOUBLE EFFECT TO SELF-DEFENCE

Numerous philosophical discussions of the Principle of Double Effect have focused, rightly, on whether its distinction between an intended and a foreseen effect of an agent's act is defensible and morally important in problem cases.[3] Direct consequentialists usually dismiss this distinction as confused or morally irrelevant. Also, many who hold that factors such as an act's being of a particular type (e.g. an injustice), and the agent's intention, enter independently into the moral evaluation of acts, nevertheless reject Double Effect. Those in this latter group are often concerned to reject the general, exceptionless moral prohibitions which gave rise to the Principle, rather than to argue that the Principle's central distinction is not morally relevant. Some advocates and numerous critics also misunderstand the Principle's purpose in its Thomistic context, which is to rule on the permissibility of acts with foreseen effects of a type that, according to adherents, one must not intend. The Principle does not maintain, implausibly, that we are not responsible for the foreseen bad effects of our voluntary acts provided these effects are unintended. I have argued in detail for these interpretive points elsewhere,[4] and others have argued along similar lines; nevertheless, these misunderstandings of Double Effect persist.[5]

The view that homicide in self-defence is justified in terms of the Principle of Double Effect is an influential, important strand of natural law thinking on this issue. This seems to me

---

[3] See, e.g. Jonathan Bennett, 'Whatever the Consequences', reprinted in *Killing and Letting Die*, edited by Bonnie Steinbock (Englewood Cliffs, New Jersey: Prentice-Hall, 1980); G. E. M. Anscombe, 'Modern Moral Philosophy' and 'War and Murder'; H. L. A. Hart, 'Intention and Responsibility', reprinted in Hart, *Punishment and Responsibility* (Oxford University Press, 1968); Philippa Foot, 'The Problem of Abortion and the Doctrine of Double Effect', reprinted in Foot, *Virtues and Vices* (Oxford: Basil Blackwell, 1978); Jonathan Glover, *Causing Death and Saving Lives* (Harmondsworth: Penguin Books, 1977), ch. 6.

[4] 'The Doctrine of Double Effect', *The Thomist*, vol. 48, no. 2, 1984, pp. 188–218.

[5] See, e.g. Campbell and Collinson, *Ending Lives*, p. 153.

a sufficient reason for carefully assessing this claim. However, the Principle's possible relevance to the morality of homicide in self-defence is not confined to natural law. A number of writers have argued that utilitarian considerations warrant our adopting, as a 'practical absolute', the moral prohibition of intentional homicide of innocent persons.[6] I do not find this particular line of argument persuasive.[7] But those who accept some form of indirect consequentialism may regard the Principle's central distinction as important to the morality of self-defence against morally innocent threats, and also to the morality of foreseen killing of non-threats in the course of self-defence. Recently a number of philosophers who are not institutionally committed to the Principle of Double Effect and exceptionless moral rules, have urged the general relevance to the moral evaluation of acts, and to the specification of the limits of moral obligation, of a distinction between what we aim at and what we foresee will result from what we do.[8] Their arguments are important, and provide an additional reason for deciding whether foreseen homicide in self-defence is always plausibly characterized as unintended killing. Many people regard the intentional killing of innocent persons as intrinsically wrong, and as normally very seriously wrong; further, they view the agent's intention to inflict such injustices, and not simply the infliction of them, as relevant to the moral evaluation of any such act. It is important, at least in some circumstances, to decide whether homicide in self-defence is unintended killing.

[6] For example, Philip E. Devine, 'The Principle of Double Effect', *The American Journal of Jurisprudence*, vol. 19, 1975, pp. 44–60. Richard Brandt has also maintained that absolutism about compliance with rules governing warfare can follow from rule-utilitarianism, 'Utilitarianism and the Rules of War', reprinted in *War and Moral Responsibility*, edited by Marshall Cohen, Thomas Nagel, and Thomas Scanlon (Princeton: Princeton University Press, 1974).

[7] See my article 'The Doctrine of Double Effect', p. 208, n38.

[8] See, e.g. R. A. Duff, 'Intention, Responsibility and Double Effect', *Philosophical Quarterly*, vol. 32, no. 126, 1982, pp. 12–13; Philippa Foot, 'Morality, Action and Outcome', in *Morality and Objectivity: a Tribute to J. L. Mackie*, edited by Ted Honderich (London: Routledge and Kegan Paul, 1985); Thomas Nagel, *The View From Nowhere* (Oxford University Press, 1986), p. 179.

I say in some circumstances, because where the agent's intention is said to be relevant to the morality of foreseen killing, what is now commonly thought to be morally offensive is the intentional killing of an *innocent* person. As I noted in chapter 3, Aquinas maintained that a private person must never kill anyone intentionally; hence the need to appeal to 'double effect' as a justification of all private homicide in self-defence. Some modern exponents of the Principle of Double Effect also hold this unqualified prohibition of intentional private homicide.[9] However, other writers regard the qualified prohibition of intentional homicide as having general application – as constraining permissible intentional private homicide as well as intentional homicide by public authorities. And the natural law prohibition of intentional private homicide is also sometimes expressed in this qualified way. On this qualified prohibition of intentional private homicide, whether the agent's intention is crucial to the permissibility of homicide in self-defence will depend on how the qualification 'innocent' is explained.

Some writers suggest that the relevant sense of 'innocent' is 'causally innocent' or 'currently harmless': that 'innocent' is opposed not to 'guilty' but to 'doing harm'.[10] However, 'caus-

9 Anscombe, for instance, maintains that the qualified prohibition – that the innocent must not be killed intentionally – applies only to rulers and those under their command. Innocent persons are never permissibly killed intentionally, by anyone; however, unjust aggressors can permissibly be killed intentionally in war, 'War and Murder', pp. 53–4.

10 Anscombe suggests this sense in 'Mr Truman's Degree', reprinted in *Collected Philosophical Papers*, vol. III, p. 67 and p. 69; however, Anscombe is speaking of warfare, not private defence. Philip E. Devine, *The Ethics of Homicide*, p. 152, suggests 'those who are doing no harm' as the sense of 'innocent' relevant to the justification of private defence. See also Thomas Nagel's discussion in 'War and Massacre', p. 19. Nagel urges the moral relevance of a distinction between what one (deliberately) does to people and what merely happens to them as a result of what one does, pp. 9–11. This distinction seems to straddle two distinctions which Shelly Kagan discusses as part of his critique of 'ordinary morality': the distinction between doing and allowing and that between intending and foreseeing, *The Limits of Morality* (Oxford University Press, 1989), chapters 3 and 4. In discussing self-defence as seriously problematic for the constraint against intending harm, Kagan himself appears to take 'not innocent' to mean 'culpable', pp. 134–5.

ally innocent' interpreted as 'currently harmless' is too broad to mark the desired *moral* boundary between those who are thought impermissibly killed intentionally and those who are not considered immune in this way.[11] As I pointed out in chapter 3, a person against whom force is used *in self-defence* is him- or herself an immediate threat: he or she is not currently harmless. Thus, *all* homicide in self-defence, irrespective of the rights and wrongs of the conflict, would seem to fall outside the scope of this interpretation of the prohibition of intentional killing. Consider a case in which A is conducting an unjust attack on B, and A defends herself against B's use of force in self-defence. Some people would excuse A's self-defence here; some might (like Hobbes) even think it permissible. But those who believe that it is wrong to kill the innocent intentionally should feel extremely uncomfortable with the implication that in these circumstances A is freed of the constraint not to kill B intentionally simply because B is not currently harmless to A.

The relevant sense of 'innocent' in the qualified moral prohibition or constraint needs to be more explicitly and strongly normative than is 'currently harmless'. 'Blameless' is too narrow. 'Unoffending' – i.e., not an unjust threat – marks a more defensible moral boundary. (Because there can be blameless unjust threats, it is better not to use 'innocent' to mean 'unoffending'. But here my concern is not terminological clarity, but the substance of the distinction between 'innocent' (unoffending) persons and others.) In chapter 3, I remarked on the difficulty in some cases of identifying someone as a threat in the sense relevant to acting in self-defence, and also on the additional difficulty of specifying the conditions under which someone is an unjust threat. A prohibition of intentional homicide of unoffending persons creates harder cases than a prohibition which invokes the

11 Some might consider 'currently harmless', taken strictly, also to be too narrow to mark the limit of permissible intentional killing. Think of the example (from 3.2) of the instigator of a contract killing who is killed as a means of self-defence against the hit man. Anscombe, 'Mr Truman's Degree', p. 67, comments 'that "what someone is doing" can refer either to what he is doing at the moment or to his role in the situation'.

broader distinction between the currently harmful and the currently harmless. Nevertheless, unless the scope of the prohibition or constraint is meant to exclude *all* homicide in self-defence, irrespective of the rights and wrongs of the conflict, the more difficult of these two distinctions needs to be maintained. The less difficult distinction – that between those who are currently harmless and those who are not – is too descriptive to mark a boundary of such professed intrinsic moral importance. Further, to reiterate another point from chapter 3, the need to defend a distinction between offending and unoffending persons is not confined to natural law accounts: something like this distinction is crucial to the justification of self-preference in the case of foreseen homicide in self-defence. In the final section of this present chapter, I highlight the significance of the justification of self-preference to the justification of homicide in self-defence. In chapters 5 and 6, I explain what I consider to be the necessary terms of this issue's resolution.

The more modest points which need to be emphasized at this stage can be summarized as follows: If the qualified prohibition of intentional homicide applies to private homicide, and 'innocent' refers to someone who is currently harmless, then appeal to Double Effect seems irrelevant to the permissibility of homicide in self-defence. (However, on this view, Double Effect will be crucial to the permissibility of foreseen homicide in the course of self-defence, and also to the permissibility of foreseen homicide in cases of necessity.) Alan Donagan, for instance, claims that the Principle is superfluous to the justification of self-defence if we accept (as he does) that someone 'who uses violence upon others forfeits his own immunity to violence to whatever extent may be necessary in order to protect them'.[12] If, alternatively, 'inno-

---

[12] Alan Donagan, *The Theory of Morality* (Chicago: University of Chicago Press, 1977), p. 163. Donagan takes this claim about forfeiture to be akin to Aquinas' view on the matter. However, Aquinas' remarks on the moral implications of the forfeiture of human dignity refer to cases of sinning: they are made in the context of his discussion of capital punishment. Aquinas invokes the notion of 'double effect' in the case of private

cent' in the prohibition means 'not guilty' (blameless), then Double Effect will be important to the justification of self-defence against morally innocent aggressors, as well as to the permissibility of killing in the course of self-defence and in cases of necessity. More plausibly, 'innocent' in the qualified prohibition of intentional homicide might refer to someone who is unoffending, not an unjust threat.[13] In this case, Double Effect could be relevant to the morality of self-defence against those who are not clearly unjust threats, and possibly to the moral permissibility of self-defence against some just threats. However, if private homicide *is* constrained by the qualified prohibition that the innocent not be killed intentionally, and 'innocent' means 'unoffending', then Double Effect is not essential to the justification of homicide in self-defence against an unjust threat.

It is often assumed that the aggressor's death is unintended when lethal force is used in self-defence; and many people take this to have an important bearing on the moral permissibility of homicide in self-defence. The description of the aggressor's death as a 'side-effect' of homicide in self-defence is invoked outside natural law justifications.[14] This line of thought about the justification of homicide in self-defence thus warrants close critical attention. I argue in 4.2 that despite sophisticated arguments to the contrary, homicide in self-defence is not always plausibly characterized as unintended killing. However, my interest in the Double Effect justification of homicide in self-defence extends beyond its being a highly influential view, the central claim of which I do not endorse. As I illustrate in 4.3, the evaluation of a particular range of acts of foreseen self-preferential killing under the conditions of the Principle of Double Effect highlights some-

homicide in self-defence because he holds that it is impermissible for a private person to kill *anyone* intentionally.

[13] Anscombe suggests this sense in 'War and Murder', p. 53 (again, she is speaking of warfare, not private self-defence).

[14] See, for instance, the legal theorist George Fletcher, 'The Right to Life', p. 139. Fletcher also maintains that lack of intention to harm is part of the legal consensus about the elements of Self-Defence, 'Passion and Reason in Self-Defense', p. 649.

thing very important about the justification of homicide in self-defence: namely, the significance to the justification of self-preference of the fact that lethal force is defensive and directed against an unjust aggressor.

4.2 IS HOMICIDE IN SELF-DEFENCE UNINTENDED KILLING?

Traditional statements of the Principle (or Doctrine) of Double Effect outline four conditions under which it is said to be morally permissible for a person voluntarily to bring about a foreseen bad effect of a type never permissibly intended. These conditions are:

(1)The act itself must be morally good or at least indifferent; (2)The agent may not positively will the bad effect but may permit it. If he could attain the good effect without the bad effect he should do so. The bad effect is sometimes said to be indirectly voluntary; (3)The good effect must flow from the action at least as immediately (in the order of causality, though not necessarily in the order of time) as the bad effect. In other words the good effect must be produced directly by the action, not by the bad effect. Otherwise the agent would be using a bad means to a good end, which is never allowed; (4)The good effect must be sufficiently desirable to compensate for the allowing of the bad effect. In forming this decision many factors must be weighed and compared, with care and prudence proportionate to the importance of the case. Thus, an effect that benefits or harms society generally has more weight than one that affects only the individual, and an effect sure to occur deserves greater consideration than one that is only probable; an effect of a moral nature has greater importance than one that deals only with material things ...[15]

Condition 1

In general to seek to preserve one's own life is a morally legitimate end. Some people also regard it as a duty. But unless one holds that self-preservation, and more particularly

[15] *New Catholic Encyclopedia*, vol. 4 (New York: McGraw-Hill, 1967), pp. 1020–2.

self-defence, is always one's overriding obligation, whether a particular act for this end is justified will depend on factors such as the nature of the threat to one's life (e.g. that it is unjust, imminent, and cannot otherwise be avoided without unreasonable cost), the means used to defend oneself (that they are necessary for defence, and that they do not impermissibly infringe someone else's rights), and the foreseeable consequences of self-defence (that the harm done is proportionate to that prevented). Conditions 2, 3, and 4 of the Principle are meant to guide decision on matters such as these, and also on the crucial issue of intention.

Condition 2, necessity and intention

It is certainly wrong to assume that an agent can avoid intending a foreseen bad effect of his or her act simply by directing his or her *attention* away from it at the time of acting.[16] The sense of 'intention' relevant to the Principle is outlined in conditions 2 and 3: an agent is said to intend *that which he or she positively wills as his or her chosen end* (condition 2) *or as a means to that end* (condition 3).

Before I discuss the applicability of this notion of intention to homicide in self-defence, it is worth pointing out that deliberation under condition 2 illustrates something important about the more general requirement of necessity to which I drew attention in chapter 3. The second condition states: 'The agent may not positively will the bad effect but may permit it. If he could attain the good effect without the bad effect he should do so.' The second sentence of this condition seems meant to illuminate the first to some extent. And indeed, the fact that particular harm is caused where it could have been avoided, and the stated end still achieved, can be a strong indication that this harm too was intended, part of the agent's aim. For instance, if I am physically very strong and I know that I could easily and harmlessly restrain a particular aggressor with my bare hands, but I choose instead

[16] Anscombe, 'War and Murder', pp. 58–9.

to pick up a gun and shoot him, then it is implausible to claim that it was no part of my intention, my aim, to harm him.

The suggestion of a strong link between an agent's voluntarily causing unnecessary harm, and his or her intending that harm, arises from the stipulation that the agent not inflict unnecessary harm. This stipulation is an important moral and legal condition of justified self-defence. But as with this more general requirement of necessity, the Principle's requirement that, if possible, the agent obtain the good effect without the bad, to be reasonable, cannot be interpreted absolutely literally: it must itself sometimes involve an evaluation of relative costs and the reasonableness of alternative courses of action. The agent must believe that the act which will cause the foreseen harm is necessary in the circumstances; but this condition must allow that sometimes an agent can reasonably regard the act which will cause this particular harm as indispensable even though there are alternative means available for achieving the desired end which will not cause *this* harm.

If condition 2 were to require that the act with the foreseen bad effect be the agent's sole available means of achieving the good effect, then the Principle would be extremely limited as a possible guide to moral decision. This very restrictive interpretation would mostly confine the Principle's use to cases which are not really morally perplexing. This cannot be what is meant. Rather, condition 2 places the onus on the person who would cause harm in the achievement of some good end to consider less harmful alternatives and to justify the harm caused as unintended and reasonably judged necessary in the circumstances.

I now come more directly to the issue of intention. Given what I argue below, it is important that I say clearly at the outset that sometimes it is perfectly appropriate to call a foreseen bad effect a side-effect or an unavoidable concomitant of an act or activity aimed at something else. People who undergo chemotherapy for cancer suffer nausea and hair loss which, although foreseen bad effects of the treatment, are no part of its aim. Similarly, weight gain is often a foreseen side-effect of some oral contraceptives, fluid retention is a foreseen side-effect of immuno-suppressant drugs, and thinning of the skin and puffiness are foreseen side-effects of the use of anti-inflammatory steroids. More relevantly, there are cases in which a foreseen death can be either a side-effect of an act aimed at something else (e.g. a civilian death which occurs when a bomb is dropped on a military target located near a house), or an unintended effect foreseeably brought about (e.g. where a doctor operates (say) by transplanting organs, as the only hope of saving someone's life, realizing that the surgery or its effects will probably kill the patient).

Nevertheless, it is important to specify the conditions under which an effect of an act or activity is a *side-effect* or a *concomitant*, because the very common use of these terms to describe the bad effect in cases of double effect can mislead us about that feature of a foreseen bad effect which conditions 2 and 3 take to be morally crucial; and this can also unnecessarily restrict the Principle's possible useful application. The Principle is paradigmatically used to distinguish intended effects from incidental effects which are foreseen as being certain. But (as illustrated by examples below) the Double Effect distinction is arguably also morally relevant to cases of justified risk taking in which the bad effect is foreseen as highly probable rather than certain.

Both 'side-effect' and 'concomitant' are terms of everyday discourse and may be somewhat imprecise, but obviously each can be used appropriately or inappropriately. The Oxford Dictionary describes a side-effect of an act as a secondary (usually undesirable) effect. Secondary effects are sometimes indirect effects, but an act or activity can have direct side-effects. The hair loss which results from chemotherapy, and the fluid retention caused by immuno-suppressant drugs, are paradigm side-effects. Side-effects are often, but are not necessarily, unwelcome. If I take on a manual job in order to earn extra money, a side-effect of this might be that I become much more physically fit, something about which I should be very pleased. The important consideration in describing the fitness as a side-effect is not that it is unwelcome, but rather that it was not my reason or part of my reason for doing this work. (If the increased fitness is a reason for taking the manual job, with the extra money being the primary reason, then fitness is a secondary or subordinate motive, not a side-effect.) Also, most often when we describe an effect as a *side*-effect, another effect (the aim with which the act was done) has been achieved, at least to some extent. This is necessarily so with 'concomitant' which means accompanying thing. If the person for whom I am doing the manual work goes broke and I am not paid, I might console myself with the thought that at least I got fit as a result of the work. If I undergo chemotherapy and this has no short or long-term therapeutic effect, then I am likely to complain that all the treatment did was cause nausea and make my hair fall out. The fitness and the hair loss in these examples could still be described as side-effects, bearing in mind what the activities which caused them were intended to achieve alongside these effects. But neither is a concomitant of the intended effect. Lastly, an act or an effect of an act which in the circumstances contributes to the achievement of the aim – that is, something by means of which the aim is brought about – is not a side-effect, nor merely an unavoidable concomitant. Side-effects and unavoidable concomitants are not essential, either as part of the aim or the means to its achievement in the circumstances, even when the agent believes they will certainly occur. Undoubtedly this is the reason for the common use of the terms 'side-effect' and 'unavoidable concomitant' to describe the bad effect of actions said to be of double effect.

The above discussion identifies that feature of side-effects and unavoidable concomitants which conditions 2 and 3 require of the foreseen bad effect. This requirement is that the bad effect be *incidental*: it must not be either part of what the agent aims to do or bring about, nor part of the means of achieving the agent's aim in the circumstances. This requirement can be fulfilled where the bad effect is not, because of other features of these two concepts, appropriately described as an unavoidable concomitant or a side-effect. Consider the above example of the surgeon who operates in a desperate attempt to save someone's life, knowing that the surgery will probably kill the patient. Predictably in the circumstances, the patient dies. Here the patient's death is neither an unavoidable concomitant nor a side-effect of the surgery. This is not because it is a direct result of the surgery. (Death may have been due to tissue rejection or infection, and even if the surgery itself has killed the patient, side-effects can be direct effects.) Rather, it is because the patient's death is entirely incompatible with the aim of the surgery, and hence cannot accompany the aim (be a concomitant) or be caused alongside the aim (be a side-effect). Nevertheless, the doctor's action fulfils conditions 2 and 3, and seems permissible under the Principle's other conditions. In other cases too, Double Effect would appear to allow acts which will probably themselves directly kill someone – and indeed to identify the reasons why these acts are cases of justified risk taking – when it is nonsense to describe the death as a concomitant or a side-effect.[17] One such case is where a parent throws her child out of a burning building as the child's only hope of not being burnt to death, hoping to save the child's life but realizing that the fall may well kill it.[18]

---

[17] R. A. Duff makes a similar point in *Intention, Agency and Criminal Liability* (Oxford: Basil Blackwell, 1990), pp. 97–8. He makes the milder comment that *'pure* side-effects' are those effects 'whose occurrence is *wholly* irrelevant to the success or failure of the action' (emphases original). In my view, a foreseen effect the occurrence of which is wholly incompatible with the agent's aim is not an *impure* side-effect: such an effect is *incidental* to the agent's aim, but it cannot be a side-effect.

[18] This example, and the risky surgery case, are cited in the Law Reform Commission of Victoria's Discussion Paper No. 13, *Homicide* (1988), in connection with the question of allowing the defence of Necessity to murder in cases of justified risk taking. Such examples bring out that some foreseen effects of an agent's act are not intended because they are wholly incompatible with the agent's aim. Where this is so, one way of allowing the accused a defence to murder could be to recognize this distinction in the legal notion of intention in murder. (See also Duff, *Intention, Agency and Criminal Liability*, pp. 97–8.) The required distinction is clear enough, and would need to be drawn anyway in pleading Necessity to murder in a case of risk taking. Finnis, 'Intention and Side-Effects', p. 51, proposes that the mental element in murder be defined disjunctively, as 'either intention in its ordinary sense or certainty ("knowledge") that death would be brought about by an act that one does without lawful justification or excuse'. Finnis also maintains that judges have rejected the view that 'an agent who foresees con-

So, although 'double effect' implies, and is mostly taken to refer to, two *actual* effects, one intended and the other not, the descriptions 'side-effect' and 'unavoidable concomitant' are too restrictive as characterizations of what conditions 2 and 3 require and allow. Side-effects and unavoidable concomitants are incidental both to the aim of an act or activity and to the means of its achievement in the circumstances. But some incidental effects of acts and activities which are aimed at some good purpose are neither side-effects nor unavoidable concomitants. Thus, the terms 'side-effect' and 'unavoidable concomitant' can be misleading, and their use in some cases can make what is arguably an important moral consideration seem very implausible. In assessing the applicability of the distinction between what is intended and what is merely foreseen – to homicide in self-defence and in general – it is far better to specify that the foreseen bad effect be *incidental*. The foreseen bad effect must not be necessary, either as part of the agent's aim or the means of achieving that aim in the circumstances.

sequences as *probable*, or at least as highly probable, intends those consequences', p. 45 (emphasis original).

Ought Necessity be an admissible defence to murder in cases in which the foreseen death *is compatible with* the achievement of the agent's aim? Here is a case where so-called justificatory Necessity, if admissible, would be strongly arguable: a driver whose brakes fail swerves into a pedestrian on the footpath, killing him, rather than running into a group of people on a level crossing. Here is a case where so-called excusatory Necessity, if admissible, would be strongly arguable: a driver whose brakes fail runs into a pedestrian crossing the road, killing him, rather than steering into a steep embankment. To allow Necessity as a defence to murder might seem a practical way of avoiding the difficulty of satisfactorily incorporating a more general 'double effect' distinction in the legal notion of intention. However, this difficulty would still have to be faced at some point if 'justificatory' and 'excusatory' Necessity in the examples just given are to be distinguished from (say) a surgeon's killing one person in order to use parts of his body to save another or others. To disallow Necessity altogether as a defence to murder, and to rely instead on the good judgment of prosecutors to ensure that people are not unfairly or inappropriately charged in cases of risk taking, is a way of avoiding the difficulties of the 'double effect' distinction. But it is not a wise solution in my view.

Intention and homicide in self-defence

This particular distinction between what is intended and what is merely foreseen can be clearly stated. Further, sometimes this distinction can be drawn with some point. But can foreseen homicide in self-defence always plausibly be characterized as unintended killing?

It can always rightly be claimed about homicide in self-defence that the aggressor's death is not *strictly required*, provided this means only that it would be sufficient for self-defence if the aggressor could be, or were to be, warded off or stopped without being killed. But the agent who acts in self-defence *intends to use necessary force* against the threat, and it is most important that we do not equate *necessary force in the circumstances* with what is strictly required for self-defence (the latter will always be only that the aggressor be warded off or stopped). Necessary force is not determined simply by what is strictly required in the above sense. Necessary force is, rather, *the degree of force that it is necessary for a particular agent in a particular set of circumstances to use in order to stop the threat*. Necessary force in a particular set of circumstances depends not only on the nature of the threat, but also on the capabilities of the self-defending agent and what defensive measures are available at the time. If someone is shooting at me, for example, it is strictly required for self-defence only that I stop the bullets hitting me. It is not strictly required that I kill the gunman nor even that I harm him. (If available, far less violent measures, e.g. the use of a shield, might be perfectly adequate to stop the shots hitting me until help arrives.) Nevertheless, it could be necessary in some circumstances that I use force on a gunman in self-defence, and sometimes the degree of necessary force will be lethal (e.g. explosives thrown at someone in a bunker).

The standard of what is strictly required for the achievement of the agent's aim is sometimes invoked by exponents of Double Effect as sufficient to determine whether a foreseen bad effect is part of the agent's intention. The answer to the question, 'Would the agent's end or aim in any way be thwarted if the bad effect did not occur?' identifies what is strictly required. Thus the answer to this question sometimes marks an important difference between what the agent aims at and what he or she merely foresees (e.g. the chemotherapy case). But this question is too narrow as it stands to mark the outer limit of intention where the agent's aim is specified as 'the good effect' (whatever it might be). This test would classify as unintended cases of killing in which the death of the person killed is *perceived by the agent as necessary in the circumstances*, although not strictly required, for the achievement of the good effect. One such example is where a terminally ill patient requests direct euthanasia because he is suffering unbearable, seemingly unrelievable pain, and the doctor complies by giving this person what is normally a lethal dose of a drug; against all expectation the patient survives the dose and the drug eliminates the pain.[19] It is not then necessary for the doctor to achieve *her aim of ending this patient's suffering* (good effect) by ensuring that the patient dies some other way. Here, in giving the patient the drug the doctor intended to kill him (the doctor gave the patient what she believed was a lethal dose in order to bring about death). Exponents of the Principle of Double Effect typically, and rightly, maintain that this is so.[20]

However, at least one prominent twentieth-century natural law philosopher, Germain Grisez, employs the criterion of what is strictly required for the agent's aim in determining the agent's intention under condition 2. Thus, Grisez maintains that the aggressor's death is not the agent's intention in any case of genuine self-defence because it contributes nothing

---

[19] This example is a variation of one suggested to me by Peter Singer.
[20] See also Duff, *Intention, Agency and Criminal Liability*, pp. 62–3. Duff points out that 'the test of failure' ('Would the agent's intention be thwarted ... ?') must be applied in light of the agent's beliefs at the time of action. Duff argues that this test does then distinguish an action's (paradigm) *intended* effects (those which the agent acts in order to bring about) from its foreseen side-effects (some of which Duff thinks can be said to be done *intentionally*). However, I doubt that Duff would accept that the aggressor's death is always a foreseen side-effect of self-defence on this test, pp. 89–91. See also Duff's 'Intentionally Killing the Innocent', *Analysis*, vol. 34, 1973, pp. 16–19.

directly to the agent's objective (to stop the threat), but is only a contingent fact.[21] Numerous other moralists, including many sympathetic to Double Effect, have objected to what they regard as the sometimes sophistical manoeuvre whereby the agent's intention is specified under the description of what is strictly required for the achievement of the agent's aim (e.g. the termination of pregnancy in the first trimester by the removal of the foetus from the womb) and not under another description (killing the foetus). But in order to resist this sort of distinction as a distortion of the Principle, they need to appeal to something like Philippa Foot's suggested 'criterion of "closeness" ... (whereby) anything very close to what we are literally aiming at counts as if part of our aim'.[22] Philip Devine argues that we should be able to refer to a 'non-fantastic scenario' in which the good effect is achieved without the bad.[23] Devine's requirement is too restrictive, because under the Principle's conditions 2 and 3 an agent can be said not to intend an effect of his act which is certain to occur. (This seems right, e.g. with the side-effects of some drugs.) Foot's suggested criterion of 'closeness' (which she does not develop) is important, and I take it up below.[24]

Condition 2 should, it seems to me, yield the following position on homicide in self-defence:

(i) In all cases of genuine self-defence the agent's aim is to stop the threat. The *death* of the person posing the threat is not strictly required for the achievement of this aim; that is to say, the aim of *stopping the threat* is logically distinguishable, and may be practically distinguishable under different circumstances, from killing the person who is the source of the threat: it is logically possible, and may in other circumstances be practically possible, that this aim be achieved without this death. (Grisez argues, more generally, that a 'performance

[21] Grisez, 'Toward a Consistent Natural Law Ethics of Killing', p. 76.
[22] Foot, 'The Problem of Abortion', p. 22.
[23] Devine, 'The Principle of Double Effect'.
[24] Warren S. Quinn's 'Actions, Intentions, and Consequences: The Doctrine of Double Effect', *Philosophy and Public Affairs*, vol. 18, no. 4, 1989, pp. 334–51, esp. pp. 337–43, is relevant to the following discussion of condition 2.

may be *divisible by thought* or divisible in the sense that *under some other conditions it could be divided*, yet *remain practically indivisible* for a given agent here and now'.)[25]

(ii) The *logical* distinguishability, or practical divisibility under *other* conditions, of what is strictly required for the achievement of the agent's aim, from an effect of the agent's act which the agent perceives as necessary in the circumstances for the achievement of his or her aim, cannot confine the agent's actual intention to what is strictly required. *An agent intends those aspects and effects of his or her act which he or she believes are necessary in the circumstances for the achievement of his or her aim.* And some aspects and effects of an act are too close to what the agent believes necessary to achieve his or her aim in the circumstances not to count as part of the agent's intention. Closeness is not merely a matter of empirical certainty: some genuinely incidental effects can be certain to occur. Rather, some so-called effects are too close to what the agent is literally aiming to achieve in the circumstances to be plausibly described as distinguishable effects. As Foot says, I cannot maintain that I did not intend to kill someone, but simply to blow him to pieces.[26] *Pace* Grisez, I cannot say that I did not intend to kill a foetus, but only to terminate the pregnancy in the first trimester by removing it from the womb by suction. In these cases, the intended degree of force (blowing someone up, removing a foetus by suction) and the result (killing) are the same event; the degree of force intended as necessary in the circumstances and the foreseen killing are not distinguishable effects of the same act.

(iii) Force used in self-defence is *directed at* the threat, and the *degree of force* that the agent believes *necessary in the circumstances* to stop the threat is *not incidental* to the agent's intention. Given this, we can maintain that the aggressor's death is not intended by the self-defending agent only if the degree of force intended as necessary in the circumstances to stop the threat is, from the self-defending agent's point of

---

[25] Grisez, 'Toward a Consistent Natural Law Ethics of Killing', p. 88 (my emphases).

[26] Foot, 'The Problem of Abortion', p. 21.

view, not expected to kill the aggressor. For example, although it is foreseeable that a person could die if I shoot her in the leg, or if I push her down an embankment, or if I attempt to shoot near her to frighten her and accidentally hit her, my stopping the threat in any of these ways, if in fact I kill in self-defence, need not be intentional killing.

In other, admittedly more difficult cases, an aggressor's death may be an *expected* effect of the agent's use of the necessary degree of force in self-defence, and yet be *incidental to the degree of force necessary in the circumstances* to stop the threat. Here I think of the following example. We are alone on top of a tall building admiring the view. Suddenly you rush at me obviously intending to push me off the building. You catch me off guard and are almost on top of me, but I am much stronger than you and provided I can ward off the very immediate threat, either by stepping out of your path or by pushing you a very short distance away, I will be out of danger. In the circumstances it is necessary for my defence only that I step sideways, or that I avoid your full impact by pushing you just a very short distance away. I can easily do either of these things. Unfortunately for you, however, the circumstances are such that if I step sideways, or push you away, you will go off the edge of the building. Now, were it necessary in the circumstances for me to defend myself *by pushing you off the building*, it would be strongly arguable that in intending to save myself in this way I intend to inflict lethal force. But this is not so in this example. Rather, the degree of force necessary for self-defence in these circumstances is only *my stepping sideways or my pushing you away*; in this case it is incidental to the necessary degree of force that it will cause you to go off the building.

I think that condition 2 is met in this last case. It is met where there is a plausible distinction between the degree of force necessary for self-defence in the circumstances (the infliction of which the agent intends), and a foreseen, unavoidable effect which is incidental to that degree of force. How can we say in a particular case that this distinction is plausibly drawn? Above I rejected the question, 'Would the agent's end or aim (confined to that which is strictly required) be thwarted if the bad effect did not occur?' as too narrow to determine that the agent did not intend the bad effect. But of course a variation of this test uncontroversially (because trivially) identifies something (e.g. a degree of force) as intended by the agent as necessary in the circumstances to achieve what is strictly required. For instance, if I intend only to step out of your way or to push you away, either of *these* intentions will be thwarted if I don't manage to step out of your way or to push you away. But neither of these intentions will be thwarted if I do not, in stepping sideways or in pushing you away, cause you to go off the building. However, if I aim to eliminate you as a threat by pushing you off the building, *this* intention is thwarted if you do not go off the building. Similarly, if I try to stop you shooting at me by blowing you up, *this* intention is thwarted if you do not get blown up; if I intend to terminate a pregnancy by removing the foetus from the womb by suction, *this* intention is thwarted if the suction does not remove the foetus; if I intend to give someone a lethal dose, *this* intention is thwarted if the person doesn't die. Foot's criterion of 'closeness' then determines whether I must be said to intend to kill in acting on the following intentions: to push you off the building, to blow the gunman up, to remove the foetus from the womb by suction, and to give the patient a lethal dose. (Of these I think that only the first intention of necessary force is arguably not an intention to kill. In the example, I know how tall the building is, and that there is nothing to break your fall, etc., and necessary force in these circumstances is my *pushing you off*, because I am otherwise defenceless. Nevertheless, closeness is a matter of degree; necessary force in these circumstances need not be as close to my killing you as it is in circumstances in which necessary force is my blowing you up, because *the very same degree of force* (my pushing you off the building so that I am out of range) would be all that is necessary were there to be something (e.g. a ledge) below to break your fall.)

The distinction between the intended degree of force and unintended effects of that force can sometimes be very difficult to draw in practice, and there are obviously borderline cases. Nevertheless, there are examples in which it is simply sophistical to deny that an agent's intention to use necessary force is an intention to kill. Whenever my honest characterization of my intentional act of *directing at this threat the degree of force I believe to be necessary in the circumstances to stop it* is a description of an act that is itself a foreseen killing (e.g. 'I am stopping her by blowing her up'), then I cannot plausibly maintain that I did not intend to kill. Homicide in self-defence is sometimes intentional killing.[27]

Condition 3, means and ends

Some who accept, as I do not, that genuine self-defence always meets condition 2, nevertheless argue that some killing in self-defence does not comply with condition 3. Grisez notes that heavy criticism has focused on condition 3, because if a chosen means is as intended as one's objective, then this 'seems to exclude killing in self-defense because the force used as a means of self-defense is effective to that end only in virtue of the fact that it first harms the attacker. If the required form and level of defensive force will be in fact deadly, then the one defending himself is safe only when the attacker has suffered a death-dealing counterattack. Reasoning thus, many who hold the principle of double effect do not apply it to the case of killing in self-defense. Instead they say that in such cases the intentional killing of an unjust assailant is justified.'[28]

Condition 3 requires that good effect be produced directly by the act, not by the bad effect. In discussions of whether the Principle of Double Effect permits some cases of abortion, for instance, advocates often say that there is a difference in intention between the act of removing a foetus (thereby killing it) in order to save a woman's life, *where the foetus itself constitutes the danger* (impermissible), and removing a cancer-

---

[27] See also Charles Fried, *Right and Wrong* (Harvard University Press, 1978), p. 44.
[28] Grisez, 'Toward a Consistent Natural Law Ethics of Killing', p. 79.

ous womb (thereby killing the foetus it contains) in order to save the woman's life, *where the cancer constitutes the danger* (permissible). The woman's life in the second case is saved by the removal of a cancerous womb, the presence of the foetus and its removal from the woman's body being irrelevant (incidental) to this aim and to the means of achieving it.

This distinction between a good effect produced directly by the act, and a good effect produced through the foreseen bad effect, can be clearly drawn. (Although many, including myself, would reject it as morally decisive in the above cases, and I doubt very much that it can consistently be applied to all abortions now usually said to be permissible under the Principle's conditions, e.g. terminations of ectopic pregnancies.)[29] Further, this distinction, like that between what is aimed at and what is incidental to the agent's aim, seems inapplicable to some very straightforward examples of homicide in self-defence. Something like Foot's criterion of 'closeness' must be important not only to the interpretation of condition 2, but also in determining whether or not the bad effect is a means to the agent's aim. For example, where my only available means of stopping an aggressor is to blow him up, then *this act of blowing the aggressor up* is in the circumstances *the way in which I stop him*. I stop him *by* blowing him up, and *this* is too close to killing the aggressor for his death not to be intended as a means.

If some advocates of Double Effect maintain that even in such a case the aggressor's death is unintended, or (very implausibly) is a side-effect, then the Principle's notion of intention seems indefensible and so narrow that it admits a great deal more killing as unintended than exponents usually want to allow.[30] Traditionally, where the removal of a foetus from the womb in order to terminate a pregnancy is what is strictly required, and the foetus is so premature that its chance of survival outside the womb is as remote as that of someone directly hit by dynamite, or where, more to the

[29] See my article 'The Doctrine of Double Effect', pp. 209–11.
[30] Ibid., p. 208.

point here, the chosen method of removal kills it, exponents of Double Effect have held that the foetus' death is intended.

Grisez maintains otherwise, and in evaluating his sophisticated interpretation of condition 3 it is important to note that his argument goes well beyond his initial use of the somewhat vague phrase 'happens to involve', where he says that 'the death of the attacker is not the *means* of self-defense; rather, the means of self-defense happens to involve the attacker's death'.[31] He urges that this distinction is not vacuous because the aggressor's death does not contribute anything directly to the objective of self-defence. In maintaining this, Grisez appeals to what would need to be done to achieve the agent's aim where, contrary to expectation, the attacker is put out of action without being killed.[32] (Above I rejected this sort of question as invariably a satisfactory test of lack of intention.)

As I understand Grisez's argument, the essential parts of which I now explain in words very close to his own, he maintains: (i) that we must distinguish between a unified performance, one which is practically indivisible for a given agent here and now, and a performance which is divisible by the agent, and (ii) that a performance may be divisible by thought, or divisible in the sense that under some other conditions it could be divided, yet remain practically indivisible for a given agent here and now. My lighting a cigarette with a match is a performance which is practically divisible by me: I could ignite the match without lighting the cigarette, and I could light the cigarette a number of different ways. (So, lighting the match is my chosen means of lighting the cigarette.) But the fact that one can distinguish by thought, or because under some other conditions they could be divided, 'between moving one's fingers and a match's igniting *does not*

---

[31] Grisez, 'Toward a Consistent Natural Law Ethics of Killing', p. 76 (my emphasis). Also, Grisez maintains that abortion which doesn't strictly require the death of the foetus is unintended killing. He argues, unsuccessfully in my view, that abortion is mostly impermissible under condition 4. His argument for this explicitly assumes that the same rules must apply to the killing of foetuses as to 'any other persons'.

[32] Grisez, 'Toward a Consistent Natural Law Ethics of Killing', pp. 76–7.

necessitate the restriction of the human act, which is a means, to the movement of one's fingers. The reason is that one *cannot choose* to move one's fingers in that way without also choosing the igniting of the match.'[33]

We should, it seems to me, say the following about Grisez's match example. Provided I am holding a match in a certain way in my fingers, and I am holding the match very near and at a certain angle to the igniting side of a match box, and I am presently aware of how matches work and know that if I move my fingers in this way the match will ignite, then I cannot choose to move my fingers in this way without also choosing the igniting of the match. Under all these conditions, we do not restrict the human act, which is a means, to choosing to move my fingers in this way, because my choosing to move my fingers in this way is also my choosing to ignite the match. All the same, I can say that I ignite the match *by* moving my fingers in this way (rather than in some other way, and even if there is no other way). Further, under these conditions, even if I choose to move my fingers in this way for some reason which has nothing to do with the ignition of the match, in choosing so to act I choose to ignite the match. Similarly, if I know that I am in a gas-filled room, and I know what will happen if I ignite a match, then I cannot choose to ignite a match (for whatever reason) without choosing to blow myself up. Here, in choosing to ignite the match I choose to blow myself up. Nevertheless, you can say that I blew myself up *by* igniting the match (rather than in some other way, and even if there was no other way).

Grisez's own explanation of condition 3 is both very dense and, in some respects, lacking in the sort of detail which would be helpful in applying the more theoretical discussion to the cases of self-defence in question. Grisez does not say, for instance, exactly what he takes my intended act to be in those cases of self-defence in which it is necessary that I use lethal force. Is it my stopping the aggressor, which in the circumstances I cannot practically divide from my killing the

[33] Ibid., p. 88 (emphases original).

aggressor? Or is it, rather, my using *this* degree of force (lethal) on the aggressor in order to stop him, which is practically indivisible from my killing him? I take Grisez to mean the latter, because condition 3 raises the problem of means to ends in cases of self-defence in which it is necessary for me to use lethal force on the aggressor (i.e., to kill him) in order to stop him. Here Grisez is not arguing that I cannot stop the aggressor without killing him, although this needs to be so for Double Effect to apply. Rather, he claims that if I stop the aggressor by killing him, my killing him (bad effect) *need not be a means* to my stopping him, thereby saving myself (good effect).

The need to work through these details of Grisez's argument brings out something important, and that is that discussions of Double Effect too often take for granted that the agent's act or activity, and the good and bad effects of this, are clearly identifiable and distinguishable. In some cases this assumption is perfectly reasonable. For example, where the activity is a course of chemotherapy, the foreseen effects are both therapeutic (desired effects) and hair loss and nausea (unwanted effects). In the risky surgery case the surgery (activity) may have the desired effect (patient's life is saved) or the undesired effect (patient dies). But as Grisez recognizes, we also often engage in elision when speaking about human acts and their effects, and we describe what is either an effect of an agent's more basic act, or a further act, as itself the agent's act. In the previous paragraph I mentioned a number of examples – some unified performances and some not – in which such elision is appropriate: I move my fingers in this way (act) and the match ignites (effect), or I ignite the match (act); I ignite the match in this gas-filled room (act) and I get blown up (effect), or I blow myself up (act); I ignite the match (act) and then I light the cigarette (further act), or I light the cigarette (act). Sometimes the elision of more basic acts is inappropriate.[34] But we should note for future reference that the appropriateness of the elision of more basic acts

[34] See D'Arcy, *Human Acts*, pp. 18–19.

in the case of a unified performance does not depend on the agent's having strictly required the effect. I can ignite the match, and blow myself up, without intending to do so, even in Grisez's narrow sense of what I intend, i. e. , what I strictly require.

When we speak of means and ends we often, probably most often, have in mind a non-unified performance, a sequence of causally related acts rather than a unified performance in which a number of acts supervene on a common more basic act. Grisez gives the example of one's igniting a match (act) as a means to lighting the cigarette (further act). Other examples are where I boil the kettle in order to make a cup of tea, and where I study regularly in order to pass my exams. Nevertheless, we can speak of means and ends in a perfectly straightforward way in the case of unified performance. I can say that I ignite the match *by* moving my fingers in this way (rather than in some other way, and even if there is no other way), and you can say that I blew myself up *by* igniting the match (rather than in some other way, and even if there was no other way). To describe an act, X, as having been a means to an effect, Y, is to answer 'X' to the question, 'How was Y achieved or brought about?' When we describe an act, X, as having been a means to an effect, Y, we often also imply that the agent did X *in order* to achieve Y. But this implication is not necessary: Y can be brought about *by means of* X even where the agent does not do X in order to achieve Y. For instance, I can become physically fit by means of doing manual work, even though I do this work solely in order to earn extra money.

Further, condition 3 requires that the bad effect not be essential to the achievement of the good effect. This requirement is stated in the *New Catholic Encyclopedia* in (imprecise) causal terms: the good effect must 'flow from', in 'the order of causality', the action as immediately as the bad effect; the good effect must be 'produced by' the action and not by the bad effect. We may think that it is more appropriate to speak of supervenience rather than causation in the case of a unified performance. Even so, the stipulation of condition 3 is clear: it

117

is that the bad effect must not mediate between the more basic act and the good effect. The bad effect must not be essential; it must be incidental both to the aim (condition 2) and to the way in which the aim is achieved in the performance (condition 3). In the unified performance in which I blow myself up by igniting a match in a gas-filled room, my igniting the match (act) and my blowing myself up (act) both arise from the more basic act of my moving my fingers in a particular way. But my act of blowing myself up supervenes on my act of igniting the match. The occurrence of the latter *explains how* the former occurred. In contrast, where in igniting a match I illuminate the area around the candle (act), and singe a hovering mosquito (act), both acts supervene on a common more basic act, and the occurrence of one is not part of the explanation of *how* the other was achieved.

The important point here is that in unified performances of double effect in which a description of the agent's *act* can include the bad effect (e.g. she killed the aggressor), the bad effect must be a distinct supervenient act. The bad effect must be distinguishable, in a defensible way, not only from the good effect, but also *as an effect* of a more basic act on which the good effect supervenes independently of the bad effect. If the latter distinction cannot plausibly be maintained, then the good effect will arise through the bad effect, which is illegitimate under condition 3. To make the point more broadly, in *any* case of double effect where the agent's act has two effects which can both be described as what the agent did, in order to comply with condition 3 we must be able to describe the agent as having performed two distinct acts based on the one more basic act, with one of these two acts having been intended and the other not. Further, although in the circumstances the intended act will have been the agent's reason for doing the unintended one, the unintended act must not explain why or how the intended act was done.

The last, negative condition arguably needs refinement in some cases. For example, if I need to penetrate the innocent shield of a threat in defending myself, my shooting through the shield is part of the explanation of how in the circumstances I stop the threat. Harm to the shield, then, seems to be a means to my end. However, in discussing the permissibility of harming shields, Shelly Kagan distinguishes (as possibly helpful to a non-consequentialist moral constraint he is criticizing) between what he calls stronger and weaker means to ends.[35] Where my shooting *through* the shield is necessary in the circumstances to accomplishing the end of stopping the threat, the harm to the shield is a means to an end which I would have been able to achieve even were it not for the existence/state of the shield (weak means). (For example, an attacker is standing behind a hostage.) This is different from a case in which I harm the shield as a means of stopping the threat and where without the shield I would have been incapable of stopping the threat (strong means). (For example, I stop an attack by firing at a human shield who is tied to the aggressor's vehicle, splattering the shield's blood all over the aggressor's bullet-proof windscreen.) Some might take Kagan's distinction further, and argue that a case of weak means (my shooting *through* the shield of a threat, as distinct from my using someone as a shield against a threat) need not violate condition 3. In a case of weak means, harm to the shield can be incidental to necessary force in the circumstances, provided the shield is purely a *moral* shield, i.e., one whose purpose is to deter defence on moral grounds. (For example, I have an anti-tank gun but there is a hostage strapped to the front of the aggressor's tank.) However, given my available means of defence, if the shield functions in any degree as a physical protection of the threat, one which I must penetrate as a means of success (e.g. the aggressor is on foot and holds the shield in front of him in order to stop my bullets), then harm to the shield is not incidental to necessary force in the circumstances.[36]

---

[35] *The Limits of Morality*, pp. 140–4.
[36] The moral rationale of Kagan's distinction could be that with strong means I use a person in an offensive way – I harm him as a means of improving the position of myself or others – whereas with weak means I do not. Kagan argues that, although problematic, a modified constraint that forbids only use of strong means might be defensible. It can allow me to shoot through the shield, and it also allows self-defence because

The conditions outlined in the paragraph before last are fulfilled by those acts most plausibly said to be permissible under condition 3. Very clear cases are those in which 'double effect' might describe two possible, incompatible effects. For instance, even though when the patient undergoing the highly risky surgery dies we can say, truly if harshly, that the surgeon killed the patient (act), surgery (act) could have produced recovery (good effect), although surgery (act) in fact worsened the patient's condition (bad effect). One or other outcome would have produced a different act on the part of the surgeon (the surgeon's having saved the patient, or the surgeon's having killed him). So the bad effect, even though it can be included in a description of what the

harm done to an aggressor in self-defence is typically a *weak* means: the use of force in self-defence does not put the agent in a better position than had the threat never come along in the first place. However, Kagan argues, unless the modified constraint can be analysed *differently* it admits too much; for instance, it admits my pushing a bystander off a cliff, enabling me to stand in safety where the bystander is currently standing.

Unlike some writers, I do not assume that it is clearly permissible that I shoot through the innocent shield of a threat. Why is this self-preferential killing permissible? I return to these issues later in this chapter, and in chapters 5 and 6. But I should like to make two points here. First, if a constraint against harm as a strong means can be satisfactorily explained and defended, it does not follow that harm is permissible provided it is a weak means. (Kagan notes this, p. 152.) Secondly, it is necessary in my view that any distinction between strong and weak means be analysed normatively against a *status quo* which distinguishes between persons who are *threats* and those who are not, or not clearly so. Use of *defensive* force as a means against a threat would then be a weak means; whereas use of force as a means against a non-threat would be a strong means. The intrinsic moral offensiveness would consist in the use of strong means against people who are not unjust threats: it would consist, as many hold, in the intentional harming of unoffending persons. I think this moral offensiveness extends to intended harm to innocent shields of threats, and clearly includes intended harm to the bystander who is pushed off the cliff so that I can stand in safety. One problem, though, in deciding how we should regard the shield is that, although not himself the source of the threat, the shield is arguably being used as part of an unjust threat. The bystander on the cliff is arguably a passive threat (standing between me and safety); but in standing where she does she is not offending (an unjust threat). There will be other difficult cases, of course: it is not always easy to say whether or not someone is a threat or an unjust threat.

surgeon did, is clearly distinct from, and not a means to, the achievement of the intended good effect.

The same can be said about cases of double effect in which the agent expects both the good and the bad effect, and can be said to have 'done' both. For example, the bombardier can be said to have killed the civilian in the house next to the military target (act); but harm to the civilian (bad effect) does not bring about the achievement of the good effect (destruction of the munitions base). Thus, the bombardier in dropping the bomb (more basic act) both destroyed the munitions base (supervenient act, includes good effect) and killed a civilian (supervenient act, includes bad effect); the surgeon by removing the uterus (more basic act) both removed the cancer (supervenient act, includes good effect) and killed a foetus (supervenient act, includes bad effect); and the doctor both saved the patient with the better prognosis (supervenient act, includes good effect) by giving her the scarce drug (more basic act), and let the weaker patient die (supervenient act, includes bad effect).

On the other hand, in the case of self-defence the good effect (stopping the threat, thereby saving my life) arises from the intentional use of the necessary degree of force on the person posing the threat. Where the necessary degree of force is foreseen as lethal, the act on which the good effect supervenes is too close to a description of the bad effect (killing the person) not to *be* the so-called bad effect. *This* is Grisez's problem with the means: Double Effect's condition 3 requires that the act produce the good effect directly, and not through the bad effect. But where it is necessary to use lethal force to stop a threat, the act (that which produces the good effect) *is* the so-called bad effect, *unless* it is somehow possible to distinguish this bad effect from the agent's act. Grisez's proposed solution maintains that practically indivisible performances can be divided as acts by reference to the agent's intention. (Grisez quotes Aquinas as holding that 'moral actions are characterized by what is intended'.[37] But Thomists

---

[37] Grisez, 'Toward a Consistent Natural Law Ethics of Killing', p. 71.

typically interpret this as meaning that in cases of double effect the agent's intention determines the *moral quality* of the agent's act (e.g. whether or not a homicide is murder),[38] and not, as Grisez appears to maintain in the case of practically indivisible acts, the description of the act itself (e.g. whether an act of self-defence is homicide).)

Alongside unity of performance, Grisez identifies the agent's intention as the other source of unity of action, although he in fact emphasizes the 'divisive effect of intention'. (' "Intention" here refers not merely to intention of the end' (in Grisez's narrow sense of what is strictly required), 'but also the meaning one understands his act to have when he chooses it as a means to an intended end'.)[39] First, as Aquinas says, the same act in the order of nature can belong to two different *moral* categories,[40] regardless of its unity of performance, depending on the agent's intention. Grisez does not give an example here, but my igniting a match could be intended simply to illuminate the area where I stand so that I can locate the light switch (morally innocent), even though in igniting the match I blow myself up because the room is filled with odourless gas. Alternatively, where I know about the gas, my igniting the match may be intended as a way of killing myself (for Aquinas, morally culpable). Secondly, where a performance is known by the agent to be divisible, he may be responsible for an omission if he fails to divide it, even though he does not choose the elements of the complex separately. A person may choose only to do X, which will cause preventable harm to others, and be responsible for that harm if he (negligently) fails to prevent it. Grisez claims that here there are two *moral* acts (my emphasis), one determined by the choice to do X and the other determined by the negligent omission. Similarly, 'although a performance may be actually indivisible, a duality of action may arise from the fact that an alternative performance could have been chosen

---

[38] See, e.g. Joseph Rickaby, *Moral Philosophy* (London: Longman's Green & Co. Ltd, 1929), p. 202.

[39] Grisez, 'Toward a Consistent Natural Law Ethics of Killing', p. 88.

[40] Ibid., p. 89 (my emphasis).

that would have served one's purpose without the foreseen harm'. Thus, a doctor who negligently prescribes a drug which may have a dangerous side-effect instead of an equally effective, safe drug, 'would both prescribe medication and negligently omit due care in treating the patient'. (Condition 2 disallows unnecessary harm, as explained above.)

However, Grisez argues, if 'in fact, the agent has only a single intention ... and if there is not a related omission, then the act will be a single unit so far as the unity is determined by intention'. '... an act that is both one from the point of view of intention and from the point of view of the performance is one absolutely. *What specific action it is*, will be determined by the scope of intention, not by parts of the performance that remains a whole indivisible by the agent.'[41]

We should remind ourselves that according to Grisez a foreseen effect is not within the scope of my intention if it contributes 'nothing to my objective or to the process of its realization'.[42] I argued above that the divisibility by thought, or by appeal to what might be practically divisible under other conditions, is an inadequate criterion for distinguishing intended effects from those which are really incidental in the circumstances to the agent's aim. Grisez concludes that 'a good effect which in the order of nature is *preceded in the performance* by an evil effect need not be regarded as a good end achieved by an evil means, provided that the act is a unity and only the good is within the scope of intention ... *From the ethical point of view*, all of the events in the indivisible performance of a unitary human act are equally immediate to the agent; *none is prior (a means) to another.*'[43]

Grisez believes that homicide in self-defence, as Aquinas explains it, complies with condition 3 as Grisez interprets it. He also maintains that according to his interpretation, 'a woman might interpose herself between her child and an attacking animal, since the unitary act would save the child as well as unintentionally damage the agent'. But 'she could not commit adultery to obtain the release of her child, because the

41 Ibid., p. 89 (my emphasis).   42 Ibid., p. 77.
43 Ibid., p. 90 (my emphases).

good effect would be through a distinct human act, and she would have to consent to an adulterous act as a means to the good end ... Again, a starving party of explorers might divide available food among the stronger members, allowing the weaker to die, since the same act would benefit the one group and harm the others. But if the stronger killed one of the weaker to cannibalize him, the killing would be a bad means, chosen in a distinct act, since killing and eating are divisible and the act is therefore not unitary.'[44]

I am unpersuaded by Grisez's attempt to include as a case of double effect an act of stopping an aggressor which in the circumstances *requires* lethal force to be used against the aggressor. Remember, the objection Grisez is addressing is that in this case the bad effect is *a means to* achieving the good effect, and thus impermissible under condition 3. The question which Grisez poses to focus this objection is: 'if an *effect* in the order of nature *contributes to the fulfillment of a human purpose*, must the natural *cause* of that effect be viewed as a means in the order of human action?' (my emphases). I take this question to be asking the following about self-defence: If an effect in the order of nature (stopping the aggressor, putting him out of action) contributes to the fulfilment of a human purpose (saving my life), must the natural cause of that effect (use of lethal force, aggressor's being killed) be viewed as a means in the order of human action? Grisez says that usually condition 3 is 'interpreted in a way that assumes an affirmative answer to this question', and he adds that sometimes, indeed, the requirement states '... *provided that the evil effect does not first arise and from it the good effect*'.[45] His overall argument is intended to show that this interpretation of the requirement is mistaken.

But which interpretation is this? The one which assumes the affirmative answer to the question about whether the natural cause of an effect which contributes to the fulfilment of a human purpose is a means? Or the interpretation which

[44] Ibid., p. 90.
[45] Ibid., p. 87. Grisez quotes Henry Davis, *Moral and Pastoral Theology*, 5th ed. (London: 1946), vol. 1, p. 14 (Grisez's emphasis).

says that the evil effect must not arise first and from it the good effect? The *New Catholic Encyclopedia* carefully excludes the latter interpretation of condition 3 in stating: 'the good effect *must flow from the action at least as immediately (in the order of causality, though not necessarily in the order of time) as the bad effect*. In other words *the good effect must be produced directly by the action, not by the bad effect'* (my emphases). Whether or not the bad effect occurs prior to, simultaneously with, or after the good effect is irrelevant if the good effect arises *directly from a common more basic action* (permissible) rather than *by means of the bad effect* (impermissible). Thus it is a distraction for Grisez to say that 'a good effect which in the order of nature is *preceded in the performance* by an evil effect need not be regarded as a good end achieved by an evil means, provided that the act is a unity and only the good is within the scope of intention ... whether the good or evil effect is prior in the order of nature is morally irrelevant ... all of the events in the indivisible performance of a unitary human act are equally immediate to the agent; none is *prior (a means)* to another' (my emphases). The relevant question is: 'if an effect in the order of nature *contributes to the fulfillment of a human purpose*, must the natural *cause* of that effect be viewed as a means in the order of human action?' (my emphases).

Grisez says that we must distinguish between cause and effect in the order of nature on the one hand, and on the other, means and end in the order of human action.[46] His argument appears to be that where I stop the aggressor by killing him, my killing the aggressor is not a means to stopping him if, (i) in the circumstances I cannot stop him without killing him, and (ii) my intention is (only) to stop him. But surely a means to an end in the sense required by condition 3 is the act *by which the end is brought about*. Where I believe that a certain degree of force is *necessary* to stop a threat, then in self-defence I intend to stop the aggressor by directing that particular degree of force at him. If the act of stopping (which is aimed at inflicting the necessary degree of force on the

46 Ibid., p. 87.

aggressor) is itself a foreseen killing, then I intend to stop the aggressor *by killing him*.

The statement of condition 3 in the *New Catholic Encyclopedia* disallows in a perfectly straightforward way Grisez's example of the woman's adulterous act to save her child, and also the act of killing and cannibalism, and it admits in a perfectly straightforward way the division of food among the stronger members of the stranded explorers. The act of the mother who interposes herself between her child and an attacking animal seems as straightforward a case of means (interposition) to end (saving the child) as one could find. For this mother *uses* her interposition, she makes herself into a shield, *as a way of* saving her child. Yet I think that condition 3 arguably allows the woman to interpose herself between her child and the attacking animal. To be sure, the woman puts herself at very great risk in order to deflect harm from the child. But she does not commit suicide in order to save the child; and her interposition, not her death, explains how the child is saved. Appeal to condition 3 can create a very fine line in some cases. But such a line can sometimes be viable, for instance in the case that I discussed in connection with condition 2, in which you are attacking me on top of a tall building and I need in my own defence only to push you a short distance away so that I avoid your full impact. In these circumstances, my intended action *of pushing you a short distance away* itself provides the degree of force necessary for self-defence. My foreseeably killing you in this case, where you go off the building because I push you, does not violate condition 3. Here, my more basic act of pushing you a short distance away so that I avoid your full impact, both saves my life and, independently, sends you off the building to your death, provided that only my pushing you a short distance away, and not my pushing you off the building, is what I intend as necessary to defend myself in the circumstances. Thus, this case is also distinguishable in terms of condition 3 from one in which *my pushing you off the tall building* (or my blowing you up, etc.) is in the circumstances what I need to do in order to eliminate the threat you pose.

Anscombe concedes that 'there are borderline cases, where it is difficult to distinguish, in what is done, between means and what is incidental to, yet in the circumstances inseparable from, those means'.[47] And as it becomes increasingly difficult to distinguish the bad effect of an agent's act *as a distinct act produced by a more basic act which also produces the good effect independently of the bad effect*, so the applicability of condition 3 becomes increasingly doubtful. We should not shirk cases in which a description of a person's voluntary act of self-sacrifice is itself a description of a foreseen killing of him- or herself (e.g. she threw herself directly in front of the high-speed train). One's own death may be necessary in the circumstances in order to save someone else, and intended as such (e.g. the woman who interposes herself between her child and an attacking animal might not be shielding the child, but rather offering herself as a meal to the animal who would otherwise eat the child). In such cases, it seems to me that death *is* intended, whether or not death itself is strictly required for the achievement of the agent's aim, and consistency requires that such acts be disallowed by a moral theory which forbids the intentional killing of an innocent person, including oneself.

All the same, there is a difference between an act of self-sacrifice such as that Grisez describes and the type of self-defence cases which seem to violate condition 3. Say the woman's more basic act is to shield her child by interposing herself between the attacking animal and her child. This act is divisible in thought, and under some circumstances practically divisible (someone shoots the animal before it reaches the woman), but not practically divisible for this agent *from the effect* of her being grievously harmed by the animal. If the woman knows these things, she cannot choose to interpose herself without also choosing to be grievously, even fatally, wounded by the animal. Nevertheless if she dies, the more basic act of interposition has both caused her own death (bad effect) and, if her aim succeeds, saved the child (good effect).

[47] 'War and Murder', p. 59.

But in the cases of self-defence at issue, it is necessary in the circumstances for me to use lethal force on the aggressor (my intended more basic act) in order to stop him (effect). So it is not that a common more basic act *both* kills the aggressor (bad effect) and, independently of the act of killing, stops him (good effect).

Grisez emphasizes that where acts done for a good end, which also have a bad effect, are practically indivisible by the agent, it makes a difference to ends and means that *the very same act* (e.g. feeding the stronger) produces both the good effect (those who are fed live) and the bad effect (those not fed die).[48] In my view, this is so when 'the very same act' is some more basic act which produces both the good and bad effects as distinct acts. For instance, although my more basic act of feeding the stronger both saves the stronger and lets the weaker die, it is not the deaths of the weaker, nor even my not feeding them, which saves the stronger. The stronger are saved by my act of feeding them. If I give another snake-bite victim all my supply of antivenene in order to save her life and die myself as a result, it is not my letting myself die which saves this other person (I could have let myself die by pouring the antivenene down the sink or by giving it to a third person). She is saved by my act of giving her the antivenene.

But what is 'the very same act' in a case of self-defence in which stopping the aggressor requires the use of lethal force? The act which produces the good effect (whether this effect be described as stopping the aggressor or, more broadly, as saving my life) in these circumstances is *the use of lethal force against this person*: this *is* killing the aggressor, the so-called bad effect. Where the act of stopping the aggressor in this way is not practically divisible by the self-defending agent from killing the aggressor, Grisez's argument relies on my action not being 'I killed him', but rather 'I stopped him', and this in turn depends on (i) my intention being determined by what is strictly required, and (ii) the description of my *act* being determined by intention in the case of a unified performance.

[48] 'Toward a Consistent Natural Law Ethics of Killing', p. 90.

However, neither (i) nor (ii) is right. What I intend to bring about includes what I aim at as necessary in the circumstances for the achievement of my aim. Intention cannot be confined to what is strictly required for the achievement of my aim. The description of my act (what I do), in cases of double effect and in general, extends beyond what I intend in Grisez's narrow sense, i.e., what I strictly require. In cases of double effect, and especially in the case of a unified performance, what I can be said to have *done* certainly also includes the bad effect where this is either a foreseen direct effect of what I voluntarily do (my more basic act) in order to bring about what I strictly require (good effect) or a foreseen direct effect of the strictly required good effect. I can voluntarily and foreseeably *kill* someone or *allow him to die*, even though I do not strictly require his death either as an end or a means. Here I am responsible for killing him, or for allowing him to die, in the sense that I am morally answerable for what I have done.[49]

The detailed discussion of this section has focused on the central feature of the Double Effect justification of self-defence – the claim that the use of lethal force in self-defence is not intended killing. Some cases of the use of lethal force in self-defence are not plausibly characterized as unintended killing; such cases cannot be justified under the conditions of Double Effect. In my view, the intentional use of necessary and proportionate lethal force in self-defence against someone who poses an unjust immediate threat is not intrinsically morally offensive; and the use of lethal force in self-defence can be permissible intended killing. Sometimes homicide in self-defence *is* unintended killing; but where homicide in self-defence does meet the central condition of the Principle of Double Effect, this is insufficient to establish that it is justified. Any justification of homicide in self-defence requires

---

[49] See my article 'The Doctrine of Double Effect', pp. 211–18. For another critical discussion of Grisez's interpretation of Double Effect as applicable to all homicide in self-defence, see Donagan, *A Theory of Morality*, pp. 160–3. Finnis also rejected Grisez's interpretation of intention, in 'The Rights and Wrongs of Abortion', reprinted in *The Philosophy of Law*, edited by R. M. Dworkin (Oxford University Press, 1977), p. 144.

that self-preference be justified, and as I shall argue shortly (4.3), this requires a particular interpretation of proportionality (the Principle's condition 4) which distinguishes between offending and unoffending persons.

4.3 SELF-PREFERENTIAL HOMICIDE AND DOUBLE EFFECT

The Principle of Double Effect and plausible variations of it do not maintain that a good intention is sufficient to permit foreseen killing. The application of Double Effect to homicide in self-defence implies that the foreseen killing of the aggressor is not irrelevant to the act's moral permissibility: the aggressor's being killed is a foreseen bad effect which must be evaluated under a separate proportionality condition (condition 4).[50] Those who appeal to Double Effect as justifying homicide in self-defence *per se* must hold that self-preferential killing is justified. The explanation of why, in using lethal force, I can be justified in giving my own life priority over the life of the aggressor needs to refer to a moral asymmetry between myself and someone who him- or herself poses an unjust threat.[51] In the case of homicide *in self-defence*, the

[50] Duff, 'Intention, Responsibility and Double Effect', pp. 3–16, argues that the Principle has two different applications: cases in which a foreseen bad effect enters into the agent's moral deliberation as a reason against doing the act, and cases in which the agent regards the foreseen bad effect as morally irrelevant to what he or she is permitted or obliged to do. Exponents of the Double Effect justification of homicide in self-defence should regard this as a case of the former application, given the nature of the bad effect. The Double Effect view is typically combined with the belief that there is a general duty to preserve life: self-defence is neither permissible nor obligatory irrespective of the consequences for others. I think Duff's distinction is important. However, his category of acts for which consideration of the foreseen bad effect is believed irrelevant to the act's moral permissibility or obligatoriness does not, presumably, require condition 4.

[51] Depending on what is considered proportionate, homicide in self-defence which complies with condition 4 could be restricted to warding off someone who threatens death, or it could also include defending oneself against serious bodily injury, rape, loss of liberty, and even loss of property in some circumstances.

required moral asymmetry arises from the fact that the person against whom lethal force is used is an unjust immediate threat.

Condition 4, proportionality

The claim that the Double Effect justification of self-defence relies on a moral asymmetry between the self-defending agent and the unjust aggressor certainly needs detailed explanation and defence (which I provide below), because the *combined* conditions of the Principle purport to rule on the moral permissibility (allowability) of an act with a foreseen bad effect of a type not permissibly intended; they do not say that an act which meets these conditions is morally justified in the stronger sense (right).[52] Thus, as I noted in chapter 3, some explications of the Principle maintain that the fourth, proportionality condition – that the good effect be sufficiently desirable to compensate for the bad effect – does not require an asymmetry: they claim that it does not require that the foreseen bad effect be *outweighed* by the intended good effect, but only ever that the good and bad effects be *comparable in order of magnitude*.[53] I shall refer to this claim as the never-more-than-comparable-magnitude interpretation of condition 4. In chapter 3, I claimed that, given fulfilment of the Principle's other conditions, the never-more-than-comparable-magnitude interpretation is too weak to establish the permissibility of my foreseeably killing a bystander in the course of self-preservation (e.g. swerving my car into a child in order to avoid hitting a boulder on the road). A more complex interpretation of condition 4 is necessary, as I now explain.

---

[52] According to the Principle, an act which fails to meet each of the four conditions is *impermissible*. Helga Kuhse, *The Sanctity-of-Life Doctrine in Medicine* (Oxford University Press, 1987), p. 120, misconstrues the Principle's first three conditions as sufficient to establish the permissibility of an act of double effect and fulfilment of condition 4 as determining that such an act is justified (right).

[53] See, e.g. Campbell and Collinson, *Ending Lives*, p. 156.

Rejection of the never-more-than-comparable-magnitude interpretation   The first point to make in rejecting the never-more-than-comparable-magnitude interpretation of proportionality is that the Principle, thus interpreted, would set an inadequate standard of moral permissibility were it always to require only comparable *types* of effects: that is, were it only ever to require that the bad effect be of the same *order* of magnitude as the good effect, without ever taking into account the comparative numbers of people who will suffer and benefit as a result of an act of double effect. Philippa Foot's much discussed example of the choice faced by the driver of a runaway tram[54] is useful in explaining that sometimes it would be unacceptable if deliberation under condition 4 ignored the numbers of people affected for better or worse by an act of double effect. This is because in Foot's example relative numbers determine comparable harm. In the example, the driver cannot stop the tram, but he can steer it either onto track A, foreseeably killing one man working on track A, or else onto track B, foreseeably killing five men working on track B. (So as not to complicate matters unnecessarily here, I assume that all the men on the two tracks are strangers to the driver.) The Double Effect conditions permit the driver to steer onto track A. Moreover, this act would be the better choice; indeed, many people would hold that in these circumstances the driver *ought* to steer onto track A in order to avoid killing as many people as possible. Nevertheless, we can ask whether the Principle's conditions also permit the driver to steer onto track B rather than onto track A. If condition 4 only ever requires that the agent compare *types* of harm (in this case, causing death and avoiding death), then the answer to this question is yes. The greater number of people who will be killed on track B would not make the driver's steering onto track B impermissible under condition 4 *thus interpreted*. (Condition 2 does require that

[54] Foot, 'The Problem of Abortion and the Doctrine of Double Effect', p. 23. This example is often referred to as 'the trolley problem'. See Judith Jarvis Thomson's detailed discussion, *The Realm of Rights* (Camb. Mass: Harvard University Press, 1990), ch. 7.

where possible the agent obtain the good effect (saving one person) without the bad (killing five), and *this* the driver can do by steering onto track A. But in the circumstances the driver cannot save one *particular* person – the man on track A – without killing those on track B.) In this example, as with some other acts of double effect, the driver foreseeably infringes the equal right to life of whomever he kills in the act of saving another or others. In general it is impermissible that an agent foreseeably infringe someone's rights, especially very weighty rights such as the right to life, in the act of saving or benefiting another or others, without a morally sufficient reason. However, it might be argued, a morally sufficient reason can be given for the driver's infringing the right to life of *each* of the men on track B. It can be said of each of these men, '*His* right to life was not infringed impermissibly: it was infringed in preventing comparable harm to someone else, the man on track A.' No individual man trapped on track B can rightly complain, as the tram hurtles towards him, that in infringing *his* right to life the driver is not also preventing harm of comparable magnitude to someone else.[55]

[55] This suggested response is based on Anscombe, 'Who is Wronged?', *The Oxford Review* 5, 1967, pp. 16–17. (I do not know that Anscombe would argue in this way about *killing* the five in the act of saving the one.) In my view, I do *wrong* (because I infringe the right to life of) any unoffending person whom I kill in the act of saving another or others. But if I am Foot's tram-driver, I do so justifiably in the circumstances if I steer onto track A. In another example of Foot's, to which Anscombe is replying, a person is faced with distributing a scarce drug. Say there are six persons who need the drug to survive; five of these people will be saved if they each get one-fifth of the available supply of this drug, and the sixth person's life will be saved only if he receives all of the available supply. Anscombe's point is that if it is up to me to distribute the drug, I do not *wrong* any of the five if I choose to give the drug to the one. This may well be so; none of the five individuals need have a stronger right to the drug than the one, or any right at all to it. All the same, in these circumstances I can *act wrongly* in giving the drug to the one. Anscombe is wrong to suggest that I could not act wrongly in giving the drug to the one provided no one was wronged.

For my purposes, Foot's tram example has the advantageous feature that all the trackworkers have an equal right to life. The example also has the possible disadvantage that, because the tram is runaway, some will feel that any death caused is not clearly an effect of the driver's act. The scarce drug case eliminates this disadvantage, and could be elaborated so

This last piece of reasoning misses the point that the Principle purports to give an *overall* ruling on the permissibility of acts of double effect. In Foot's example, the foreseen effects to be considered and compared under the Double Effect conditions are the killing of the one man on track A and the killing of five men on track B. A defensible interpretation of condition 4 must take numbers into account in a case such as this. While none of the men on track B may be able to appeal to the presence of the other four as a reason why it is impermissible that *his own* right to life be infringed in these circumstances in the act of saving another person, morally speaking there is a sense in which there can be safety in numbers. If the driver steers onto track B, anyone can rightly complain that in this case the driver foreseeably brought about a bad effect without bringing about a good effect sufficiently desirable to compensate for it. For in saving the man on track A the driver killed five others on track B, each of whom had an equal right not to be killed.[56]

as to make clear that I do wrong any of the six to whom I do not give an adequate supply of the drug (e.g. each of the six has taken out health insurance to secure a quantity of the drug adequate to save his or her life in an emergency, and an inadequate supply for each of the six turns up). Nagel remarks that in the scarce drug case *I do not kill* those who die because I give the drug to others, 'War and Massacre', p. 11. But it does not follow from this that Double Effect is superfluous in this case. Clearly one can bring death about intentionally by omission (e.g. by deliberately failing to warn someone of imminent danger, *in order to bring about his death*), and surely the prohibition includes such acts.

[56] I emphasize unavoidable rights violation in this case, because I am not suggesting that greater numbers are always decisive in cases of double effect, nor that in such cases one is morally required always to save as many people as possible. In making the particular point I want to make here, Foot's example is not complicated by the driver *shifting or deflecting* harm from one person onto another or others. Shifting or deflecting harm to a smaller number can be permissible. (See, e.g. Nancy Davis' variation of Foot's example, where the driver *diverts* a runaway tram onto another track in order to avoid killing as many people as possible, 'The Priority of Avoiding Harm', in *Killing and Letting Die*, edited by Bonnie Steinbock (Englewood Cliffs, New Jersey: Prentice-Hall, 1980), p. 193.) However, if as a result of driving at high speed, I and a passenger in my car can avoid hitting a tree only by my swerving the car into a child playing on the footpath, who will then be killed, comparative numbers do not morally require that I do this. Further, my swerving into the child, although it might be partly excusable in the circumstances, is not even morally permissible in my view. I discuss similar cases below.

Secondly, the never-more-than-comparable-magnitude interpretation of condition 4 is not implied by the fact that the standard of no-more-than-comparable-magnitude satisfies condition 4 in *some* cases of double effect (most obviously where the effects of alternative acts are, from the agent's perspective, morally indistinguishable). For example, I might face a choice between act A which will both avoid my killing one person, Y, and kill another person, X, and act B which will both avoid my killing X and kill Y. Either act will avoid my killing one person and also kill someone else who has an equal claim not to be killed by me, and *nothing* is known to me which would be a morally defensible basis on which to distinguish in either X's or Y's favour.[57] Even so, where *different people* will be harmed and saved/benefited by a particular act of double effect (say act A), comparable types of effects and comparable numbers will still be *insufficient* to establish the moral permissibility of this particular act unless a morally defensible selection procedure is used to choose those to be saved/benefited and those to be harmed. (This need not be the same procedure in all such cases. Where, as in the example just given, either act unavoidably involves rights violation, and I know nothing about X and Y which morally distinguishes the alternative acts, a random procedure is morally appropriate. But in another case, where something morally relevant is known, it might be appropriate to select on the basis of personal circumstances, e.g. the fact that one person has dependants and the other does not.) In the case of X and Y, the good effect of my doing act A or (alternatively) act B is sufficient to compensate for the bad, without the bad effect having to count as less weighty than the good effect. In this case either A (with the intention of saving Y) or B (with the intention of saving X) is permissible all things considered, provided the procedure for choosing which person to save at the other's expense is morally defensible. Given equal

---

[57] This could be a variation of Foot's tram example (one person on each track), or a variation of the diabolic machine example discussed by Michael Tooley in *Abortion and Infanticide* (Oxford University Press, 1983), p. 189.

numbers, and harms of comparable magnitude to X and Y, it is not *then* morally permissible for me to save Y at X's expense (or vice versa) on some morally irrelevant, unfair, or otherwise morally indefensible basis, such as that Y is better looking than X, or that my acting to save X would involve my chipping a fingernail, or the fact that I owe X money.[58]

The never-more-than-comparable-magnitude interpretation of condition 4 can perhaps seem reasonable at first because acts with foreseen bad effects are *impermissible* where the foreseen bad effect is *disproportionate* to the intended good effect. For example, it is morally impermissible that I dump highly toxic chemicals into a river in order to avoid paying for their safe disposal, and it is morally impermissible that I maim someone in the act of protecting some trivial interest of mine. But it does not follow, of course, that it is always morally *permissible* to bring about any foreseen, unintended bad effect provided it is *not disproportionate* to the intended good effect. Whenever (as in the case of self-defence) an act of double effect foreseeably injures someone other than the person(s) whom it saves/benefits, it is unacceptable that condition 4 require only that the good and bad effects not be disproportionate (given comparable numbers of people saved/benefited and injured).

I argue further for this last claim below. But let me say here that if condition 4 were always to require only that the foreseen good and bad effects not be disproportionate, then when an act of double effect injures and saves/benefits different people the Principle would establish only the very minimal ruling that the act is not *necessarily* impermissible. That is to say, against the background prohibition, the Principle's conditions would establish that the act is not morally out of the question in the circumstances. In the absence of a morally defensible selection criterion, or an additional, morally relevant reason on the side of saving someone at another's expense, the Principle is not only too weak to establish that it is morally right that an agent save someone by

---

[58] Anscombe, 'Who is Wronged?', p. 17, makes the point that I act wrongly if my 'preference signalizes some ignoble contempt'.

an act which foreseeably kills another person, but too weak even to establish that such an act is morally permissible.

Moral permissibility and moral justification   Some conceptual reminders, and some more general further remarks about moral permissibility and moral justification, are necessary before I add more detail to the claim that we should reject the never-more-than-comparable-magnitude interpretation of proportionality where (as in the case of self-defence) acts of double effect injure and save/benefit different people. These conceptual reminders and more general remarks about per-missibility and justification might at first seem a diversion from the issue at hand, but directly below I apply them to what the Principle's proportionality condition requires in the case of homicide in self-defence.

In chapter 2, I distinguished a justified act (permissible or right) from an excusable act (wrongful, but the agent is not blameworthy or not fully so). I also distinguished an act's being morally permissible or right from the perspective of the agent in the circumstances (justified^{ii}) from that act's being morally permissible or right from an objective perspective (justified^{i}). An agent's act can be justified^{ii} without being justified^{i} (mistaken beliefs are compatible with an act's being justified^{ii}). But justification^{ii} is necessary to the justification^{i} of an agent's act. (If an act is not morally justified from the agent's perspective, then the agent does not *act* justifiably even if from a more objective perspective the agent does the right thing.) I also pointed out that although permissibility is a justification and not an excuse, there is a weaker (permissible act) and a stronger (right act) standard of justification. If an act is permissible it is allowable; if an act is justified in the stronger sense it is right in the circumstances. Because this is so, permissible acts need not be morally justified in the stronger sense: permissible acts need not be positively the right thing to do. These distinctions form the background of the necessarily more complex account of moral permissibility and justification that I now give.

'Permissible' and 'justified' are frequently not distinguished in moral assessment, and sometimes they need not be. Certainly if an act is morally justified in the stronger sense (right) then it is morally permissible. But very many acts (e.g. the exercise of liberties such as the right to marry, to paint one's house, to undertake a higher degree, to dine out, etc.) are optional and morally permissible, and can be justified in *this* sense without being morally the right thing to do. With the exercise of many liberties what is required for the moral justification of a particular act need not go beyond the fact that it was permissible. Where this is so the act's permissibility is sufficient to establish that it is, if not positively the right thing to do, justified in the sense of *not being wrong*. In this (weaker) sense, I might justify my actions in reply to the accusatory question 'What were you doing driving her car?', by establishing that it was permissible for me to act as I did: by saying, 'She lent me her car for the evening.' In the stronger sense, I might justify those same actions by replying, 'I borrowed her car to take a dangerously ill person to hospital; it was an emergency.' So there are at least four senses in which we can speak about moral justification, because alongside the distinction between justification[i] and justification[ii] there is a (weaker) sense in which to say that an act is morally justified is simply to say that it is not wrong, and a (stronger) sense in which to say that an act is morally justified means that it is positively the right thing for the agent to do.

A morally *permissible* act can fail to be, as the agent judges it to be, justified in the stronger sense of objectively the right thing to do. This is conceptually and morally unproblematic, because justification[ii] establishes agent-perspectival permissibility. As I argued in chapter 2, it can be morally permissible for someone to act in a particular way (hand over money from the till) on the basis of her justified belief that this is the right thing to do, even though from a more informed perspective this act is not the right thing to do (the threat is a bluff). A morally permissible act can also fail to be, as the agent (or anyone else, given available knowledge) reasonably judges it to be at the time of action, justified[i] in the weaker sense of not wrong. Say, for example, a woman reasonably believes that

138

her having another child would be morally permissible and optional, and she decides to go ahead. Although prior medical tests reveal no problems, the pregnancy causes the woman to have a stroke which kills both her and the foetus, and so leaves her other children motherless, etc. Given the woman's reasonable beliefs at the time of deciding to conceive, it was morally permissible for her to act as she did. But her decision was wrong[i], wrong from a more informed (later) perspective. Were she to have had good reason at that time to expect the actual outcome of her pregnancy, her decision to conceive would not have been a morally defensible option, it would also have been wrong[ii].

As I have said, some permissible acts are morally optional, and hence need not be justified in the stronger sense of being positively the right thing to do. But could a particular act be permissible and yet the wrong[ii] thing for the agent to do in the circumstances? We might at first think that the answer is obviously no. It seems inconsistent to say of a particular agent's act that although it was permissible it was wrong[ii], wrong from the perspective of the agent in the circumstances. (As I have said, sometimes the justification of a particular act need go no further than what was permissible in the circumstances.) However, we need to remember that although permissibility is a justification, and *justification* is always an all-relevant-things-considered evaluation of whatever is said to be justified, sometimes the ground on which a particular act is said to be permissible is narrower than those considerations which its justification[ii] should take into account. And this can be true of justification[ii] not only in the stronger sense (the right thing to do), but also in the weaker sense (not wrong). Someone may have a particular permission, e.g. a right, to do something that it is wrong[ii] for him or her to do all things considered. We can fail to notice this because in the everyday moral defence of acts it is commonly, wrongly, assumed that the existence of a particular permission is sufficient to show that the act in question was permissible all things considered. For instance, in reponse to a criticism such as 'You ought to have let her keep the piano when you parted. It meant a great deal to her, she can't afford to buy another one, and you never use it', 'But it's mine' is a familiar sort of reply. The obvious rejoinder, however, is: 'Yes; given it's yours, it was permissible for you to take it. All the same, you were wrong not to have left it with her.' The following four examples, I believe, also illustrate that acts which can be said to be permissible in this narrower, somewhat legalistic, sense can be the wrong[ii] thing to do in the circumstances all things considered. (No doubt not everyone will agree that each of the examples shows this, but I think most will accept that at least one of them does.)[59]

(i) I greatly admire a rare book of yours that you treasure. Because of your feelings for me you give me the book saying, 'Here; I'd like you to have it.' I accept your very generous gift, knowing that even though you want me to have the book, you are forgoing something you treasure and would otherwise keep. Later, someone you hardly know (say my brother), whom I want to please more than I want to keep the book, greatly admires it. I am very tempted to give it to him. It would be permissible for me to give the book to my brother: you gave it to me unconditionally and I am free to give it away. But another consideration is relevant in the circumstances to deciding whether it would be wrong to give my brother the book. In coming to the view that it would be wrong, I ought to weigh very heavily the fact that you treasured the book but gave it to me because I admired it and you wanted *me* to have it.

(ii) On the last day of a hike it is permissible for me to eat all my adequate (because carefully managed) food rations myself, rather than relieve your moderate hunger pangs by sharing them with you, if you have, knowing what was to come, irresponsibly fed much of your food to birds early on. But this is probably in the circumstances a very nasty thing to do.

[59] Thomson points out that some acts which do not inflict injustice can involve quite serious moral wrong, 'A Defence of Abortion', reprinted in *The Philosophy of Law*, edited by R. M. Dworkin (Oxford University Press, 1977).

(iii) You and I survive a bad fall while walking in a remote area. You are hurt and may not be able to look after yourself adequately without my help. You might not survive if left alone, and your chances of survival will be very greatly enhanced by my staying and looking after you. However, my best chance of survival is to set out immediately on my own, rather than staying with you in the hope that help will arrive soon. If I stay with you for a day or so, I do somewhat (although not dramatically) increase the risk of not surviving myself. In these circumstances, although it is permissible for me to set out on my own, it would be wrong of me not to stay with you.

(iv) I lend you a computer that I rarely use and you promise to return it as soon as I ask to have it back. Months pass. Use of the computer becomes extremely important to you in writing your thesis and you could not replace it if I asked you to return it. I don't really need the computer, although I would now prefer to have it back because it would help me entertain a child who will be in my care for a few weeks. Although it is permissible for me to ask you to return my computer now, it would be wrong of me to do so in the circumstances given the cost to you.

'Permissible' represents a standard which is often, but not always, sufficient for an act's not being wrong[ii] all things considered. In the examples just outlined, it is of course also permissible for you to leave your ex-partner the piano, and permissible that I, (i) not give your generous gift to my brother, (ii) share my remaining rations with you, (iii) stay and look after you for some time, and (iv) not ask you to return my computer. *These* permissible acts are the right thing to do in the circumstances, and the opposite acts can be said to be permissible but wrong all things considered. When an act is said to be permissible according to a narrower set of considerations than those that are relevant to judging that the act is not wrong[i] all things considered, permissibility is insufficient to establish that the act is justified[ii] even in the weaker sense. The fact that a particular act is wrong[ii] all things considered can be consistent with its being permissible on some narrower basis.

Three possible positions on proportionality and homicide in self-defence The Principle's conditions purport to establish the *permissibility* of some acts of double effect, and the application of the distinctions I have just drawn gives us three possible positions to consider in the case of homicide in self-defence. (What holds for (weaker and stronger) justification[ii] will also hold for (weaker and stronger) justification[i], of course, provided the circumstances are as the self-defending agent believes them to be.) First, the four conditions might be held jointly to establish that self-defence *per se* is justified in the stronger sense (positively the right thing to do). If this is so, the self-defending agent must justifiably regard the good effect of saving him- or herself as outweighing the bad effect of killing the aggressor. This is because *self-preferential killing needs to be positively right.* (Depending on the reason why self-preference is regarded as right, this position might imply that *not* to defend oneself would, other than in exceptional circumstances, be wrong.)

Secondly, the Principle's conditions might be held to establish that self-defence is justified in the weaker sense (permissible all things considered, i.e., not wrong). If this is so, homicide in self-defence might *also* be positively right where there are considerations on the side of saving oneself *additional* to those required for the judgment that self-defence is permissible all things considered. But on this second view, self-defence is permissible and morally optional all things considered in the absence of such additional considerations. I argue below that this weaker position on self-defence would also be insufficiently supported if condition 4 were to require only foreseen good and bad effects of comparable magnitude.

The third possibility is that the Principle's four conditions merely establish a narrow permission, one not based on an overall judgment that self-defence is permissible. Whether the Principle (within its own terms) establishes a narrow permission – such as the minimal ruling that homicide in self-defence is not morally out of the question – does depend on what condition 4 requires. However, a permission of this type, one compatible with self-defence being wrong all things

142

considered *despite* its meeting the Principle's conditions, is not what advocates of Double Effect intend. On the contrary, they believe that acts of double effect which meet the Principle's conditions are permissible all things considered. For this reason we should reject interpretations of condition 4 which could yield only the third, weakest ruling.[60]

I now argue that in order for the Principle clearly to establish even the weaker of the other two positions – that homicide in self-defence *per se* is not wrong – condition 4 must require more than foreseen good and bad effects of comparable magnitude.

Permissible and impermissible self-preference Most people would consider foreseen homicide in self-defence to be very clearly morally permissible in the example I shall now outline. An aggressor threatens my life, so the foreseen bad effect of my self-defensive act (the aggressor's death) is uncontroversially of the same order of magnitude as the good effect. I do not go beyond necessary force in defending myself. There is only one aggressor; the aggression is, and is reasonably believed by me to be, unjust and culpable. The aggressor alone will suffer direct injury from my act of self-defence. In the circumstances the proportionality comparison can reasonably be confined to the two immediate, very specific direct effects of self-defence (i.e., to the killing of the aggressor and the saving of my life); it does not include foreseen indirect effects (such as the effect of either my death, or the aggressor's, on others), and there are no other known complicating factors (such as that I am bound to be killed in

---

[60] Nancy Davis accepts this third interpretation of the Principle. She states condition 4 as requiring only (ever) that the good and bad effects not be 'morally disproportionate', and she sees the Principle as intended to determine whether or not an act of double effect violates the relevant deontological constraint (e.g. that the innocent must not be killed intentionally), 'The Doctrine of Double Effect: Problems of Interpretation', *Pacific Philosophical Quarterly*, vol. 65, 1984, pp. 108–10. Davis' interpretation is too weak, since fulfilment of the Principle's first three conditions is sufficient to establish that an act of double effect does not violate the relevant deontological constraint.

some other way even if I succeed in stopping the aggressor,[61] or that I am terminally ill, etc.). Even in *this* case, the proportionality condition would be insufficient to establish the moral permissibility of homicide in self-defence were this condition to require only that the intended good effect and the foreseen bad effect be comparable in order of magnitude. The reason is, as indicated above, that in *any* case to which Double Effect applies, it must be legitimate, all things considered, for the agent to protect or promote one interest at the expense of another. In any circumstances, including those of self-defence, in which an interest of my own which I protect is uncontroversially of the same order of magnitude as a foreseeable injury which my act directly inflicts on someone else, it is permissible that I inflict this foreseeable injury on someone else only if *self-preference* is permissible in the circumstances.

Most people would take for granted the clear permissibility of self-preference in the example just outlined. The reason is, I think, the assumption that *given* foreseen good and bad effects of comparable magnitude, the injury I do the aggressor is morally outweighed in these circumstances by my preventing the harm he or she would otherwise wrongfully do me. It may be that the assumed very clear permissibility of self-preference in this case relies not simply on the other person's being technically 'in the wrong' – an unjust immediate threat – but on his or her being actively or culpably so. (George Fletcher, for instance, maintains that 'the factor which skews the balance of evils in favor of the [victim] is the aggressor's culpability in starting the fight'.)[62] In chapter 5, I discuss the moral significance of unjust aggression and the aggressor's culpability to the justification of homicide in self-defence. The important point arising from this present discussion is this: a moral asymmetry between the parties must be explained and defended by advocates of the Double Effect justification, in order that even the above 'model' case of permissible homi-

[61] Devine notes that futile self-defence is unjustified, *The Ethics of Homicide*, p. 165.

[62] *Rethinking Criminal Law*, p. 859.

cide in self-defence be morally distinguished from examples of morally impermissible and dubiously permissible self-preferential homicide, such as those I shall outline shortly. These examples of morally impermissible and dubiously permissible self-preferential homicide are meant to show that an agent cannot simply assume the permissibility of self-preference provided the following conditions are met: (i) the act has a good intention (self-preservation); (ii) the good effect cannot be achieved without the bad, and the bad effect is neither the agent's aim nor a means to its achievement in the circumstances; and (iii) the injury the agent inflicts and the good achieved are uncontroversially of comparable magnitude. In each of the examples, if I do what is necessary in the circumstances to preserve my own life one other person will die, and (as in the 'model' self-defence case) I will foreseeably *kill* this other person in acting to save myself. (Since I am concerned to highlight what permissible self-preferential homicide requires *given* fulfilment of conditions (i)–(iii), I shall simply assume that each of the examples clearly meets condition (ii), i.e., the Principle's conditions 2 and 3.) My central claim is that where I can save my own life only by an act that foreseeably kills an *unoffending* person, self-preferential killing is not morally permissible on the basis of (i)–(iii) alone.

Without a justification of self-preference, conditions (i)–(iii) are insufficient to establish the permissibility of my killing an unoffending person in the course of self-defence or in the course of self-preservation. Say someone, Alan, fires a missile at me and my only available means of self-defence is to use a device which will deflect Alan's missile. I know that if I use this device Alan's missile will be deflected to an innocent bystander, Brian, who will then be killed.[63] Here Alan unjustly threatens my life; but then Brian's life will be unjustly threatened if I deflect the missile to Brian. In the absence of a justification for saving myself at Brian's expense, my deflecting the missile to Brian is not morally permissible.

[63] Judith Jarvis Thomson discusses this sort of case as one of Substitution-of-a-Bystander, 'Self-Defense', *Philosophy and Public Affairs*, vol. 20, no. 4, 1991, p. 289.

Further, in my view the conditions of justified self-preference are more stringent where I foreseeably *kill* some unoffending person in saving myself, than in a case in which I foresee that an unoffending person will be *protected* from harm issuing from some other source only if I do not act to save myself. Say I could save myself simply by moving out of the trajectory of Alan's missile; but if I do this the missile will hit Conall who is standing behind me. If I *deflect* Alan's missile, I kill Brian; whereas if I *duck* Alan's missile, I do not kill Conall. If Brian acts against me, to thwart my deflecting Alan's missile to him, Brian acts *in self-defence* against me, an unjust immediate threat. In the varied example, where I am between Conall and the threat (Alan's missile), although my ducking Alan's missile can be said to endanger Conall, Conall's acting to prevent my ducking (so using me as a shield) is not self-defence against me; rather, Conall would be attacking me in the course of self-defence against Alan. No doubt act-consequentialists will regard my ducking Alan's missile knowing that it will then hit Conall, and my deflecting Alan's missile to Brian, as morally indistinguishable. They will argue that if my ducking the missile is permissible, then so *equally* is my deflecting it: that if in saving myself I can choose either to deflect the missile to Brian, or to duck it knowing that it will hit Conall, it is morally irrelevant whether I deflect or duck. However, I do not consider these acts to be morally indistinguishable. I am under a moral constraint not to inflict unjust harm on Brian, an unoffending person. This constraint might or might not be outweighed by the cost to me of not deflecting Alan's missile. But if Alan fires a missile at me and in the direction of Conall, I am not obliged to shield Conall; I am not obliged to protect Conall from Alan's missile, given the cost to me.

Nancy Davis' view, that the relevant moral distinction is between killing and allowing to be killed, takes us along the right lines in evaluating such cases.[64] (This is so despite the

---

[64] Davis, 'The Priority of Avoiding Harm'.

argument that *some* duckings are killings.)[65] However, not all impermissible deflections are, strictly speaking, killings. Christopher Boorse and Roy A. Sorensen discuss an example in which, being trapped and knowing that someone is looking to kill me, I surreptitiously swap my identification papers with those of the person sitting next to me, with the result that the person sitting next to me is killed instead of me. Here I am partly responsible for this person's death, but I do not kill her. This can also be true when I use an innocent person as a shield against an aggressor, and the shield is killed.[66]

Similarly, (i)–(iii) alone do not permit me to steer my car into someone's front garden, foreseeably killing a person who is sleeping there, in order to avoid being hit by an oncoming boulder on the road. Consider another example, in which I am driving a heavy truck down the Bulli Pass near Wollongong.[67]

[65] Christopher Boorse and Roy A. Sorensen argue that some duckings are killings, 'Ducking Harm', *Journal of Philosophy*, vol. 85, no. 3, 1988, pp. 115–34.

[66] My discussion of these matters is by no means exhaustive. The justification of these distinctions in terms of a theory of obligation and agent responsibility is difficult and very important. But it has to remain unfinished business as far as this book is concerned. The distinction critically discussed by Boorse and Sorensen is that between my ducking harm to another and my using another as a shield. (In my view, my using Brian as a shield violates Double Effect's condition 2, whereas my *deflecting* harm to Brian need not.) Boorse and Sorensen also argue that 'on standard accounts of homicide' the one who ducks harm seems to have no defence to murder or manslaughter, p. 117. This is doubtful in my view, given the general principle concerning *novus actus interveniens* expressed in *Pagett* [1983] 75 Cr. App. R. 279: 'A reasonable act performed for the purpose of self-preservation, including a reasonable act of self-defence, does not operate as a *novus actus interveniens* ... ' Further, *Pagett* would suggest that in my example I am not *legally* causally responsible for Brian's death if I *deflect* Alan's missile to Brian. (See also, more generally, Eric Colvin, 'Causation in Criminal Law', (1989) 1 *Bond Law Review*, pp. 265–70.) However, on ordinary principles of agent causation I do cause Brian's death if I deflect Alan's missile to Brian, as long as this *deflection to Brian* is an act on my part, even an instinctive or reflex one. (Attribution of causation would be different if Alan's missile hit my protective armour and so was deflected to Brian.)

[67] This sort of example is taken up in the Law Reform Commission of Victoria's Report, *Homicide*, p. 102, in the context of a discussion of Necessity as a defence to murder.

For much of this very steep, narrow mountain road there is a sheer drop on one side and a cliff face on the other. The brakes fail and the truck quickly accelerates. Unless I steer off the road I'll almost certainly run over a cyclist travelling in the same direction in front of me. The cyclist cannot get out of my way; I cannot avoid running over the cyclist other than by steering over the sheer drop or into the cliff face at great speed. Either way of avoiding the cyclist would almost certainly kill me; but if I manage to keep the truck on the road I'll be able to stop it once I reach a safety ramp some way ahead. I can see that there is no one but the cyclist between me and the ramp. Given fulfilment of conditions (i)–(iii), my running over the cyclist is not permissible self-preference if the brake failure is my fault. Even where the brake failure is not my fault, given conditions (i)–(iii) alone, my running over the cyclist is not clearly morally permissible self-preferential homicide. (It might be argued that the cyclist in this example *is* a threat – albeit a passive, morally innocent one, akin to the person mentioned in chapter 3 who happens to be in the way of my escape – in that he comes between me and safety. If the cyclist is arguably a passive threat, she is certainly not offending, not an unjust threat. However, the cyclist is not a threat such that my killing her would be homicide in self-defence. The cyclist does not create, instigate, or force the conflict (I do so, even if blamelessly); and she is not identifiable as the source of the danger to me. My running over the cyclist in keeping on the road is insufficiently a case of resisting, repelling, or warding off an immediate threat to be a case of homicide in self-defence. It is, rather, a case of homicide in the course of self-preservation.)[68]

[68] Some writers would take self-preference to be clearly morally permissible in each of the above two examples. Montague, for instance, asserts that it is 'quite clear' that I am 'at liberty' to save myself by diverting a trolley onto a siding where it will run over a child sitting on the tracks, 'Self-Defense and Choosing Between Lives', p. 209. But the permissibility of self-preference here is not at all clear, since I would infringe the equal rights of the child in acting in this way. It is by way of uncritically assuming the clear permissibility of self-preferential killing in this kind of case that Montague goes on to claim that self-defence and self-preservation cases involving innocent (i.e. blameless) victims are all 'in very

Conditions (i)–(iii) can be fulfilled across a spectrum of examples in which I foreseeably kill one other person in acting to save my own life. The particular spectrum I have in mind ranges from a starting point at which I kill someone who is clearly a non-threat (e.g. an innocent bystander), and progresses through examples in which my killing someone else is arguably in self-defence (e.g. I remove someone who stands in the way of my escape), towards uncontroversial examples of homicide in self-defence (e.g. I resist an attacker). As we move through this spectrum in this direction, the claim that self-preferential killing is morally permissible in any particular example strengthens as it becomes increasing plausible to regard the other person as *offending*, as an unjust immediate threat against whom force is used in self-defence. Consider a version of the sinking plank case, a familiar example in discussions of necessity.[69] The details of this example could place it in the middle of the spectrum, on the boundary of self-defence and necessity. Say you and I are shipwrecked, and we happen to reach a plank and cling to it at the same time, each of us needing the plank in order not to drown. Unfortunately the plank cannot support us both. Is it permissible that I simply go ahead and push you off the plank, given only that, (i) self-preservation is a laudable aim, (ii) your death is not strictly a means to saving myself, and (iii) the good effect (I am saved) is of the same order of magnitude as the foreseen bad effect (you drown)? If neither of us acts, both will drown; and it seems reasonable to save someone rather than no one. But these considerations alone do not warrant self-preference rather than self-sacrifice. Although your clinging to the plank endangers me, my presence equally endangers you; further, the situation in which we are both endangered results from legitimate acts on both our

much the same moral boat' (i.e., equally permissible – but why?), and that the right to use force in self-defence derives from the aggressor's culpability, pp. 211–18.
69 See William Blackstone, *Commentaries on the Laws of England*, vol. iv, p. 186; also Immanuel Kant, *The Metaphysics of Morals*, transl. by Mary Gregor (Cambridge University Press, 1991), p. 60.

parts. In the absence of either a fair selection procedure or some additional, morally sufficient reason on the side of saving myself at your expense, my saving myself by pushing you off the plank is not morally permissible. Interestingly, given fulfilment of conditions (i)–(iii), if the sinking plank example is changed in just one respect, so that in clinging to the plank I am a threat to you (you reached the plank well before me), my pushing you off in order to save myself is more clearly impermissible self-preference. We move in the direction of permissible self-preference if I am clinging to the plank first, and in order to save myself I push you away as you attempt to cling to it too.

An example mentioned in 3.2, where more survivors climb into a lifeboat than the boat will carry, is similar to my first version of the sinking plank example. But in this lifeboat case there is time to require that those who are endangered engage in a morally defensible selection procedure before the casting out of particular people can be morally permissible as necessary for the good of the others. Probably the urgency of many situations similar to those outlined in the previous two paragraphs would mostly prompt 'automatic' acts of self-preference. No doubt many people would view acts of self-preference in such circumstances as simply instinctive, and similarly regard analogous cases in which we save loved ones at the expense of strangers. (Preference for loved ones at the expense of strangers could be viewed as an extension of self-preference. All the same, we should recognize that *self*-preference on the basis of conditions (i)–(iii) alone is more likely to seem impermissible to us where the person who endangers us on the plank is someone we know.)

In the examples I have been discussing, extenuating considerations such as instinct, fear, and the urgency of the situation, are certainly relevant to the question of whether self-preferential killing is morally excusable. Further, as Kant claims, these factors can also render legal punishment irrelevant in such cases. But, of course, the moral excusability or legal unpunishability of a particular homicide is not a justification.[70] And we should be generally suspicious of ready access to the claim that acts are morally legitimate because instinctive. As others have pointed out, morality can sometimes require that we curb some of our instincts, if instincts they be.[71] Claimed instincts aside, it is undoubtedly true that typically we *care* much more about our own life, and about the lives of those who are close to us, than we care about the lives of others, especially strangers. This *preferential valuing* of ourselves and those with whom we have close personal ties seems essential to self-development and to important personal relationships, such as love and friendship, which we have with particular people and which most of us regard as necessary to living a worthwhile human life. If we acknowledge that from an impersonal perspective, the lives of strangers are as important, as worthy, *as valuable,* as our own and the lives of those close to us, it remains true that from the perspective of the individual persons we are, living particular lives and involved in particular relationships, we do not *value* these other lives equally with our own life and the lives of those close to us.[72] The moral difficulty here concerns the grounds on which, and the limits within which, it is morally legitimate that we act on this preferential valuing.[73]

[70] *The Metaphysics of Morals*, pp. 60–1.
[71] In discussing what sense there is in calling the natural (animal) instinct of self-preservation a right, Ritchie remarks that natural instinct can be furthered by reflection, and it may come to be thought a duty to preserve life. On the other hand, natural instinct may be overcome by reflection, and it may come to be thought a duty not to preserve life, or only a secondary duty, subordinate to others. Even in the absence of reflection, the instinct to preserve life often gives way to other instincts, e.g. the desire to preserve offspring or even the desire to gratify passion, *Natural Rights*, pp. 119–20.
[72] See also Susan Levine, 'The Moral Permissibility of Killing a "Material Aggressor" in Self-Defense', *Philosophical Studies*, vol. 45, 1984, p. 73.
[73] Some suggested *impersonal* justifications of acts of self-preference – such as the claim that our judgments about our own interests and the interests of our 'nearest and dearest' are likely to be much more accurate than our judgments about the interests of strangers – clearly fail in cases which involve inflicting injustice or serious harm on others. And in other contexts, as a defence of preferring to direct our own time or resources to those with whom we have close personal ties, such claims (where persuasive) seem an impersonal gloss on an independently motivated,

In the absence of an impersonal justification of self-preference, it might be argued that *within moral limits* (for instance,
given fulfilment of conditions (i)–(iii)), a universalizable,
agent-relative permission warrants self-preference in the
above examples and also in the case of self-defence.[74] But, of
course, agent-relative permissibility cannot simply be
invoked *ad hoc*: the basis of such a permission needs to be
explained and defended. Grisez, for instance, draws attention
to the importance to Aquinas' justification of self-defence of
the general background claim that as individuals we are
naturally inclined towards self-preservation. As Grisez notes,
the existence of this natural inclination would be insufficient
by itself to justify self-preference. In fact Aquinas maintains
something stronger: he says that each person is more strongly
bound to safeguard his own life than that of another. Grisez
remarks that the claim that individuals have a paramount
obligation to take care of themselves is crucial to Aquinas'
account of self-defence: 'if there were no moral responsibility
for oneself, an inclination to preserve one's life by using force
deadly to another could never be justified'.[75]

Surely this supposed stronger obligation to ourselves must
be held to operate within moral limits. Aquinas is discussing
self-defence against unprovoked attack, and it is reasonable
to assume that this context is important to the justification of

essential ingredient of a subjectively worthwhile human life. (See, e.g.
Frank Jackson, 'Decision-theoretic Consequentialism and the Nearest
and Dearest Objection', *Ethics*, vol. 101, 1991, pp. 461–82.) In *Reasons and
Persons* (Oxford University Press, 1984), pp. 31–40, Derek Parfit discusses
consequentialist evaluation, consequentialist-inspired motives, and
cases of what he calls 'blameless wrongdoing' (e.g. saving one's own
child rather than several strangers). However, Parfit's examples do not
suggest that one is saving one's own child by harming or killing otherwise unendangered strangers, but rather that one is saving one's child
instead of saving similarly endangered strangers. Parfit discusses self-
preferential harming of others in 'Innumerate Ethics'.

74 Universalizable in that each person is permitted to save him- or herself.
75 Grisez, 'Toward a Consistent Natural Law Ethics of Killing', p. 75. See
also Finnis, 'The Rights and Wrongs of Abortion', p. 146. If this particular
normative background is necessary to the Double Effect justification of
self-defence against unjust aggression, then this justification does not
easily extend to defence of others.

self-preference where this involves *killing* another person. A more general obligation to prefer ourselves would be too strong: it would permit self-defence, but it would also imply an obligation to defend or protect ourselves at another person's expense. Aquinas, unlike some later natural law theorists, may have considered us obliged to defend ourselves, especially against culpable aggression. But, presumably, he did not intend his claim that individuals have a paramount obligation to take care of themselves to imply that one has an obligation foreseeably to kill, if necessary, an *unoffending* person (e.g. the cyclist) in saving oneself. It is one thing to maintain that if *your* life is in peril through no doing of mine, and I am more strongly bound to safeguard my own life than I am to safeguard yours, then I am not obliged to risk or sacrifice my life in order to save you. (This is the claim that I am not obliged, e.g. to deflect to myself a missile aimed at you, or to give you my heart or even one of my kidneys, even if you cannot survive unless I do.) But it is another thing to claim that I have an obligation to deflect existing danger (Alan's missile or the failed brakes) from myself to you, an unoffending person, where this is necessary to save myself. (This is the claim that if my life is in peril, and this is not your doing, then I am obliged foreseeably to kill you if necessary in the act of saving myself.) One very important difference between these two claims is this: in the former cases, in not sacrificing myself (not deflecting the missile to myself, not giving you my heart), I do not thereby *wrong* you; whereas in the latter cases (deflecting Alan's missile to you, running over you if you are the cyclist) I do. If you defend your life against me in the latter cases it will be self-defence on your part against my unjust threat to you; whereas I am not a threat to you, unjust or otherwise, in the former cases.

Conditions (i)–(iii) are met if I run over the cyclist, if I swerve my car into the person in the garden, or if I deflect Alan's missile to Brian. If Aquinas' background justification of self-defence – that we have a stronger obligation to safeguard our own lives than we do to safeguard the lives of others – *requires* that I act on the basis of self-preference in these examples, then I do not accept that we have this obligation. (I expect that many, including most advocates of Double Effect, would agree.) To be plausible, a justification of self-preference must be consistent with its also being permissible in these examples that I not save myself at the expense of an unoffending person (even a stranger). Given fulfilment of conditions (i)–(iii), the permissibility of my not deflecting Alan's missile to Brian, of my not running over the cyclist, of my not swerving into the person in the garden, is clear.

An alternative, more defensible interpretation of Aquinas' background justification of self-preference might be this: although self-sacrifice is permissible where self-preservation would involve killing an unoffending person, given fulfilment of conditions (i)–(iii) it is also permissible that I save myself on the basis of natural inclination, simply because I do not have a stronger obligation to safeguard the life of another person than I have to safeguard my own life. But even this weaker piece of justificatory reasoning is insufficient to establish that, as in the above examples, self-preferential killing which *wrongs* another person is permissible provided conditions (i)–(iii) are met. Another interpretation of the background justification of self-preference is the claim that self-preference is permissible at the expense of an unoffending person simply because it would be *unreasonable* to expect me to act otherwise – unreasonable not because I cannot act otherwise, but because this would require of me too great a sacrifice. This permission of self-preference, too, would need to be defended (why is it too great a sacrifice?). And although this permission is universalizable, it is necessarily agent-relative.

The important points of this section can be summarized as follows: fulfilment of conditions (i)–(iii) is insufficient to establish the permissibility of my violating the equal rights of an unoffending person in saving myself. Where the good I achieve in saving myself is not disproportionate to the injury I foreseeably inflict on someone else, the Double Effect conditions can *permit* saving myself only if I can legitimately weigh my own interests more heavily. The grounds of legitimate self-preference need not be the same in all cases to which Double Effect applies. Sometimes the permissibility of self-preference can derive from what is likely to do the most good; sometimes it can depend on whether or not in protecting myself I am violating someone else's equal rights. Self-preference might be legitimate, for example, if the other person in need of the limited supply of antivenene is in a weaker condition than myself and less likely to survive; self-preference may be permissible in Pufendorf's lifeboat example because others have waived certain rights by agreeing to the casting of lots. The use of force in self-defence is, I argue in chapter 5, legitimate self-preference because the person against whom force is used is an unjust immediate threat.

A very important, often suppressed element of the Double Effect justification of homicide in self-defence – the legitimacy of self-preferential killing – connects with, and appears to depend upon, something akin to the distinguishable type of justification which I discuss in chapter 5, that is, the view that in so far as the right to life entails the right not to be killed, a person who is an unjust immediate threat to life does not have a right to life equal to that of an unoffending person.

Chapter 5

The right of self-defence

The justification of homicide in self-defence requires that self-preferential killing be justified. I argued in 4.3 that lack of intention to kill (where plausibly invoked), together with the requirements of necessary and proportionate force, are insufficient to justify preserving my life by an act which foreseeably kills another person. The conditions of necessary and proportionate force – and, according to some, lack of intention to kill – are moral limits of the right of self-defence: they cannot *ground* a positive right of self-defence. This is because, as John Finnis stresses, the use of force in self-defence involves an act which would normally be a grave injustice to its victim.[1] In my view, unjust harm is inflicted when an unoffending person is justifiably foreseeably killed as the lesser evil, e.g. where an innocent bystander is killed in the course of defending a group of people, or in the case of necessity where a driver of a runaway vehicle steers into one person rather than several. Even when such foreseen killing complies with the conditions of the Principle of Double Effect, it nonetheless *wrongs* its unoffending victim in infringing his or her right to life. Unlike justified killing in the course of self-defence or in circumstances of necessity, the use of necessary and proportionate force against an unjust threat *in self-defence* does not violate its victim's right to life.[2] Because this is

[1] 'The Rights and Wrongs of Abortion', p. 149.
[2] My positive account of the right of self-defence is similar in some important respects to Judith Jarvis Thomson's most recent outline of the permissibility of self-defence, 'Self-Defense', see esp. p. 302.

156

so, the justification of self-preference in the case of homicide in self-defence distinguishes self-defence as an exception to, rather than a justified infringement of, the prohibition of homicide.

In the paradigm case of justified homicide in self-defence that I described in 4.3, the unjust aggressor is culpable. As others have commented, an unjust aggressor's culpability is an agent-neutral ground of discrimination by the victim in his or her own favour: one which can, in principle, extend to a justification of defence of the victim by a third party. The fact that an unjust aggressor is dangerous to more than one person would be an additional, and in the absence of culpability on the aggressor's part (e.g. a madman firing a gun indiscriminately), an alternative agent-neutral ground on which to defend oneself or someone else.[3] Although the aggressor's culpability and his danger to others obviously strengthen the justification of self-preference, neither of these grounds of discrimination is necessary to the positive right of self-defence. It does not follow from this, however, that the right of self-defence against an unjust immediate threat who is neither culpable nor dangerous to others is an agent-relative permission – confined to the person who is him- or herself threatened – and that the right to defend another person depends on agent-neutral grounds such as those just mentioned.

In 5.1, I explain the right of self-defence as a right to use necessary and proportionate force against an unjust immediate threat. I defend a unitary right of self-defence, one that grounds the justification of the use of force in self-defence against culpable and non-culpable, active and passive unjust threats. I claim in 5.2 that the positive right of self-defence is best characterized and defended as part of a more general permission to use necessary and proportionate force directly to block the infliction of irreparable unjust harm, such as the violation of an unoffending person's right not to be killed. Throughout this chapter, I argue that the permissibility of

---

[3] See Davis, 'Abortion and Self-Defense', p. 191.

acting directly to block an unjust immediate threat does not derive from, or depend upon, culpability on the part of the unjust threat; nor does the permissibility of using force against an unjust immediate threat to a particular person depend on other people also being threatened. Further, this permission is not, of itself, agent-relative: its scope includes defence of others; indeed in some circumstances it can amount to an obligation to assist or defend others.

In 5.2, I also address the relevance of a theory of forfeiture to the positive right of self-defence. Something akin to a theory of forfeiture of rights is necessary to the justification of self-preference in the case of self-defence. The justification of homicide in self-defence requires a particular specification of the right to life as entailing the right not to be killed. I discuss the theory of forfeiture and this particular specification of the right to life in chapter 6.

5.1 THE RIGHT OF SELF-DEFENCE

In this section I take up two basic issues, identified in chapter 3, which must be addressed in giving an account of the right of self-defence as a right to use necessary and proportionate force against an unjust immediate threat. The first is an explication of the conditions of immediate threat relevant to the use of force *in self-defence*; the second concerns the conditions under which someone is an *unjust* immediate threat.

The use of force in self-defence

In chapter 3, I distinguished homicide in self-defence from homicide in the course of self-defence. (Similarly, homicide in defence of another person is distinguishable from homicide in the course of defending another person.) Someone who is not an immediate threat, who is killed as either a means or an incidental effect of resisting, repelling, or warding off an immediate threat, is killed in the course of self-defence. Force used *in self-defence* resists, repels, or wards off someone who is him- or herself an immediate threat.[4] Persons against whom force is used in self-defence are commonly called aggressors. But as I pointed out in chapter 3, I can use force against an aggressor (e.g. the instigator of a contract killing) and not be acting in self-defence: I use force in self-defence against an aggressor only if he or she poses an immediate threat. Further, I can act in self-defence against some immediate threats (e.g. some passive threats) who are aggressors only in a stretched sense, and I can act in self-defence against immediate threats who are not aggressors (e.g. as a hijacker I can defend myself against the police sharp-shooter). I can use force in self-defence against someone if he or she poses an immediate threat; but under what conditions do I act in self-defence against persons who are passive or involuntary immediate threats? Do I act in self-defence in using force against a contingent threat, such as someone who happens to be in the way of my escape? What are the conditions of immediate threat relevant to acting in self-defence?

Although 'immediate threat' is more accurate than 'aggressor' in referring to someone against whom force is used in self-defence, the common use of 'aggressor' in this context signifies something deeper than the assumption that most persons against whom force is used in self-defence are aggressors properly so called. There is an important conceptual link between aggression and the conditions of immediate threat relevant to the use of force in self-defence. Aggression is essentially *offensive* conduct: it initiates harm or conflict. A central sense of 'aggression' is 'unprovoked attack'. In contrast, the essential feature of force used in self-defence is, of course, that it is *defensive*: it resists, repels, or wards off a threat. Some immediate threats which might be resisted, repelled, or warded off are not offensive: an aggressor might repel the harm her victim is about to inflict in self-defence. Nevertheless, force is used in self-defence against those types of threats which might be resisted, repelled, or warded off.

---

[4] In 5.2, I note and comment on a possible deviant sense of acting in self-defence.

This point is being made when persons who pose such threats are called aggressors.

Against what types of immediate threats is the use of force *defensive*? In my view, the most illuminating answer to this question is: attacks and assaults. For reasons I shall give shortly, 'attack or assault' is too restrictive in identifying the type of immediate threat against which force can be used in self-defence. All the same, the conditions of immediate threat relevant to the use of force in self-defence are best explained in terms of the concepts of attack and assault.

Attackers, assailants, and problem cases   An attack is an offensive act, initiating harm or conflict. An attacker is someone who acts against another with force, or acts harmfully or destructively on another; in so acting, an attacker seeks to hurt or defeat another. This seeking to hurt or defeat another need not be unjust (e.g. pre-emptive strikes can be just). And an unjust act which seeks to hurt or defeat another need not be culpable (e.g. excusable cases of mistaken identity). Someone can attack a *particular* person unintentionally when acting under a mistaken belief (e.g. you mistake me for your enemy), and even involuntarily (e.g. you hit me because you are dreaming that you are attacking your enemy). However, a person who uses force against, or acts dangerously or harmfully on another, but who does not seek to hurt or defeat *anyone*, is not an attacker properly so called. 'Attacker' usually implies a particular mental element – seeking to hurt or defeat. ('Aggressor' also typically implies this mental element.) I am not attacking you if I use force against you in order to protect you; someone who is accidentally or unwittingly about to fire a weapon at me is acting dangerously or harmfully on me, but she is not attacking me; a truck driver is not attacking me if his brakes fail on a hill and he steers in my direction in order to avoid hitting a group of children on a pedestrian crossing.

On the other hand, there is a sense in which 'attack' can simply mean 'act harmfully or destructively on' (seeking to hurt or defeat is not necessarily implied), whereas 'assault' is sometimes defined as 'hostile attack' (implying a belligerent motive). Yet in the example of the truck driver just mentioned, and also where you strike me not realizing what you are doing, it seems right to deny that there is an attack, although not wrong to say that there is an assault. This is because 'attack' usually implies the mental element of seeking to hurt or defeat, and 'assault' often simply means to hit or strike.[5] Where 'assault' simply means to hit or strike, an unprovoked assault need not be an attack: an involuntary act can be an assault in this sense. I can assault someone when I am asleep and dreaming that I am defending myself against a lion; I can assault someone when I hit out madly because being attacked by bees.

Where 'assault' simply means to hit or strike, whether an act is an assault is an objective matter, in the sense that it does not depend on the agent's perception (reasonable or otherwise) of what he or she is doing. There is a sense of 'attack' of which this is also partly true. Where an agent seeks to hurt or defeat another, an act which is in fact offensive (it initiates harm or conflict) can be an attack in this sense even though the agent does not perceive it as such. Say I hit you, mistakenly believing that I am *defending* myself against you. In hitting you, I am initiating harm or conflict and I intend to harm or defeat you; in fact I am attacking you, even though this is not what I think I am doing. However, the subjective element of being perceived by the agent as an offensive act is necessary to another legitimate sense of 'attack'. In this second, more subjective sense, I might say of the example I have just given that because I (mistakenly) believe myself to be engaged in defence, I am not attacking you, even though it probably seems otherwise to you. Further, 'attack' might sometimes invoke an entirely subjective notion of offensiveness. And according to this third sense, an act which in fact resists, repels, or wards off an imminent threat can be an attack if the agent perceives his or her act as offensive. Such a case would be where I use force on you believing that I am

[5] This is not the legal notion of assault, which is an unlawful personal attack even if only menacing words.

attacking you; in fact you were about to hit me and my act repels your imminent threat.[6]

I act *in self-defence* (as distinct from putative self-defence) in resisting, repelling, or warding off an *actual* threat. Hence below, in specifying the conditions of immediate threat relevant to the use of force in self-defence, I use 'attack' in the sense which invokes the central objective requirement of being an act which is dangerous or harmful to another.[7] An attack initiates harm or conflict, whether in fact or from the agent's perspective. 'Attack' also includes the subjective requirement that the agent seek to hurt or defeat another in so acting.

Force can be used in self-defence against an involuntary act which is an attack or assault (e.g. against the sleepwalker about to knife me); force can be used in self-defence against voluntary non-culpable attacks or assaults (e.g. in resisting a just pre-emptive attack, or in deflecting the driver who steers towards me rather than into a crowd). However, even if we allow that 'assault' can simply mean to hit or strike, 'attack or assault' is still too restrictive to identify the conditions of immediate threat relevant to the use of force in self-defence. This is because, first, force can be used in self-defence against some immediate threats (e.g. some passive threats) which are not attacks or assaults because they are not *acts* on the part of the person who poses the threat. Strictly speaking, 'attack' and 'assault' (and also 'aggression') imply an act (voluntary or

---

[6] I am not *acting in self-defence* in this case, for the reasons I gave in 2.2.

[7] In some cases I can be attacking you if I intend my acts to harm or defeat you, although my acts (even if unchecked) can have no such effect. However, in the relevant cases the appropriateness of describing my acts as an attack depends not simply on my beliefs about the effects of my acts, but also on the nature of what I am doing (i.e. using force on you, acting dangerously or harmfully on you). For instance, I am not attacking you if, under the delusion that I have extraordinary powers, I sit in an armchair at home and wish you dead. Am I attacking you if I pick up a dummy gun, believing it to be a real gun, and fire it at you intending to harm you? Not really. However, I am attacking you if, e.g. I launch a missile at you, even though (unbenown to me) the missile has a design fault which will cause it to explode in mid air. This latter case is a failed attack; the first two examples fail to be attacks.

involuntary). In its widest sense, an act is something about which the agent can say 'I did it': 'I dropped the plate; hit the girl; struck out; spluttered it out; coughed it up; jumped in; etc'. (Omissions, too, are properly described as things we do. And animals act in this wide sense. Of course an animal cannot say of itself 'I did it'. But we can say of an animal 'It did it' (it chased the man; it clawed him to death; it ate him; etc); and we distinguish this, as with our own acts, from 'It happened to it' (it was thrown; it became stuck; its heart stopped).) In explaining this wide sense of act, I draw upon Eric D'Arcy's characterization of act and his distinction between an act and an action: 'As a general rule, an action is called an act only when it can be described in a proposition with a personal subject ... Every act, then (whether voluntary or involuntary), is an action; but not every action is an act. The sense of the term 'action' which applies to bodily movements which are not acts is rather akin to the sense of the term 'action' in which it is used in the language of processes.' In isolating those actions which are acts, D'Arcy draws on Wittgenstein's distinction between things that simply happen to us, such as the subsidence of a violent thudding of the heart, and things that we do, such as raising an arm.[8] This is a useful way of making the point; but we need to emphasize that in the wide sense of 'act', involuntary bodily movements such as tripping over, flailing about while having a fit, hitting out because being stung by bees, and coughing, are things that we do – not things that happen to us.

This very wide sense of 'act' might allow that some so-called passive threats are assaults. If the man now hurtling down the well at me has jumped (even involuntarily), in warding him off I am resisting an assault. Arguably, 'act' in this wide sense stretches sufficiently to include, for example, someone who poses a threat by tripping; some such threats might then be described as assaults in the sense in which 'assault' means to hit or strike. However, strictly speaking, someone is a passive threat on account of something that

[8] *Human Acts*, pp. 6–7.

happens to him rather than in virtue of anything he voluntarily or involuntarily does. And someone who threatens harm *only as an object* (as a stone might), and not as an agent even in the widest sense, is not an assailant. The man in Nozick's example who has been thrown down the well at me is not himself an assailant or an attacker, yet he is an immediate threat of a type that might be resisted, repelled, or warded off. I can *defend* myself against immediate threats posed by dangerous inanimate objects, as well as those posed by agents.[9]

A second reason why 'attack or assault' is too restrictive in identifying the conditions of immediate threat relevant to acting in self-defence is that force can be used in self-defence against some *active* immediate threats which are not assaults, and are not attacks because, although dangerous or harmful and intended to harm or defeat, they are not offensive acts. For example, as an aggressor I might defend myself against my victim's self-defence by preventing the victim from cutting off my air supply. Thirdly, to restrict the conditions of immediate threat relevant to acting in self-defence to those of assault and attack would beg the question of whether force can be used in self-defence against a contingent threat, such as someone who stands in the way of my escape, or whose coughing will reveal my hideout to the secret police who will shoot on sight. Persons who pose such contingent threats are not themselves attackers or assailants, yet they presently endanger me by exposing me to an attack or an assault.

The conditions of immediate threat relevant to the use of force in self-defence   In the light of the above discussion, I shall adopt the following specification. Force is clearly used in self-

---

[9] Examples of persons trapped in a threat (e.g. passengers in a plane crashing in a populated area) test the conditions under which someone is a passive threat. These cases can be conceptually grey in my view. The infliction of harm on a person whose presence is strictly incidental to the threat itself (e.g. a trapped passenger) is distinguishable from force used in self-defence on a passive threat itself (e.g. someone who has been thrown at me). Nevertheless, in some cases a person trapped in a threat might be so inextricably bound to the threat itself that he seems to be part

defence against an immediate threat who is an assailant; or an attacker; or someone who would be assaulting me were the threat he poses to be an act on his part; or someone who is not attacking me only because his acts are not offensive, or only because he does not intend to harm or defeat me.[10]

In this specification, 'assault' means to hit or strike; 'attack' implies an offensive act which is dangerous or harmful to another, and intended to harm or defeat. The justification of this specification of the conditions of immediate threat relevant to clear cases of acting in self-defence is the *requirement of defensiveness*: force is used in self-defence if it resists, repels, or wards off an immediate threat.[11] Paradigm acts of self-defence against persons resist, repel, or ward off immediate threats posed by voluntary or involuntary attackers or assailants. As I illustrate below, the requirement of defensiveness, and the degree to which an immediate threat resembles an attack or an assault in the specified senses, clarify the conditions under which force is used in self-defence against passive threats, and against active threats which are not attacks or assaults. Further, the requirement of defensiveness, together with the conditions under which an act is an attack, also highlight the relevant and competing considerations involved in classifying the use of self-protective force against contingent threats.

The above specification explicitly includes the use of force against some *passive* threats. The requirement of defensiveness is clearly met where a passive threat would be an assault were it to be an act on the part of the person who poses an immediate threat. The person thrown down a well at me is a passive threat; I act in self-defence in warding him off because he would be assaulting me were the threat he poses

of the threat. Certainly, the infliction of harm on someone trapped in a threat is far closer to resisting or warding off the immediate threat itself than is, e.g. deflecting a threat to oneself to a bystander.

10 This revises the specification I suggested in 'Self-Defense and Natural Law'.

11 To avert possible misunderstanding, perhaps I should stress here that the conditions of immediate threat relevant to acting in self-defence do not settle the issue of *unjust* threat. Assaults and attacks need not be unjust.

to be a voluntary or involuntary act on his part. (I would also act in self-defence in using force against the person about to throw the man down the well, since this person is about to strike me with an object. Ditto someone whose falling will trigger a mechanism that will kill me.) The use of force against other passive threats is not explicitly included. The requirement of defensiveness arguably admits further cases, others will lie on the borderline of self-defence and necessity. Some passive threats are excluded by the requirement of defensiveness; for instance, the infamous fat man who is stuck in the mouth of a cave, trapping the pot-holers within as the tide rises,[12] does not meet the conditions of immediate threat relevant to acting in self-defence. If the pot-holers use dynamite to remove this obstruction, they act on the wider principle of necessity.

The above specification also allows that I can use force in self-defence against a variety of *active* immediate threats which are not assaults or attacks, but which would be attacks were they to be offensive acts, or were they to be intended to harm or defeat me. For instance, I noted above that as an aggressor I might defend myself against my victim's self-defence by preventing the victim from cutting off my air supply. Here, I am not being assaulted or attacked, yet I am under an immediate threat of a type which might be resisted, repelled, or warded off. My victim is acting dangerously or harmfully on me, and she intends to harm or defeat me; she would be attacking me were the threat she poses to be offensive. Force can also be used in self-defence against some active immediate threats which *create* danger or harm, but are not attacks because they are not intended to harm or defeat me. For instance, I can use force in self-defence against someone who is accidentally, carelessly, or unwittingly about to fire a gun at me, or to push me in front of a moving train, or to light a match when we are surrounded by petrol fumes. If I am already clinging to a lifebuoy that will support only one, then I act in self-defence in pushing someone away who tries to

[12] Foot discusses this example, 'The Problem of Abortion and the Doctrine of Double Effect', pp. 21–2.

cling to it too. Also included are examples in which another person's acts *exacerbate* existing danger; for instance, another trapped person uses our limited air supply unnecessarily quickly because he panics and lights a fire; another occupant of the lifeboat goes berserk, violently rocks the boat, staves in the hull. These threats are not attacks or assaults, yet they are immediate threats of a type which might be resisted, repelled, or warded off. They are offensive acts which are themselves dangerous or harmful to me; they would be attacks were they intended to harm or defeat me.

The remaining problem cases – contingent threats – are the most difficult to classify. Someone is a contingent threat because his acts *expose* me to an immediate threat; unlike a bystander, a contingent threat is presently doing something which endangers me. The acts of someone who exposes me to an immediate threat are not irrelevant to the success of the immediate threat; someone is a contingent *threat* in virtue of the fact that he or she facilitates an immediate threat (whether involuntarily, unwittingly, or deliberately). Indeed, in some cases (e.g. where someone's coughing will reveal my hideout to the secret police) it might be that the immediate threat would not succeed but for this particular exposure. Where I use self protective force against a contingent threat, provided there is no other room for escape, it might seem reasonable to say that I act in self-defence. Further, I do seem to act defensively in, e.g. pushing someone out of the way of my escape or putting my hand over the cougher's mouth. On the other hand, the use of force against some contingent threats seems much more like an attack on them. Consider a case of ducking harm similar to that discussed in 4.3. I am standing behind Colin, and Adam fires a missile in our direction. Colin can avoid the missile by ducking; I will be protected provided Colin stays put. In these circumstances, Colin's ducking Adam's missile exposes me to Adam's missile. But in preventing Colin's ducking, I am not defending myself against Colin; rather, I am using Colin as a shield. In so doing, I am attacking Colin as a means of defence against the immediate threat, which is Adam's missile.

167

A person who happens to be in the way of my escape from an assailant, someone whose coughing will reveal my hideout to the secret police, and someone whose ducking will expose me to a missile that someone else has fired, all endanger me in the particular circumstances, but *indirectly*: their acts expose me to immediate danger or harm initiated and inflicted by another agent. In using force against contingent threats I am stopping, or trying to stop, what they are doing, or about to do, because their acts endanger me. But their acts (standing in the doorway, coughing, ducking) endanger me only because of someone or something else (the assailant hot on my heels, the secret police outside, Adam's missile) which in the circumstances we identify as the immediate threat. This strongly suggests that force is used against a contingent threat *in the course of self-defence* against the immediate threat itself. Generally, this is the right response to such cases in my view, *provided* a contingent threat merely exposes me to something or someone else which in the circumstances we identify as the immediate threat. My preventing Colin's ducking Adam's missile is a clear case. (This is not to say, I hasten to add, that the use of force against a contingent threat in the course of self-defence is always unjustified. The use of self-protective force on a contingent threat in the course of self-defence might be justified as the lesser evil, e.g. the person in the way of my escape might suffer some bruises as the result of my assault, whereas my life is at stake.)[13]

The proviso – that something or someone else be identifiable as the immediate threat – is necessary to my general classification of the use of force against contingent threats, because under some conditions it does seem appropriate to regard someone whose acts expose me to a threat as himself the immediate threat, or part of the immediate threat, against which I can act in self-defence. Hence, the above specification of the conditions of immediate threat relevant to acting in

[13] Where not the lesser evil, as suggested by the example of my using Colin as a shield against Adam's missile, self-preference is not justified in my view, although the use of self-protective force might be excusable in some circumstances.

self-defence allows that force can be used in self-defence against a contingent threat which is itself either an attack or an act which would be an attack were it intended to harm or defeat me. The first condition – where a contingent threat is itself an attack – arises when someone deliberately exposes me to danger which will be inflicted by another agent, intending thereby that I be harmed or defeated. This person is an aggressor – he is not simply facilitating, but is assisting an attack on me. (This is so even if he is indifferent to my welfare and exposes me because he is curious about the outcome of the impending conflict.) We could take the view that even though this person is an aggressor, he is not an immediate threat. In that case, in (say) pushing the doorblocker out of my way, I am using force against this person in the course of self-defence against the immediate threat, the assailant. (On this view, the fact that this contingent threat is assisting the unjust attack would be relevant to the justification of using force against this person in the course of self-defence.)[14] But there are also grounds for taking a stronger view of the status of someone who is presently assisting an immediate threat, that is, for including his actions as a part of the immediate threat against which I can use force in self-defence. If, intending to harm or defeat me, someone deliberately blocks my escape, or coughs in order to reveal my hideout, or ducks in order to expose me, then he becomes both an aggressor and a party to an assault or attack on me. Someone can be an aggressor and a party to an attack or assault (as is the instigator of a contract killing), yet not be an immediate threat. But the present acts of the doorblocker, the cougher, and the missile ducker, endanger me; and if they are intended to harm or defeat me by assisting an assault or attack, these acts are themselves attacks against which I can act in self-defence. (Someone whose acts endanger me by exposing me to an attack by another agent is part of the immediate threat *only*

14 This is Pufendorf's view. He maintains that I may regard some of those killed out of necessity in the same way as I would an aggressor who threatens my life; for instance, I may regard in this way someone who 'insolently and inhumanly' blocks my flight.

169

because he is an attacker – an aggressor who is presently assisting an attack; whereas someone who strikes me down, pushes me in front of a train, or transmits a fatal disease by coughing in my face, is an immediate threat *whether or not* he intends to harm or defeat me.)

The distinction between someone who is himself an immediate threat and someone who merely exposes me to an immediate threat, is the difference between, on the one hand, someone who initiates danger or harm by, e.g. launching a missile at me or locking me in a room full of poison gas, or exacerbates it by making a missile speed faster towards me or turning up the gas, and on the other, someone who exposes me to someone else's missile by ducking it. However, the second condition under which force is (at least arguably) used in self-defence against a contingent threat arises because sometimes another person's acts can *create* a threat simply by exposing me to danger. And where this is so, we might sometimes be inclined to identify this person's acts, rather than the danger to which these acts expose me, as the immediate threat. Say I am working in a railway tunnel. Approaching trains blow a whistle before entering the tunnel in sufficient time for me to stand in a small alcove (there for this purpose) until they pass. Someone else enters the tunnel and stands in the alcove; a train approaches and I cannot get out of its way. One way of responding to this example is to say that in my job I am frequently exposed to serious threat from approaching trains, which an established procedure allows me to avoid. When the intruder stands in the alcove, he endangers me by exposing me to an immediate threat, the approaching train. In pushing the intruder out of the alcove I am not defending myself against him; rather, I am attacking him in protecting myself from the train. An alternative response to this example is to say that approaching trains are a danger, but normally not a threat. The approaching train is a threat in the particular circumstances due to an anomalous factor, namely, someone else standing in the alcove. This person's standing in the alcove causes me to be threatened by the train. Certainly, the case for identifying the person's standing in the alcove as an immediate threat, against which I can use force in self-defence, is strengthened if his standing there is an attack on me. (He wants me dead and deliberately exposes me to the train.) But even if his acts are not an attack (he just wanders into the tunnel, hears the whistle, and takes refuge in the alcove), there are grounds for identifying his acts as a threat: they create the threatening circumstances, and would be an attack on me were they intended to harm or defeat me. Even though the harm will be inflicted by the train, the person who stands in the alcove is arguably on a par with someone who swerves a missile in my direction.

Undoubtedly the grounds on which we identify someone's conduct as a threat are normative. (Colin would be a threat to me were he to deflect Adam's missile to me, whereas he is not the threat in ducking it. Someone who has no right to be in the tunnel alcove arguably creates the threat given the train, whereas someone who is entitled to stand in a doorway does not create the threat given the assailant hot on my heels.) But the considerations to which I have appealed in identifying the conditions of immediate threat relevant to the use of force in self-defence are not strongly normative. In an important, detailed discussion of coercion, Nozick argues that in classifying what someone *says* to another person as a threat rather than an offer, we sometimes take as the *status quo* the morally expected course of events.[15] However, in describing A as acting in self-defence against B, we do not judge that B poses a threat to A against a background of the morally expected course of events. As I noted in chapter 3, the police sharp-shooter about to pick off the hijacker holding hostages is an immediate threat to the hijacker, even though the police sharp-shooter has a right to act as he does and the hijacker is entirely in the wrong. In shooting the police sharp-shooter, the hijacker is acting in self-defence.

Hence, the conceptual points I have made above about the conditions of immediate threat relevant to the use of force in

15 Robert Nozick, 'Coercion', reprinted in *Philosophy, Science and Method: Essays in Honor of Ernest Nagel*, edited by S. Morgenbesser, P. Suppes and M. White (New York: St Martin's Press, 1969), pp. 440–72.

self-defence do not settle the moral issue of the conditions under which the use of force in self-defence is *justified*. 'It was self-defence' is often cited as a justification, of course; and those who characterize acts of self-defence in a strongly normative way – as the legitimate repulsion of unjust aggression – are citing a permission. Natural law accounts often suggest that unjust aggression is both conceptually and morally crucial to acting in self-defence: that force is used in self-defence if it resists, repels, or wards off an unjust threat, and that this distinguishing feature of self-defence grounds its permissibility. However, in my view it is important to identify the conditions under which force is used in self-defence, and to recognize that it is possible to act in self-defence against a just or rightful threat. It is then a further, morally evaluative task to determine the conditions under which the use of force in self-defence is justified.[16] In drawing this distinction between important conceptual and justificatory issues, I am saying that the fact that force is used in self-defence does not by itself warrant the presumption that it is justified. This does not mean that the fact that force is used in self-defence is irrelevant to its moral appraisal.

Unjust immediate threats

The central concern of this present chapter is to ground a unitary right *of self-defence*, one which encompasses the kinds of genuinely self-defensive acts that most of us think are obviously justified. It is important that I draw attention to the fact that the conditions of immediate threat relevant to the use of force in self-defence clearly include some involuntary and passive threats, because a unitary right of self-defence needs to take into account self-defence against persons such as the attacking sleepwalker and the man thrown down the well. Thus, in explaining a unitary right of self-defence as a right to resist, repel, or ward off someone whose conduct poses an unjust immediate threat, 'conduct' needs to be used

[16] See also David G. Ritchie, *Natural Rights*, 4th edition (London: George Allen & Unwin Ltd, 1924), p. 120.

sufficiently loosely to include a person's voluntary and involuntary acts, as well as those things that happen to him in virtue of which he would be an assailant were the threat he poses to be an act on his part.

Some writers deny that self-defence against a passive threat is part of the right of self-defence. They take the *right* of self-defence to imply the right of a third party to act in my defence, and hold that although I have a right of self-defence against a non-culpable, active unjust threat (e.g. a deranged attacker), the permissibility of self-defence against a passive threat is agent-relative. Nancy Davis, for instance, maintains that the fact that one party is an *active* unjust threat to another provides an agent-neutral reason for defence of the victim by a third party.[17] Davis' explanation of why (even involuntary) agency makes the difference between agent-neutral and agent-relative permissibility is that an active threat is 'hostile, dangerous'. But in the absence of any *wider* hostility or danger, it is appropriate to ask whether the fact that a non-culpable threat is hostile or dangerous to *this* victim can provide an agent-neutral reason for a third person's defence of the victim. My answer to this question is yes. Davis may well agree, but her examples suggest wider danger: a baby with a handgrenade, a psychotic out of control.

Passive threats can, of course, pose wider danger – there might be another person with me at the bottom of Nozick's well who will also be crushed by the one who has been thrown. However, I take the claim that the permissibility of self-defence against a passive threat is agent-relative to imply that in the absence of wider danger, a third party has no moral reason for defending the victim at the expense of the threat.[18] But surely a third party has a moral reason for defending the victim of a passive *unjust* threat. Further, a third party has exactly the same reason that she has for defending the victim of an active *unjust* threat: namely, the reason of directly blocking the infliction of serious, irreparable

[17] 'Abortion and Self-Defense', p. 191.
[18] John Harris claims this, *The Value of Life: An Introduction to Medical Ethics* (London: Routledge and Kegan Paul, 1985), pp. 70–1.

unjust harm. If this reason is sufficient to ground defence of the victim of a blameless active threat, then it is also sufficient in the case of a blameless passive threat.[19]

Consider an example of a passive threat in which *assistance* by a third party is permissible. Mick involuntarily becomes a human missile and hurtles towards the immobile Nora. Nora pleads with you for help. Say you can save Nora by moving her out of Mick's trajectory. If you move Nora, Mick will hit the ground at full speed and die. If you leave Nora where she is, she will be killed but her body will cushion Mick's fall and he will survive. Surely it would be permissible for you to *assist* Nora by moving her out of danger. Now, say you can't move Nora away in time, but you can save her life by deflecting Mick so that he lands next to Nora instead of on top of her. If you deflect Mick he will hit the ground at full speed and die. Is your deflecting Mick from Nora morally distinguishable from your assisting Nora by moving her? If you assist Nora by moving her you don't kill Mick, even though he dies as a result of what you do; whereas (arguably) you do kill Mick if you defend Nora by deflecting him. However, in deciding whether *this distinction* indicates that in these circumstances it is impermissible that you *defend* Nora, the relevant question is whether you inflict unjust harm on Mick – whether you violate his right to life – by deflecting him. According to the specification of the right to life that I give in chapter 6, you do not do so.[20] You violate Nora's right to life, however, if in

[19] See also Thomson, 'Self-Defense', pp. 306–7.
[20] The permissibility of one's deflecting a number of blameless threats, *whether active or passive*, arguably depends on these threats being sequential. If it is permissible that I deflect a number of blameless threats sequentially, it does not follow that I can permissibly deflect a threat that itself incorporates several blameless people. In the sequential case, no one act of self-defence inflicts disproportionate harm, whereas in the non-sequential case one act of self-defence might do so. It would take me too far afield to explore possible puzzles generated by this distinction, but this is not to deny their importance. Nora's self-defence would probably be excusable in the non-sequential case even if we do not regard it as justified: self-defence can require a snap decision, and someone faced with a threat to her life will often be very affected by panic or fear. However, this excusability may not extend to defence of Nora by a third party in the non-sequential case.

different circumstances in which Mick's trajectory will land him next to Nora, you *deflect* Mick *to* Nora, killing her, in order to save Mick's life.

Mick is certainly a non-just immediate threat to Nora. Is he an *unjust* threat to her? Mick's threat to Nora is involuntary and inactive, and some may well think that in this case he more clearly constitutes an unjust threat to Nora if (say) he has been fired at Nora by someone acting maliciously than if he has (say) fallen off a cliff. However, in using 'unjust threat' in the sense identified in chapter 3, I am agreeing with Thomson that in order to threaten or violate someone else's right not to be killed one need not be acting; further, one might simply be the victim of bad luck.[21] This does not, of course, identify the conditions under which someone is an unjust threat to another person. Mick is an unjust threat to Nora because his landing on her would be an assault on an unoffending person were it to be an act on his part. However, legitimate doubt can arise as to the permissibility of third-party intervention on behalf of the unoffending victim of a passive threat, especially in cases where the victim would not be acting in self-defence (e.g. where one pot-holer is trapped by the fat man). Many passive threats are not clearly unjust, they do not closely resemble assaults on unoffending persons. The important point here is that, provided a passive threat would be an assault were it to be an act on the part of the person posing the immediate threat, the *mere* fact that the threat is passive does not make the permissibility of self-defence agent-relative.

Just as there are clear and unclear cases of acting *in self-defence*, so there are clear and unclear cases of *unjust* immediate threat. Across many cases we can distinguish an unjust immediate threat (e.g. the hijacker holding hostages), from both a just immediate threat (e.g. the police sharp-shooter) and an immediate threat which is not unjust (e.g. another person struggling to grasp the lifebuoy at the same time as oneself). Clear cases of unjust immediate threat to life are not

21 Thomson takes this view in 'Self-Defense'.

restricted to cases of culpable threat. Blameless putative self-defenders, for example, unjustly threaten the lives of their victims, and the attacking sleepwalker, and the madman with the gun, involuntarily do so. Non-problematic cases of unjust immediate threat include voluntary or involuntary attacks or assaults on unoffending persons. However, as I have said, the conditions under which someone can be said to pose an unjust immediate threat to another person can be difficult, sometimes very difficult. Some of these difficulties have been identified in previous chapters. They include conflicts which arise from mistake of fact, from the victim's conduct having occasioned the threat, and from disagreements about proportionate harm. Further, people will disagree about whether some *passive* immediate threats are unjust threats. Some philosophical disputes about abortion illustrate this last point. Is a foetus which threatens a woman's life by growing, or in the process of being born, an unjust immediate threat to the woman? Are the circumstances of the foetus' conception relevant to answering this question?[22] Disagreement can also arise as to whether some *active* threats are unjust. Say I am a carrier of a highly contagious, very serious disease, and I need to cough this very instant to avoid swallowing a live wasp or a substance that will make me extremely ill. Unfortunately we are so positioned that I cough directly into your face, jeopardizing your health and perhaps your life. Does my coughing in these circumstances infringe any right you have against me?

If it is possible to develop a definitive account of the boundaries of the right to life, and other important rights, which would allow us neatly to classify contentious cases of unjust threat, I cannot provide such an account in this book.

[22] See Thomson, 'A Defense of Abortion', pp. 117–18; Finnis, 'The Rights and Wrongs of Abortion', pp. 145–50. Moreover, although abortion to save the woman's life has been discussed in terms of the right of self-defence and defence of another, we can also question whether a foetus is an immediate threat of a type that is being resisted, repelled, or warded off. (See also Davis, 'Abortion and Self-Defense', pp. 185–90.) Abortion in these circumstances seems arguably on a borderline of self-defence and necessity, rather than a clear case of the use of *defensive* force.

However, I am strongly inclined to think that, just as some immediate threats lie on a borderline of self-defence and necessity, so the distinction between an unjust immediate threat and one that is not unjust is not always clear-cut. Inevitably there will be arguable borderline cases, cases in which not all the relevant facts are known, and cases about which reasonable people can disagree. In this chapter, I set out the principle which grounds a unitary right of self-defence, and I describe the specification of the right to life necessary to permissible self-preference in the case of justified homicide in self-defence. In so doing, I appeal where necessary to what I take to be reasonably clear examples of unjust threat, and also sometimes to test cases.[23]

5.2 A POSITIVE RIGHT OF DEFENCE

In this section I explain the right of self-defence as part of a more general positive right to use necessary and proportionate defensive force against an unjust threat. The permissibility of homicide in self-defence is *grounded* in the fact that the act is one of resisting, repelling, or warding off an unjust immediate threat. The positive right to use lethal force in self-defence, and in defence of others, does not derive from culpability on the part of the aggressor, nor from the fact that an unjust aggressor can be said to have forfeited the right to life.

A right of defence

Self-defence has such prominence as a moral and legal justification of homicide that some writers understandably take the right of self-defence to be the more basic moral permission, the right to intervene in defence of another person being seen as a (more limited) corollary of the victim's right of self-defence. Judith Jarvis Thomson, for instance, once

---

[23] So perhaps I should note here that acts of self-defence and self-preservation can be excusable conduct in circumstances in which we might disagree about justification.

177

remarked that where an unjust threat is innocent (blameless), bystanders may feel that they cannot intervene but the threatened person can defend herself.[24] However, as I have maintained above, in the absence of wider danger, the fact that one party poses an unjust immediate threat to another's life can be sufficient to ground the permissibility of third-party intervention on behalf of the victim.[25] (The right of any private defence is dubious to the extent to which the immediate threat is not clearly unjust.)

The view that the right of self-defence is the more basic permission can be an easy, mistaken inference from the fact that the right to defend another person derives from the victim's right not to be killed. My right of self-defence against an unjust immediate threat derives directly from my right not to be killed. The right of a third party to defend me also derives directly from my right not to be killed; it is not merely an implication of my right of self-defence. A right of *defence* – of oneself or another – against an unjust immediate threat to life is a corollary of the victim's right not to be killed.[26] The fact that the right of self-defence and the right to defend another person are both derived from the threatened person's right not to be killed partly accounts for the assumption that the right of self-defence is the more basic right.

The assumption that the right to intervene in defence of the victim of an immediate threat is a more limited corollary of the victim's right of self-defence is also sometimes a mistaken inference from the fact that self-defence can be permissible in circumstances in which third-party intervention is impermissible. However, neither of these rights – the right of self-

[24] 'A Defense of Abortion', p. 117. Unfortunately, in Thomson's illustrative example the blameless threat is not clearly unjust: someone is trapped in a room in which she will be crushed to death by another, rapidly growing person. Is the growing person an intruder? Does she have a right to grow in the room as she does? Is the threatened person an intruder? etc.

[25] In 'A Defense of Abortion', p. 126, Thomson took this view of some interventions, viz. abortions to save the woman's life.

[26] Onora Nell (O'Neill) makes essentially this point, 'Lifeboat Earth', *Philosophy and Public Affairs*, vol. 4, no. 3, 1975, p. 274.

defence and the right to defend another person – is a corollary of the other. Rather, these two rights derive from the same source,[27] and the permissibility of self-defence and defence by a third party need not always coincide. That the circumstances of permissible self-defence do not always warrant third-party intervention is explained by the fact that my right of self-defence is not derived from another person's right to defend me.[28]

My account of the relationship between these two rights is consistent with the sorts of considerations which can make third-party intervention impermissible when self-defence is permissible. Further, my account is supported by the fact that defence of another person's life can sometimes be morally permissible, and even required, when self-defence by the victim is impermissible; whereas this fact seems inconsistent with the view that the right to defend another person is merely a more limited corollary of the right of self-defence. In chapter 2, I noted two circumstances in which third-party intervention could be impermissible when self-defence is permissible. First, should I decide against exercising my right of self-defence, someone's intervention on my behalf may well be improper. The impropriety of third-party intervention here depends on my inaction being voluntary, rather than (say) the result of my being paralysed or badly confused by panic or fear. (Someone intervening in my defence could be mistaken about my state of mind, of course. Here intervention in my defence could be justified[ii].) The permissibility of third-party intervention can also depend on what a third party would need to do to defend me. For example, I might not want to defend myself simply because my only available weapon would kill the aggressor or a bystander. In this case my decision not to defend myself allows intervention by a third party who can stop the aggressor by (say) stunning him,

---

[27] Thomson, 'Self-Defense', p. 306, now maintains that self-defence and third-party defence (even by strangers) go hand in hand and have a common source.

[28] Montague argues that the positive right of self-defence *is* so derived, 'Self-Defense and Choosing Between Lives', p. 216.

without killing the bystander.[29] There might also be cases in which my decision not to use necessary force in self-defence does not morally preclude a third party's using an equivalent degree of force in my defence. Say, again, I don't defend myself because I don't want to kill the aggressor. Here I do not exercise my right of self-defence; but in so doing I do not, with respect to the aggressor, waive my right not to be killed. (The aggressor is not about to kill me with my permission.) In this case, whether it would be permissible for another person to use lethal force in my defence can depend on the reason why I don't defend myself. Maybe I want to be defended but just can't bring myself to shoot someone. In that case third-party intervention could be permissible. Where I don't want to be defended, although my wishes in the matter are obviously highly relevant to the permissibility of third-party intervention, and may be decisive, they are not necessarily overriding. Where (say) my life is very important to many people, third-party intervention in my defence could be permissible.[30]

A third party might not be as well placed as the victim to know that there is an unjust threat and how serious it is. This was the second reason for claiming that self-defence can be

29 Where it is clear to me that a third party *can and will* defend me by using much less force than would be necessary for my self-defence, it can be improper that I defend myself. Further, third-party intervention in my defence can be morally required in the above case. However, people disagree about the extent to which my right to life itself entails obligations of assistance on the part of others, and this extends to cases in which defending me would require a third party to harm someone else. In 'A Defense of Abortion', p. 117, Thomson maintains that one has a *right* to refuse to lay hands on another person, even where it is just and fair to do so. In my view, if we have such a right, it is wrong all things considered that we exercise it in some circumstances, e.g. where I could save a helpless person's life by stunning an aggressor.

30 The fact that my wishes in the matter are relevant to the permissibility of intervention in my defence does not mean that another person's right to defend me is simply an extension of my right of self-defence. However, there are cases in which a person who defends another can be seen as exercising the victim's right of self-defence on his or her behalf. One such case is when one person defends someone in his or her care, on behalf of whom he or she has an obligation to act as moral agent, e.g. a parent defends his or her own baby.

permissible where defence by a third party is not. (However, third parties might sometimes be in a much better position than is the victim to judge the facts, including the degree of force necessary for the victim's self-defence in the circumstances.) Other considerations can also make defence of another person impermissible in circumstances where the person threatened may defend him- or herself. In 5.1, I rejected the claim that third-party defence is permissible only against an active threat, together with the classification of homicide in self-defence against a passive threat as always an agent-relative permission. However, it may be that the permissibility of homicide in self-defence against *some* threats is, of itself, agent-relative. Some writers take the view that it is permissible that I kill a blameless attacker in order to save one of my limbs (presumably where my life is not in danger), but impermissible that a third party defend one of my limbs at the expense of a blameless person's life. Again, this view does not entail that the right to defend another person's life is merely a (more limited) corollary of the victim's right of self-defence. Rather, it assumes that agent-relative values can have a bearing on proportionality.[31]

Moral limitations of the exercise of the positive right

The view of self-defence that I have outlined agrees with those natural law accounts which regard the *right* of self-defence as (what I call) a particular permission, that is, a positive right (a right to do or to refrain) the exercise of which can be wrong in some circumstances all things considered. My having a positive right (e.g. to speak my mind, to withdraw a gratuitous service, to recoup my debts) means that I am wronged (treated or interfered with unjustly) by being deprived of the relevant interest without my consent. But my

---

[31] To allow that proportionality can include agent-relative values is not to construe proportionality purely subjectively. For self-defence to be morally permissible, my judgment that it is proportionate that I kill an unjust aggressor in order to avoid *my* suffering a particular harm, e.g. loss of a limb, must be an evaluation which can be endorsed as reasonable on my part in the circumstances.

having a positive right is consistent with my acting wrongly, all things considered, in exercising or insisting on this right in some circumstances. And this can be so with the right of self-defence. The use of force in self-defence might inflict harm on the aggressor which, although proportionate to the threat, is wrongly inflicted given the very limited benefit to me (e.g. where a young child threatens my life and I am about to die from some other cause anyway). In some circumstances self-defence against an unjust threat will also directly harm unoffending persons (e.g. innocent bystanders). Contrary to what some natural law accounts appear to maintain, in some circumstances morality can require that I not defend myself.[32] The positive right of self-defence against an unjust immediate threat can also be consistent with the permissibility of another person's preventing my act of self-defence. Say I am about to defend myself by deflecting a missile aimed at me; the deflected missile will hit a bystander who will certainly then be killed. If in these circumstances I am an unjust immediate threat to this bystander, she has a right to use necessary and proportionate force in self-defence against me, and she can be justified in preventing my deflecting the missile to her if she is able to do so.

In my view, a unitary right of self-defence, one which distinguishes self-defence as an exception to the general prohibition of homicide, depends on the particular specification

---

[32] I think foreseeable harm *directly* inflicted in the course of self-defence must always be considered. But I am unsure about foreseeable harm *indirectly* inflicted. For instance, is self-defence impermissible all things considered if I am quite elderly and alone and my life is threatened by someone who has dependants (young children), or who is a highly skilled brain surgeon? Sometimes the aggressor's non-culpability seems to have a bearing on whether *indirect* harm to unoffending persons is relevant to the permissibility of acting in self-defence. For instance, in the example just given the aggressor's non-culpability might make it more appropriate that I take into account indirect harm to her dependants, or serious loss to the community. The probability, the extent, and the seriousness of the indirect harm to others, and the possibility of its being mitigated in time (whereas loss of my life is irretrievable), are highly relevant of course.

of the right to life that I give in chapter 6. It follows from this specification of the right to life that I have no positive right to use lethal force on an unoffending person (e.g. an innocent bystander) in the course of self-defence or defence of another, nor in other circumstances of self-preservation or preservation of another.[33] The foreseen killing of an unoffending person in saving oneself or another person must be justified as the lesser evil. (In the event that I will kill an unoffending person whatever I do, all morally relevant factors being equal, a random selection procedure is appropriate.)

The significance of the positive right

What is the moral significance of our having a positive *right* to use force in self-defence against an unjust immediate threat if it can be wrong in some circumstances that we defend ourselves, and if in some circumstances other people can have a right to prevent our self-defence? I should hope that the discussion of 4.3, and what I have already said in this present chapter, have indicated a reasonably clear answer to this question. In order that the use of necessary and proportionate force in self-defence be distinguished as permissible self-preferential killing and, moreover, as an exception to the prohibition of homicide, we need to invoke the moral significance of the fact that the person killed in self-defence is an unjust immediate threat. Homicide in self-defence involves an assault on the body of the aggressor; but the use of force in self-defence against someone who is an unjust immediate threat to my life is morally distinguishable from my killing an unoffending person in the course of self-defence or in other circumstances of self-preservation.

[33] Onora Nell (O'Neill) is also right about this, 'Lifeboat Earth', p. 275. Thomson holds that 'there are drastic limits to the right of self-defence', 'A Defense of Abortion', pp. 116–17. But the example Thomson gives in support of this claim – that of one's torturing an *unoffending* person to death under duress from a third party – is not homicide *in self-defence*. In 'Self-Defense', pp. 289–98, Thomson maintains that, over a range of cases, bystanders are not permissibly killed.

The significance of defensive force

The view of self-defence that I have outlined is also sympathetic to those natural law accounts which hold that the positive right of self-defence *derives from* my danger, more specifically, from the fact that my life is unjustly threatened, and not from considerations such as the aggressor's culpability or the (claimed) greater general good of my surviving rather than the aggressor. *Pace* Hobbes, self-defence against a just threat is not an abiding agent-relative permission arising from each individual's absolute right to preserve him- or herself. The use of necessary and proportionate lethal force in self-defence against a just threat is a violation of the right to life of its victim. Homicide in self-defence against a just threat would need to be justified on agent-neutral grounds as the lesser evil. Rarely would such grounds be strongly arguable.

Philosophical discussions of self-defence mostly seek to establish the permissibility of homicide in self-defence along one of two lines. As illustrated in chapter 3, both of these general lines of argument can be found in natural law. The first characterizes homicide in self-defence as unintended killing and follows the reasoning of the Principle of Double Effect; the second explicitly focuses on the moral asymmetry between the conflicting parties in a case of self-defence. In response to the first line of argument, I argued in chapter 4 that homicide in self-defence is not always unintended killing. Lack of intention to kill can plausibly be invoked in some cases of homicide in self-defence; but in some other, very straightforward cases of self-defence, killing the aggressor is not incidental to the degree of force intended by the agent as necessary for self-defence in the circumstances. My discussion of the proportionality condition of Double Effect revealed that this justification of homicide in self-defence, like any other proposed justification, must justify self-preferential killing. Given proportionate good and bad effects, the (often implicit) morally crucial assumption behind the claim that homicide in self-defence is clearly permissible as a case of double effect is that the use of force is defensive: it is an act of resisting, repelling, or warding off an unjust immediate threat. Although intentional homicide in self-defence can be permissible in my view, the Principle's emphasis on the agent's intention in all cases of self-defence represents the important insight that the moral permissibility of the use of force in self-defence is *grounded* in the fact that the act is essentially defensive.

Some recent writers recognize the significance of defensiveness. Charles Fried, for instance, argues that homicide in self-defence is distinguishable from impermissible self-preferential killing in virtue of the special relationship which exists between the victim and the person who is the immediate and sufficient source of danger, the concept of defence being the morally relevant feature.[34] Provided defence is not against a just threat, this reasoning goes in the right direction in grounding both the positive right of self-defence and the right to defend others. Loosely interpreted, however, this claimed special relationship between the victim and the person who is the immediate and sufficient source of danger might exist between me and another trapped person using up a limited air supply, or between me and someone with a highly contagious disease. But for the reasons I have already given, in the particular circumstances these persons might not be unjust immediate threats to me such that my killing them, if necessary to save myself, would be permissible self-defence.[35] The relationship that grounds the positive right of self-defence against a particular person is the fact that this person is him- or herself an unjust immediate threat of a type that can be resisted, repelled, or warded off.

David Wasserman also emphasizes the moral importance of defensiveness to the permissibility of homicide in self-defence.[36] He says that the person justifiably killed in self-defence must be *presently* the threat. I accept this requirement,

---

[34] *Right and Wrong*, p. 50.
[35] *Castell v Bambridge* (1729) 2 Strange 854, involved an alleged attempt to kill someone by means of *deliberate* exposure to disease.
[36] David Wasserman, 'Justifying Self-Defense', *Philosophy and Public Affairs*, vol. 16, no. 4, 1987, pp. 356–78.

because in my view the positive right of self-defence is grounded in the fact that force directly blocks the infliction of unjust harm. But Wasserman's own speculative reasoning (in terms of agent-responsibility and our past and present selves) as to why it is permissible to use force against a present threat, is both unsatisfactory within its own terms and on the wrong track as an account of why it is impermissible that I kill someone who has culpably already inflicted unjust harm, as a means of remedying that harm.

Wasserman maintains that as the person I presently am, I am more closely identified with my present than with my past acts. This claim is not always true. And where true, it does not explain why it is permissible that you kill me, a present threat, in self-defence, whereas it is impermissible that you rectify an injury I have already inflicted by killing me and using my organs to patch yourself up. First, our responsibility as agents for our past conduct and its effects can increase with time. Consider acts done accidentally, impulsively, under provocation, or by reason of mistake of fact, which later on reflection we endorse or fail to rectify. For example, in a rage I might stab someone after being told that he has killed my closest friend; having regained my self-control I might decide to let him bleed to death rather than take him to a hospital. I might accidentally shoot someone, or shoot her under the mistaken belief that she is about to kill me; realizing what I have done (excusably in the circumstances), I might then leave her for dead out of sheer indifference. Secondly, we do not always identify conduct which is resisted, repelled, or warded off in self-defence with the *person* presently engaged in that conduct. The person whose conduct poses the threat might be, e.g. deluded or temporarily insane, and hence not responsible for what he or she does.

The permissibility of using force against (what Wasserman calls) a present threat is grounded in the fact that the act is one of defence. An act of defence against someone who is him- or herself an unjust immediate threat is not a punitive or a retaliatory act against the person whose conduct is offending. However, to remedy unjust harm already inflicted by means of selecting the culpable offender to be sacrificed for this end *is* punitive or retaliatory.[37]

Having endorsed the moral relevance of Wasserman's distinction between an act of self-defence against a present threat, and an act of penalizing someone in order to remedy unjust harm already inflicted, I must acknowledge the possible objection that sometimes we can permissibly use force in self-defence against a person whose *present* conduct does not constitute an unjust immediate threat. Consider a case in which I am exposed to a grenade about to go off which you have just triggered. The grenade is no longer under your control, but I push you on top of it in order to protect myself. Here I am defending myself against the grenade about to go off. But in pushing you onto the grenade in these circumstances, am I not also defending myself against you, an unjust immediate threat? It is arguable that in this case you are an unjust immediate threat. In support of this view, we can say that although the grenade is no longer under your control, the threat is a direct effect of your conduct.[38] (All the same, on this view surely my pushing you onto the grenade in order to protect myself is a deviant case of the use of force in self-defence against *you*.) But in my view, there are stronger reasons for saying that my pushing you onto the grenade is homicide in the course of self-defence. In pushing you onto the grenade I am not resisting or repelling you, an unjust immediate threat; rather, I am using your body to block the effects of the threat itself, the grenade. Further, in this and relevantly similar examples, the permissibility of my using you in this way, *as a means of* defence against the threat itself, may well depend not only on your having created the threat but also on how culpable you were in having done so. For

---

[37] I use 'punitive' where someone who is not a present threat is selected to suffer comparative disadvantage on account of prior culpable conduct. There is, of course, the stricter sense in which a *penalty* can only be inflicted by an appropriate authority.

[38] Whereas if you have (say) informed gangsters of my whereabouts and they come looking to kill me, I am clearly not acting in self-defence against you if I forcibly use you as a shield against these gangsters' bullets.

instance, it seems permissible that I push you onto the grenade if necessary to protect myself if you have deliberately triggered it in order to kill me, less so if you have triggered it through carelessness, and impermissible if, having taken due care, you have triggered it accidentally. But the permissibility of using force *in self-defence*, in resisting, repelling, or warding off someone who him- or herself clearly constitutes an unjust immediate threat, does not depend on the other's culpability. If, having taken due care, you trip and lunge towards my chest with an unsheathed knife, it is permissible that I use necessary and proportionate force to stop you.

The use of defensive force is an act of resisting, repelling, or warding off a threat. It is not essentially a punitive act; nor is it a piece of social engineering which penalizes the guilty; nor is it an attempt to achieve optimal results. When the threat to oneself is unjust, the use of force in self-defence directly blocks the infliction of unjust harm; and the permissibility of the use of force in self-defence and in defence of another person derive from this fact. Within moral limits, a private person has a positive right, and sometimes an obligation, directly to block the infliction of unjust harm to him- or herself or to another person. (An act which directly blocks unjust harm is not merely a case of preventing harm, although within moral limits it is also permissible, and can be morally required, that we prevent harm.) The positive right directly to block the infliction of unjust harm *does not depend on* the aggressor's culpability: it is a right of *defence* against an unjust immediate threat, and thus includes defence against some blameless threats. The positive right to use lethal force against a culpable threat *does not derive from* the aggressor's culpability: it derives from the fact that he or she is an unjust immediate threat. The fact that someone has culpably endangered another person's life does not give me a positive right to sacrifice the culpable party, if necessary, as a means of saving the victim.[39] For example, I have no right to remove a criminal's heart or kidneys on the grounds that I can put

---

[39] See Wasserman's discussion, 'Justifying Self-Defense'.

these organs to good use in saving someone else. This is so even if the criminal has, through a prior culpable attack, caused the intended recipient to require a transplant.[40] (I should note that in *other* circumstances, where (say) two people are endangered and both cannot be saved, the fact that one party has culpably endangered the other can be a legitimate ground on which to discriminate against the culpable party. For example, if a culpable attacker and his innocent victim are both critically injured in the ensuing conflict, and I can assist only one of them, the attacker's culpability is a legitimate ground on which to assist the victim. Further, the (very much lesser) comparative moral worth of someone who is not in any sense responsible for the present danger could in some circumstances be a legitimate ground on which to choose to injure or kill this person rather than someone else. For example, were the driver of Foot's runaway tram to be faced with steering either into a child who has wandered onto track A, or into a convicted, unrepentant serial killer working on track B, it seems permissible that he take comparative moral worth into account in choosing to steer onto track B. Under a slightly different set of conditions, this sort of consideration might also legitimize his deflecting the tram from track A onto track B in order to save the child, although deflection is morally more dubious on these grounds in my view.)[41]

In setting out the principles relevant to justified homicide in self-defence we must look to what is morally distinctive about the use of force in self-defence against an unjust immediate threat. Force used in self-defence is directed at the

40 However, in some weird examples it might be arguable that the culpable party is a *continuing* threat to the victim. For instance, prior to his accident the criminal may forcibly have taken the other person's one good kidney and had it transplanted in himself; the victim's other kidney fails totally and dialysis is unavailable; the criminal arrives in casualty, and the doctor can now save the kidney-owner's life by restoring to him his own kidney; etc.
41 These extreme, fairly simple examples are not meant to imply that a judgment about comparative moral worth is in general an acceptable ground on which to discriminate between lives, especially at the level of social policy (e.g. in the allocation of medical resources).

threat itself, and the use of lethal force in self-defence against an unjust threat to life directly blocks the infliction of very serious, otherwise irreparable unjust harm. However, because the permissibility of blocking an unjust immediate threat – either to oneself or to another person – has moral limits, something like a theory of forfeiture of the unjust aggressor's rights is necessary to the justification of homicide in self-defence.

The relevance of a theory of forfeiture

According to the second general line of justification of homicide in self-defence, the fact that lethal force is used to resist, repel, or ward off someone who is an unjust immediate threat to one's life is crucial to the justification of self-preferential homicide. Some moral absolutists who do not rely on the Double Effect justification of homicide in self-defence hold that it is permissible to defend one's life at the expense of someone who unjustly endangers it; whereas, they argue, it is morally impermissible to weigh the life of an unoffending person against one's own and then bring about death intentionally in the direction indicated by necessity and proportionality (as did Dudley and Stephens). Charles Fried argues that killing the innocent (unoffending) as a means to an end of one's own offends against the principle of equal respect for persons; self-defence against an unjust aggressor involves no unwarranted assertion of one's own moral priority.[42] This reasoning is traceable to natural law, but it is now invoked much more widely and extends well beyond moral absolutism. In another form, this general justification is very familiar, it being a common view that an unjust aggressor abrogates or forfeits his or her own right to life.

A theory of forfeiture in respect of an unjust aggressor's rights is often wrongly assumed to justify the use of force in self-defence. The role that a theory of forfeiture plays in the justification of homicide in self-defence is often misunder-

[42] *Right and Wrong*, p. 44.

stood. Sanford Kadish almost makes this point when he remarks that even if we can provide an account of how an unjust aggressor forfeits the right to life, this will not give us a theory of justified homicide in self-defence.[43] A theory which maintains that an unjust aggressor forfeits the right to life cannot *ground* the justification of homicide in self-defence: the fact that someone does not have a right to life does not itself give me a positive right to inflict lethal force on him or her. What is morally distinctive about homicide in self-defence is that my act of killing the aggressor is itself the use of necessary and proportionate force in directly resisting, repelling, or warding off an unjust threat to my life.[44] The positive right of self-defence derives from the fact that self-defence against an unjust immediate threat is an instance of acting directly to resist, repel, or ward off serious, otherwise irreparable unjust harm.

A theory of forfeiture is necessary to the justification of self-defence because, as I have said, the permissibility of one's directly blocking unjust harm, even grave unjust harm such as the violation of one's right to life, has moral limits.[45] The two conditions of necessary and proportionate force do not exhaust these limits. The rights, and especially the equal rights, of other people limit the positive right to act directly to resist, repel, or ward off the infliction of unjust harm. For instance, I have no positive right to defend myself by forcibly using an unoffending person as a shield against attack, or by deflecting an unjust threat aimed at me to an innocent bystander who will then be killed.[46] The relevance of a theory

---

43 Sanford Kadish, 'Respect for Life and Regard for Rights in the Criminal Law', *California Law Review*, vol. 64, no. 4, 1976, p. 884.
44 Grisez, 'Toward a Consistent Natural Law Ethics of Killing', rightly emphasizes this, even though (as I argued in 4.2) his argument about the divisibility of intention fails.
45 In civil society there are good reasons for *legally* restricting the extent to which private persons are permitted directly to block the infliction of unjust harm. Nevertheless, sometimes a private person is legally permitted so to act where the unjust harm is imminent, very serious, and irretrievable – self-defence being a paradigm case.
46 It can, of course, be permissible in some circumstances that I prevent a greater unjust harm to one person by means of inflicting a lesser unjust

of forfeiture to the permissibility of using force in self-defence is in addressing and removing this third type of moral constraint in respect of someone who is him- or herself an unjust immediate threat. And by underpinning the common assumption that the use of necessary and proportionate force in self-defence does not wrong the unjust immediate threat, a theory of forfeiture characterizes self-defence as an exception to, rather than a justified infringement of, the general prohibition of homicide.

In explaining the relevance of a theory of forfeiture to the justification of self-defence, we should also note that even if a successful theory of forfeiture is possible, it will not show that homicide in self-defence against an unjust immediate threat is always right all things considered. Kadish comments that we do not have a theory which successfully establishes that self-defence is always justified (positively right). In my view we do not have such a theory because self-defence against an unjust immediate threat is not always justified in this sense. General justifications of homicide in self-defence are overstated if they purport to establish otherwise. This is so even if we confine ourselves to agent-perspectival justification.

My account of the positive right of self-defence has two essential elements. The first is the claim that the positive right of self-defence is grounded in what is morally distinctive about justified self-defence: force used in self-defence against an unjust immediate threat resists, repels, or wards off the infliction of unjust harm. This grounds a unitary right of self-defence against culpable and non-culpable, active and passive unjust immediate threats. It also grounds a right to defend others. A unitary right of defence is not merely possible: it is implied by what is morally distinctive about the use of force in self-defence against an unjust threat.

The second element concerns the moral limits of the posi-

harm on someone else (e.g. by using your antique vase as a weapon against an aggressor), or even that I prevent unjust harm to one person by risking equal unjust harm to another (e.g. by deflecting a missile which will certainly kill you in a direction in which it is very much less likely to kill someone else).

192

tive right of self-defence. The right of self-defence is part of a wider permission to use necessary and proportionate defensive force against an unjust threat itself. The positive right of defence of oneself or another person requires something akin to a theory of forfeiture. In the case of homicide in self-defence, the justification of self-preference requires the abrogation or forfeiture of the right to life of someone who is him- or herself an unjust immediate threat to an another person's life. I take up this element of my account in the next chapter, by means of a critique of the commonly under-argued theory of forfeiture.

Chapter 6

Self-defence and the right to life

Something akin to a theory of forfeiture of rights is necessary to the justification of homicide in self-defence: it is necessary to the justification of self-preferential killing. Most philosophical discussions of justified homicide in self-defence maintain some variation of the claim that an unjust aggressor forfeits the right to life, but provide no more than a rudimentary theory of forfeiture. Nancy Davis, for instance, says that aggressors and assailants 'have in some sense done something that has weakened, forfeited or undermined their prior claims to full moral parity with the persons who are now their victims'.[1] Susan Levine assumes that an unjust aggressor's culpability would abrogate his or her moral standing compared with that of the victim.[2]

The idea that human rights, such as the right to life and the right to liberty, can be forfeited is also frequently invoked in other contexts, most notably in justifications of punishment. The strong association of forfeiture of rights with punishment can wrongly suggest that, since an unjust aggressor forfeits the right to life, homicide in self-defence is justified as a punitive act. Certainly, some writers have taken the association of forfeiture of rights with culpability to mean that a unitary account of justified self-defence cannot invoke the idea of forfeiture: they assume that since only culpable aggressors can forfeit the right to life, self-defence against a

---

[1] 'Abortion and Self-Defense', p. 202.
[2] 'The Moral Permissibility of Killing a "Material Aggressor" in Self-Defense', p. 69.

morally innocent unjust aggressor either has a separate justification or is excusable homicide. Because forfeiture of rights
is associated with both culpability and punishment, in setting
out the theory of forfeiture necessary to a unitary account of
justified homicide in self-defence I shall prefer to specify the
scope of the right to life appropriately, rather than say that an
unjust aggressor forfeits the right to life. However, I regard an
appropriate specification and theory of forfeiture of the right
to life as theoretically on a par. A forfeit is a penalty; and as I
argue below, the imposition of a penalty by way of a forfeited
right constitutes a disadvantage which need not imply the
culpability or punishment of the one who forfeits.

An account of justified homicide in self-defence must elab-
orate, rather than simply assume, a theory of forfeiture,
because important human rights such as the right to life are
typically said to be unconditional. The claimed unconditiona-
lity of human rights creates an immediate, insurmountable
difficulty for a theory of forfeiture in respect of the right to
life: an unconditional right cannot, by definition, be forfeited.
(An unconditional right can be lost, however, if the right
holder ceases to have the status in virtue of which the unconditional right is possessed.) If I forfeit my right to life when I
unjustly threaten someone else's life, then the right to life is
not an unconditional human right. Further, outside the
natural law tradition, persons are now most commonly said to
possess human rights simply *qua* humans or persons.[3] But if I

3 See, e.g. Alan Gewirth, 'The Epistemology of Human Rights', *Social
Philosophy and Policy*, vol. 1, no, 2, 1984, p. 1: 'Human rights are rights
which all persons equally have simply in so far as they are human.' Joel
Feinberg, 'Voluntary Euthanasia and the Inalienable Right to Life', *Philosophy and Public Affairs*, vol. 7, 1978, p. 97, remarks that human rights are a
class of moral rights that belong *equally and unconditionally* to all human
beings, *simply in virtue of being human* (my emphases). Davis, 'Abortion
and Self-Defense', p. 183, n18, also represents a very strong recent trend
in describing as 'attractive and natural' the 'view that we can explain a
being's possession of rights by appealing to the sort of being it is (the
individual's properties, or the essential properties of the class to which it
is a member)'. Davis does remark that this view is problematic in a
number of ways, but nevertheless she later claims, p. 183: 'if a fetus has a
right to life, then it has it in virtue of being the sort of entity that it is'. For
convenience, and following accepted convention, I use 'human rights' to

possess the right to life simply *qua* human or person, then I cannot forfeit this right on becoming an unjust aggressor. A similar problem arises with an appropriate specification of the scope of the right to life, as ceasing at the point at which one unjustly threatens someone else's life. This specification limits the scope of the right to life by reference to our conduct. And if the right to life is limited in this way, then it is not possessed equally by each person simply *qua* human or person. (It is instructive to note that the scope of other human rights is limited, and this includes rights which we are *also* said to forfeit under certain conditions. For example, I can forfeit particular liberty or privacy rights by engaging in criminal conduct; but the scope of the rights to liberty and privacy, where these rights are possessed, does not include my (say) engaging in intimate contact with others while concealing the fact that I have a highly contagious fatal disease.)

This present chapter examines the theory of forfeiture necessary to a unitary right of self-defence. In 6.1, I critically discuss recent objections to the common claim that an unjust aggressor forfeits the right to life. In that section I also give reasons (along the lines indicated above) for adopting an appropriate specification of the right to life. I go on to argue that, as an exception to the general prohibition of homicide, the use of force in self-defence does not violate its victim's right to life; as individuals we possess this right only so far as we are not an unjust immediate threat to another person's life or proportionate interest.[4] I discuss the grounding of this specification of the right to life in 6.2.

6.1 FORFEITURE OF THE RIGHT TO LIFE

Can we forfeit the right to life?

Two relatively recent philosophical discussions have questioned the common appeal to forfeiture as part of the justi-

refer to those moral rights that we are said to possess by virtue of the types of beings we are.

[4] Throughout this chapter I shall assume that the victim's life or proportionate interest is at stake.

fication of homicide in self-defence. In her thought-provoking article 'Self-Defense and Rights', Thomson explored what she took to be the odd implications of the view that an unjust aggressor forfeits the right to life, her scepticism about the relevance of forfeiture stemming partly from the recognition that if one possesses the right to life simply *qua* human, one cannot forfeit this right on becoming an unjust aggressor. In 'The Right to Life', Fletcher claims that the notion of forfeiture is totally inappropriate to the justification of self-defence. As I argue below, neither of these discussions undermines the significance of a theory of forfeiture to the justification of homicide in self-defence.[5] The value of Thomson's and Fletcher's critiques of forfeiture consists in the fact that they draw attention to those features of the right to life that are crucial to a satisfactory theory of forfeiture as part of the justification of homicide in self-defence. Our possession of the right to life is conditional, the condition relevant to the justification of self-defence being that we not be an unjust immediate threat to another person.

Thomson's critique of forfeiture centres on the example of a homicidal tank driver who forfeits his right to life as he drives his tank at me, only to re-acquire this right when he stalls the tank and breaks both ankles jumping out to investigate the problem. Here Thomson highlights the seemingly fortuitous way in which the aggressor's forfeited right to life is regained. He forfeits his right to life by unjustly threatening my life; but even if his malice remains, I violate his right to life if I kill him once his broken ankles render him harmless. As Thomson argues, we can appeal to utilitarian considerations in explaining why it is wrong that I kill the disabled tank driver: killing him is now unnecessary and would mean the loss of a life, whereas not killing him would mean no loss at all. But such considerations will not invariably rule out my killing the disabled tank driver if he has really forfeited his right to life

5 Indeed, Thomson's most recent account, 'Self-Defense', seems to take the aggressor's forfeiture, or lack of, the right to life as crucial to justified homicide in self-defence. In *The Realm of Rights*, pp. 366–71, Thomson mai~ that there can be forfeiture without fault.

by attacking me. For example, it might be possible for me to save the lives of five other people by using parts of his body. However, it is impermissible that I kill him to acquire his organs for other people; significantly, my killing him for this reason seems equally a violation of his right to life as would be my killing anyone else for his or her organs. The tank driver's forfeited right to life is restored once he ceases to be an immediate threat.

Thomson discusses what she takes to be the obvious alternative to forfeiture, that is, the view that human rights are *prima facie* (capable of being overridden by more weighty moral considerations such as the more stringent rights of others) rather than absolute (either possessed and overriding or else forfeited). On this alternative view, homicide in self-defence is permissible because the aggressor's right to life conflicts with, and is overridden by, the more stringent right to life of the victim. However, as Thomson argues, a satisfactory justification along these lines needs at least to explain why the victim's right to life is the more stringent. And it seems to me that any explanation will come down to something like a theory of forfeiture. For the aggressor sacrifices something morally very weighty when he becomes an unjust immediate threat; and if he does not forfeit the right to life itself, then he forfeits moral parity in respect of that right. Also, we must address the seemingly fortuitous way in which the right to life's forfeited stringency can be re-acquired. Once the tank driver is not an immediate threat, it is just as morally offensive that I kill him to acquire his organs for others as would be my killing anyone else for this reason.

Thomson identifies two related difficulties arising from appeal to forfeited rights as part of the justification of self-defence. The first is the general problem (noted above) with the claim that we can forfeit human rights while continuing to possess those characteristics (humanness, personhood, autonomy) in virtue of which we are said to possess these rights. In familiar discussions in practical ethics about the characteristic, or set of characteristics, which gives rise to a right to life, those outside the natural law tradition typically regard their favoured criterion as a descriptive feature of the beings that possess this characteristic – a descriptive feature which has normative implications.[6] Thomson regards the lack of a two-way necessary connection between the aggressor's forfeiture of the right to life, and his or her malice, as a second difficulty for forfeiture. She assumes that (only) culpable aggressors can forfeit the right to life;[7] but then a culpable aggressor regains the right to life when, by accident, he ceases to be an immediate threat. The difficulties with forfeiture to which Thomson's discussion draws attention are overcome once we recognize that our possession of the right to life is conditional and depends partly on our conduct. Both difficulties disappear once we accept that as individuals we possess the right to life in virtue of the kinds of beings we are and only so far as we are not an unjust immediate threat to others.[8]

Fletcher attempts to provide a definitive explanation of what he takes to be the irrelevance of forfeiture to the justification of homicide in self-defence. He points out that the legal idea of forfeit relates to material possessions and also incorporeal goods of a kind that can be transferred, such as citizenship and copyright interests. Legal rights can be forfeited voluntarily or involuntarily, and are forfeited even with regard to persons unaware of the forfeiture. If your legal right to something has been forfeited, this simply means that you are no longer the owner of the particular interest; thus, the knowledge or ignorance, and the intentions of anyone depriving you of that interest are irrelevant to the legality of the deed: putative violators of your (now non-existent) right act with impunity. The original conception of the outlaw was of someone who had forfeited the right to life. Outlaw status could be conferred by the crown on someone who had done

---

6 See, e.g. Davis, 'Abortion and Self-Defense, pp. 183–4, n18.
7 Thomson revises this in 'Self-Defense'.
8 On Thomson's most recent account, 'Self-Defense', possession of the right to life is conditional on conduct (broadly construed). Thomson does not express the point in this way, nor does she draw out the implications for her earlier discussion in 'Self-Defense and Rights'. See also her lengthy discussion of forfeiture in *The Realm of Rights*, pp. 361–71.

no wrong; and as someone who lived at the mercy of others, the outlaw could not complain of being hunted down even by those unaware of his status. But there is not, Fletcher argues, a plausible analogy between aggressors and outlaws. In modern western legal systems self-defence must be justified, and this requires a proper intention, with knowledge of the circumstances which would justify the conduct. If the aggressor really has forfeited the right to life, such justification would be irrelevant.[9]

Surely it is not always true that where a person does not in fact have a legal right to a particular interest (e.g. the right to reside in a particular place), the knowledge and intentions of someone seeking to deprive him or her of that interest are irrelevant to the legality of the deed. In requiring justification before a person may legally be evicted, detained, searched, arrested, or imprisoned, the law protects a more general interest which all persons have in not being interfered with in the absence of good reason.[10] This notwithstanding, Fletcher's claim that in modern western legal systems self-defence requires both a proper intention, and knowledge of the circumstances which would justify the conduct, is probably now an overstatement in two respects. The first respect highlights a possible difference between legal and moral justification on which I remarked in chapter 2;[11] the second concerns the use of force in putative self-defence. Fletcher holds that justified acts must be objectively and positively right, and that putative self-defence is an excuse rather than a justification. In chapter 2, I rejected this view in favour of a more complex account of justification and excuse. However, if we accept Fletcher's more restrictive view – that only actual self-defence which is objectively and positively right is justified – we cannot then agree with him that all modern western legal systems require that self-defence be justified.[12]

9 I closely paraphrase Fletcher's argument in this paragraph.
10 I owe this point to Hugh LaFollette.
11 2.1, text accompanying n22 and n23.
12 Fletcher's claim that self-defence requires a subjective belief in justification for the defence to succeed might be true of most American statutes (Greenawalt, 'The Perplexing Borders', p. 1905). But Fletcher

More important here is the fact that Fletcher's reasons for saying that forfeiture is irrelevant to self-defence draw on a very wide concept of legal forfeiture that includes forfeiture by decree. But these days if, for example, a person ceases to have citizenship not through her own doing, but merely as the result of a change in the laws of the land, we would say that the relevant legal and political rights she once possessed have been abolished or that she has been deprived of them. It would be very misleading to say that she has forfeited them. 'Forfeit' usually refers to a right lost or a penalty paid due to some crime or fault, breach (which need not be voluntary) or neglect of contract or rules on the part of the person who forfeits. The claim that an unjust aggressor forfeits the right to life is obviously intended to be analogous to this narrower concept of forfeiture; and this concept of forfeiture can coherently be extended to the right to life provided this right is sufficiently similar in the relevant respect(s) to forfeitable institutional, political, and legal rights.

Provided we acknowledge that our possession of the right to life is conditional – that it depends on our conduct – there is no conceptual difficulty in claiming that an unjust aggressor forfeits the right to life. (As I pointed out earlier, we readily assume that our possession of other important human rights, e.g. liberty and privacy rights, is conditional on our conduct.) However, at the same time, we must recognize that if we forfeit the right to life on becoming an unjust immediate threat to others, then as individuals we do not possess the right to life simply in virtue of the kinds of beings we are (humans, persons, autonomous beings).

remarks elsewhere that the Model Penal Code in the United States 'assimilates putative to actual self-defense, referring [wrongly in Fletcher's view] to both as claims of justification', 'Rights and Excuses', *Criminal Justice Ethics*, vol. 3, no. 2, 1984, p. 17. In 'The Right Deed for the Wrong Reason', pp. 293–321, Fletcher critically discusses the view that justification defences should be available irrespective of the intent of the actor. See also Paul H. Robinson's reply, 'Causing the Conditions of One's Own Defense: A Study in the Limits of Theory in Criminal Law', *Virginia Law Review*, vol. 71, no. 1, 1985, pp. 1–63.

Human rights and the theory of forfeiture

Writers who discuss issues of practical ethics in terms of rights often appear oblivious to the contradiction in their acceptance of both of the following: the view that simply *qua* humans or persons we possess human rights equally and unconditionally, and the view that these rights can be forfeited or suspended when we act immorally or dangerously.[13] However, some natural law theorists have explicitly recognized the need to reconcile their own talk of forfeitable or defeasible natural rights with their claim that we possess such rights in virtue of our human nature. There are serious problems associated with the natural law derivation of rights which I do not wish to minimize.[14] Nevertheless, attempts within the natural law tradition to reconcile the possession of natural rights with forfeiture, and also with apparent clashes of these rights, bring to the surface the fact that our possession of such rights depends partly on our conduct.

Earlier this century, the natural law theorist Jacques Maritain argued that natural rights must be inalienable (meaning non-forfeitable), 'since they are grounded in the very nature of man, which of course no man can lose'.[15] Maritain held that this (descriptive) conception of the basis on which we possess natural rights could be reconciled with his appeal to forfeiture in justifying capital punishment. His attempted reconciliation distinguishes between the possession of an inalienable right and the right to exercise that right. By sinning, Maritain argues, persons can forfeit the right to exercise an inalienable right. However, these persons continue to possess the right itself by virtue of their human nature. Maritain goes on to argue that, although we possess the natural right to life

---

13 In 'Voluntary Euthanasia', p. 111, Joel Feinberg draws on Locke and Blackstone in distinguishing an inalienable right and a non-forfeitable right. But this distinction doesn't reconcile the forfeitability of human rights with the claim that we possess these rights unconditionally simply in virtue of the types of beings we are.
14 See. e.g. L. W. Sumner, *The Moral Foundation of Rights*, ch. 4.
15 Jacques Maritain, *Man and the State* (London: Hollis and Carter, 1954), p. 92.

simply in virtue of being human, our possession of a distinguishable right – viz. the right to exercise the right to life – is
conditional on our not transgressing in particular ways.[16]

The possession and the exercise of natural or human rights
are distinguishable, and for the reasons Maritain gives.
People can possess human rights which oppressive regimes
do not allow them to exercise; further, where resources are
scarce it can be wrong that a person exercise a particular
human right, e.g. the right to procreate, or some property
right. But Maritain needs to make sense of the claim that a
person can continue to possess the right to life when he or she
has forfeited the *right* to exercise that right. And this distinction is vacuous if both of these purported rights are moral
rights. The distinction between a right itself, and the right to
exercise that right, makes sense only in terms of the further
distinction that Maritain implicitly and erroneously uses in
this context, that between political or legal rights and moral
rights. For example, if I live under a political regime in which
the legal right to exercise the right to life is conditional on
(say) my buying a license (a legal entitlement to grow or
obtain food, to defend myself, etc.), then to let my license
lapse would be to forfeit the legal right to exercise the right to
life. Nevertheless, in this case I continue to possess the moral
right to life, and I continue to possess the moral right to
exercise that right. However, to forfeit the moral right to
exercise the right to life would be to forfeit the moral right
itself.

Unfortunately, Maritain does not explain how capital
punishment is supposedly justified in terms of his distinction
between the right to life itself and the right to exercise that
right. If I have no right to exercise my right to life, then I have
no right to resist the public executioner. But my forfeiting the
right to exercise my right to life does not establish a positive

16 On this view, only serious transgressions could result in forfeiture of the
right to life. Further, these transgressions would need to endanger
others in a way which makes killing the sinner morally appropriate. See
Grisez, 'Toward a Consistent Natural Law Ethics of Killing', pp. 66–72,
on these aspects of Aquinas on capital punishment.

right on the part of public authority to kill me. The mistaken assumption that a theory of forfeiture could *ground* the justification of capital punishment is analogous to the mistake of assuming that appeal to the aggressor's forfeited right to life grounds the positive right of self-defence. Maritain's argument also represents the common shift from saying that human rights are grounded in our nature, to the claim that we possess such rights *simply* in virtue of our nature.

In support of his appeal to forfeiture as part of the justification of capital punishment, Maritain needed to maintain something closer to Aquinas' position: he needed to say that possession of the right not to be killed is conditional on our conduct. In chapter 3, I noted that Aquinas invoked an extreme forfeit view (not expressed in terms of rights) as part of the justification of capital punishment by public authority.[17] Aquinas realized that his claim that capital punishment was justified *for the common good* required him to maintain that the sinner who deserves capital punishment no longer has that quality which makes it wrong to kill someone for the good of others. This quality is free-will, which Aquinas says makes a man master of himself, and hence impermissibly subordinated to another's good. Aquinas argued that by deviating from the rational order and so losing 'his human dignity in so far as man is naturally free and an end unto himself', to that extent the sinner 'lapses into the subjection of the beasts and their exploitation by others'. Nevertheless, free-will is exercised in sinning, and because Aquinas recognized that the sinner remains a man, he held that the justification of capital punishment requires public judgment.[18] The apparent tension within Aquinas' position is partly resolved by the fact that his concept of humanness – human dignity – is strongly normative. For Aquinas, our having human dignity requires that we obey the 'rational order': we do not possess human dignity simply in virtue of the fact that we are human beings

[17] See again Grisez's critical discussion of Aquinas' justification of capital punishment. Other natural law theorists, e.g. Locke, also invoke forfeiture as part of the justification of capital punishment.
[18] *Summa Theologiæ*, 2a, 2ae, 64, 2.

with free-will. Thus, a person can forfeit human dignity by morally inappropriate conduct. Nevertheless, the fact that this person remains a human being continues to have moral implications concerning the way in which he or she may be treated.

Finnis expresses a normative conception of the basis on which we possess human rights. He holds that we have rights as human beings, and that our continued possession of these rights depends on our compliance with rules governing just interaction between persons.[19] Finnis argues that capital punishment can be justified because the guilty person forfeits the right that basic goods be respected in his person. According to Finnis, the guilty person forfeits this right by violating a system of rights which ensures the order of fairness in the community. A normative conception of the possession of rights associated with a particular descriptive status is also familiar to recent thinking outside natural law. For example, biological or social parenthood is commonly viewed as necessary but insufficient to secure parental rights: a parent must also perform satisfactorily as a parent.[20]

Finnis maintains that natural or human rights *where possessed* are absolute. He tackles the problem of the apparent conflict of rights, such as the right to life and the right to liberty, by claiming that the form in which human rights are absolute is one in which they are already subject to specification, limitation, and demarcation. He comments as follows on the specification of rights as solving apparent conflicts of rights: 'There is no alternative but to hold in one's mind's eye some pattern, or range of patterns of human character, conduct, and interaction in community, and then to choose such specification of rights as tends to favour that pattern, or range of patterns'.[21] According to Finnis, we possess absolute human rights already qualified in terms of considerations such as the equivalent human rights of others; at certain points our human rights simply cease. For example, he iso-

[19] *Fundamentals of Ethics*, p. 128.
[20] I owe the useful analogy with parental rights to Francis Snare.
[21] *Natural Law and Natural Rights*, p. 219.

lates as an exceptionless or absolute human claim-right the right not to have one's life taken directly as a means to any further end. Here specification is built into the right to life by reference to intentional killing. For Finnis, homicide in self-defence does not violate the aggressor's right to life and is justified as a case of double effect.[22]

Finnis' particular specification of the right to life cannot be part of the justification of homicide in self-defence because, as I argued in chapter 4, some cases of homicide in self-defence involve intentional killing. However, Finnis is right that specification of the right to life is the necessary alternative to a theory of forfeiture as part of the justification of homicide in self-defence. He is also right that the appropriate limitation of the scope of the right to life does not depend on the aggressor's culpability.

Forfeiture or specification of the right to life?

Partly because (I assume) he believes that *forfeiture* of a human right requires culpability on the part of the one who forfeits, Finnis opts for specification of the right to life as part of his unitary justification of homicide in self-defence. However, culpability is not conceptually or morally necessary to forfeiture; blameless conduct, and even involuntary conduct, can result in the forfeiture of rights. For example, under the regulations of some theatres my entitlement as a ticket holder to attend the first part of a performance is forfeited simply by my arriving after that performance has commenced. It is irrelevant that my late arrival is entirely blameless (it might even be commendable, e.g. I stopped along the way to help out at an accident), or that it is involuntary (e.g. someone delayed me by driving into the back of my car). In the realm of moral and political rights, my right not to have my liberty curtailed in certain respects can be forfeited by my involuntarily or blamelessly becoming a danger to others; particular parental rights can be forfeited by one's becoming insane; and so on.

[22] *Fundamentals of Ethics*, p. 132.

206

The importance of the right to life seems to lead some writers to assume that culpability must be a necessary condition of its forfeiture. But then, the distinction between culpable and blameless aggressors in respect of forfeiture usually plays no substantive role in what these writers have to say about justified self-defence. Culpable aggressors are said to forfeit the right to life; the right to life of a blameless unjust aggressor is said to be justifiably infringed.[23] The distinction between the forfeiture, and the infringement, of an unjust aggressor's right to life may be intended to emphasize that the moral asymmetry between a culpable unjust aggressor and the victim is greater than that between a blameless unjust aggressor and the victim. But if it is important to register this difference, it can, and should, be acknowledged without resorting to two justifications of homicide in self-defence – one justification claiming that a culpable unjust aggressor forfeits the right to life, the other maintaining that a blameless unjust aggressor's right to life is justifiably infringed. The permissibility of homicide in self-defence against an unjust aggressor either derives from culpability on the aggressor's part or it does not. Most who distinguish between forfeiture and infringement in the case of self-defence hold that it is permissible to use necessary and proportionate force in self-defence against a blameless unjust aggressor. In that case, it is inappropriate and distracting to posit separate justifications of homicide in self-defence based on a distinction between culpable and blameless unjust aggressors.

A distinction between the forfeiture of a culpable unjust aggressor's right to life, and the justified infringement of a

---

23 Further, some writers who distinguish between forfeiture and infringement of an aggressor's right to life also uncritically assume that killing an innocent shield of a threat is clearly permissible. In 'Self-Defense', Thomson regards bystanders as impermissibly killed; but she does not explicitly revise her earlier judgment in 'Self-Defense and Rights' about innocent shields of threats. Yet there are obvious parallels between some innocent shield cases (e.g. those discussed by Kagan, *The Limits of Morality*, pp. 140–4) and Thomson's Use-of-a-Bystander cases, 'Self-Defense', p. 290.

blameless unjust aggressor's right, might also arise from the belief that, in the absence of wider danger, self-defence against a blameless unjust aggressor is an agent-relative permission. We should reject this view. In the absence of wider danger, surely it can be permissible that I defend a helpless person's life against a maniac's attack, by using lethal force if necessary. And this can be so even when the maniac will come to his or her senses if not killed. Consider the following example. You, Barney, Fred, and I are workmates. Barney arranges to kill you by slipping a drug into Fred's drink which will take effect in half an hour, making the physically very powerful Fred temporarily homicidal. During the next half-hour Barney locks you and Fred together in a room, and Barney leaves the scene. The drug takes effect, and Fred ties you up and is about to strangle you. In the meantime, I have stumbled across the details of Fred's plan, and through a skylight I see Fred attacking you. You see me and plead with me for help. I know that Fred is blameless, and that provided I do not release Fred from the locked room before the drug wears off, the danger is confined to you. I also foresee that in defending your life I would probably kill Fred. Is it permissible that I defend your life in these circumstances? Yes. Here Nozick is right: the principle that prohibits physical *aggression* does not prohibit the use of force *in defence* against another party who is a threat, even though he is innocent and deserves no retribution.[24] Provided 'threat' means 'unjust threat', this is so whether one is defending oneself or someone else.

There is no reason in principle against developing a theory of forfeiture of the right to life as a necessary part of the justification of self-defence against an unjust immediate threat. Culpability is neither conceptually nor morally necessary to the conditions of forfeiture of a right. Further, there need be no substantive difference between saying that an unjust aggressor forfeits the right to life and, alternatively,

---

[24] *Anarchy, State and Utopia*, p. 34 (my emphases).

adopting an appropriate specification of the scope of the right to life.[25] Nevertheless, as I noted above, 'forfeiture' strongly suggests penalty – indeed this seems to be its central sense – and in the context of morality and the criminal law, penalty is widely associated not simply with disadvantage, but more strongly with punishment. Since homicide in self-defence is not essentially a punitive act, the punitive connotation of 'forfeiture', together with the fact that a theory of forfeiture based on culpability is commonly invoked in justifications of punishment, are practical reasons for preferring to speak in terms of specification of the scope of the right to life as part of the justification of homicide in self-defence.

6.2 SPECIFICATION OF THE RIGHT TO LIFE

In attending to the principles relevant to justified homicide in self-defence, we have the opportunity to correct the prevalent tendency in recent practical ethics to regard a particular characteristic or capacity (e.g. humanness, personhood, autonomy) as a sufficient condition of the possession of unconditional human rights. Alongside this tendency is often the uncritical, incompatible, invocation of forfeiture of the right to life as part of the justification of homicide in self-defence.[26] In this section I examine some reasons why specification of the scope of human rights might be more generally overlooked, and why it might be rejected as part of the justification of self-defence. I go on to outline the specification of scope of the right to life necessary to a unitary right of self-defence, and to clarify some of the more important implications of this specification.

[25] James W. Nickel comments that the conditions for alienating a right can also be specified in its conditions of possession, 'Are Human Rights Utopian?', *Philosophy and Public Affairs*, vol. 11, no. 3, 1982, p. 248.
[26] Feinberg, 'Voluntary Euthanasia', p. 112, notes that one must qualify for a forfeitable right by meeting certain standards of conduct. Feinberg thinks that aggressors can forfeit the right to life, but (as far as I know) he does not reconcile this with his view that we possess human rights equally and unconditionally simply in virtue of being human.

Why specification is overlooked or rejected

The practical moral problems of racism, political oppression, poverty and starvation, unjust discrimination, abortion, euthanasia, the treatment of non-human animals, our obligations to future generations, and so on, have focused much of our conceptual thinking about rights in the latter half of this century on the question of those beings who possess (equal) human rights. This focus is morally very important, but it has tended to give rise to an overly narrow account of the basis on which as individuals we possess human rights. A number of the moral problems I have just mentioned do raise questions about the scope of individual human rights. This is because resolution of these problems requires that we determine the extent to which an individual's possession of the relevant right(s) entails obligations of non-interference and assistance on the part of others. Nevertheless, in discussing whether the right to life implies positive obligations of assistance on the part of others, and if so how far these obligations extend, or in defending or denying the existence of the right to life in some practical context (e.g. abortion), it is very easy to lose sight of an important element of the older concept of natural rights. Natural rights are grounded in our nature and are conditional rights: their continued possession, by those who possess these rights in virtue of their nature, is conditional on conduct.[27]

The justification of homicide in self-defence requires that the scope of the right to life be specified by reference to conduct. Nevertheless, an appropriate specification of the right to life might be explicitly rejected, rather than neglected, in accounts of justified self-defence on the assumption that such specification would require what Thomson has effectively criticized as 'the moral specification of rights'. In

[27] H. L. A. Hart remarks that natural rights are rights we have *qua* men, but is careful to note that this is consistent with *specification* of such rights in a way that makes their possession conditional, 'Are There Any Natural Rights?', reprinted in *Political Philosophy*, edited by Anthony Quinton (Oxford University Press, 1967), p. 53.

'Self-Defense and Rights', Thomson claims that the moral specification of human rights is circular. She points out that if the possession and content of human rights is determined by a prior view about what is and what is not morally permissible, it is then circular to explain the permissibility of particular acts, such as homicide in self-defence, in terms of the non-violation of these rights. If this circularity cannot be eliminated, it calls into serious doubt the relevance in moral argument of appeal to rights as independent permissions and constraints.

The moral specification of human rights can avoid Thomson's accusation of circularity, provided we specify the scope of such rights in terms of what is just and unjust treatment of, and interference with, the particular individuals who possess these rights. (Indeed, in my view the scope of human rights should be specified in these terms, because the point of appeal to rights in moral evaluation is to invoke considerations of just and unjust treatment of, and interference with, individuals *as individual persons*.)[28] In criticizing Thomson's rejection of the moral specification of rights, W. A. Parent specifies the right to life as the right not to be killed unjustly.[29] However, Parent does not distinguish clearly enough between unjust and unjustified acts. In excepting self-defence from the general prohibition of homicide, the appropriate specification of the scope of right to life needs to invoke the distinction between lethal force that does not inflict unjust harm on the person killed, and lethal force which inflicts unjust harm on the person killed but which is, nonetheless, justified in the circumstances.[30] I do not unjustly interfere with a crazed attacker if I push him off a building in

[28] Here I am agreeing with Foot's conception of the role of such rights; see 'The Problem of Abortion' and 'Euthanasia', both reprinted in *Virtues and Vices*.

[29] W. A. Parent, 'Judith Thomson and the Logic of Rights', *Philosophical Studies*, vol. 37, 1980, pp. 405–18.

[30] My awareness of the importance of this distinction in fact owes much to Thomson's 'Rights and Compensation'. Thomson accepts that appeal to rights does not itself determine whether or not a particular act is morally justified all things considered.

using necessary force to stop him pushing me off. This person has no right against me that I not use necessary and proportionate force in resisting, repelling, or warding off his unjust immediate threat. But if my car's brakes fail on a hill and I kill a person on the footpath, rather than steer into a group of children on a pedestrian crossing, I unjustly interfere with this person – I infringe her right to life – albeit justifiably in the circumstances. She is unoffending and the infliction of harm on *her* in preventing harm to others is offensive, not defensive. Homicide which violates its victim's right to life is unjust, but not necessarily unjustified all things considered. Homicide in self-defence against an unjust threat is not unjust, but it is not necessarily justified all things considered.

An appropriate specification of the right to life would overcome the difficulties arising from Thomson's discussion of forfeiture. However, the appropriate specification of human rights, as reflecting what is just and unjust treatment of, and interference with, individual persons, cannot eliminate conflicts of rights. Interference which inflicts unjust harm on someone can be justified all things considered, and in order to eliminate conflicts of rights, specification *would* need to be circular in the way Thomson says it is.[31] The circularity to which Thomson draws attention highlights the daunting task of providing an independent defence of the specification of human rights as reflecting what is just and unjust treatment of, and interference with, the particular individuals who possess these rights.

---

[31] Finnis specifies the right to life as the right not to be killed intentionally (for Finnis, impermissibly), *Natural Law and Natural Rights*, p. 225. On Finnis' view, my killing the person on the footpath would not violate that person's absolute right to life, because that person's life is not 'taken directly as a means to any further end'. One problem with Finnis' position is that this is also true of each of the children on the pedestrian crossing if I steer into them instead of the one on the footpath. Surely, in killing the person on the footpath I wrong this person, even if I do so justifiably in the circumstances. *Unjust* interference with an unoffending person is not avoided simply by ensuring a fairly determined distribution of harms. In this case, I inflict a lesser unjust harm in order to avoid inflicting a greater one (running into the children on the crossing): it is the lesser evil.

Self-defence and the right to life

An appropriate specification

A unitary account of justified homicide in self-defence, as an exception to the general prohibition of homicide, requires that any *unqualified* right to life be conditional. Our possession of an unqualified right to life, as entailing the right not to be killed, depends on our not being an unjust immediate threat to the equal rights of someone else: we do not have an unqualified right not to be killed if we are an unjust immediate threat to another person's life or proportionate interest.[32] A more stringent version of this specification holds that possession of *any* right to life is conditional on our not being an unjust immediate threat to another person's life or proportionate interest. The former, less stringent of these two versions can allow that someone who is an unjust immediate threat has a qualified right to life, and can be wronged if killed unnecessarily. According to this less stringent specification, if I am an unjust immediate threat to your life, I do not have a right against you that you not use necessary and proportionate defensive force. If the required degree of force is lethal, I do not have a right against you that you not kill me. However, if you use force beyond what is necessary to resist, repel, or ward me off (e.g. you can harmlessly deflect me but you annihilate me instead), then you wrong me, you violate my right to life. According to the more stringent version of the specification, you do not wrong me in going beyond what is necessary to resist, repel, or ward off the threat I pose. Nevertheless, your act is wrongful because it inflicts unnecessary harm.

No doubt even the less stringent version of this specification will strike some people as unduly hard on blameless or passive unjust immediate threats. However, a unitary right of self-defence depends on our accepting, as a minimum condition, that someone who is an unjust immediate threat to the life or proportionate interest of another does not have an

[32] The specification relevant to the use of force in self-defence need not exhaust the conditions in virtue of which we possess an unqualified right not to be killed. Other conditions of possession of this right are arguable.

213

unqualified right not to be killed. A unitary justification of homicide in self-defence assumes that the use of force *in self-defence* against a blameless or passive unjust immediate threat is permissible self-preferential killing – that the use of lethal force in resisting, repelling, or warding off an unjust immediate threat is morally distinguishable from self-preference at the expense of an unoffending person's life.

Implications of this specification

By way of four examples, I shall now bring out four important implications of the above specification of the scope of the right to life. These implications will help clarify the essential features of this specification, and also provide a useful framework upon which to restate the central features of justified homicide in self-defence which I have set out in this book.

(i) Alex is a psychopath. He and Bernard are on top of a tall building. Alex is on the point of pushing Bernard over the edge. Bernard, being unaware of this, pushes Alex over the edge as part of a plan to inherit Alex's money. In fact Bernard's act is necessary to ward off Alex's imminent attack. If Bernard's pushing Alex over the edge is wrongful, it does not infringe a right that Alex has in these circumstances that Bernard not use lethal force against him. Further, had Alex got in first, and had his using lethal force on Bernard been necessary to stop Bernard pushing him over the edge, Alex would not have infringed a right of Bernard's that Alex not use this force against him.

(ii) Clare is about to shoot Donal dead. Donal realizes this and shoots Clare dead. Donal knows that his act is necessary for self-defence, but Donal's motive is not self-defence. (Donal is generally indifferent to his own death, and in slightly different circumstances would even prefer to let himself be killed.) Rather, Donal opportunistically kills Clare in order to prevent her exposing his best friend as an embezzler. Again, if Donal's killing Clare is wrongful, this is not because it infringes a right Clare has in these circumstances that Donal not use lethal force against her.

I should address a possible denial of implication (ii). It might be argued that Donal does violate Clare's right to life, because Clare was not an unjust threat to Donal in the circumstances. Some might claim that Donal has waived his right to life, since he does not mind being killed.[33] This argument is faulty. Certainly, Clare does not infringe Donal's right that Clare not do x if this right is discretionary and, with respect to Clare, Donal has waived it. Clare's doing x does not violate Donal's right if Clare does x with Donal's permission. Donal might waive a right against Clare by action or inaction, in one of the following ways: by entering into a particular relationship with her (e.g. a partnership or agreement), by letting a particular relationship lapse, by explicitly consenting to Clare's doing x, or simply by publicly abandoning something (e.g. if Donal puts some old chairs out for the garbage collection, Clare does not infringe Donal's property rights by taking these chairs for her weekender). But Donal's being indifferent to, or even pleased about, Clare's attempt to kill him does not entail that Clare does not violate Donal's right to life because, with respect to Clare, Donal has waived this right; nor does it entail that Clare is acting with Donal's permission. One example will suffice to illustrate this point. Eamon is trying to diet. Someone gives him a large box of chocolates. Eamon resolves to keep these chocolates for guests, knowing full well that if the chocolates are in the house he'll be hopelessly weak and eat them himself. A babysitter who is minding Eamon's children raids the cupboard and eats the chocolates. Eamon is fairly easy-going, and when he comes home and discovers the chocolates gone he is pleased on balance that the temptation has been removed. Moreover, the babysitter's action has benefited Eamon: he stays on the diet. Does it follow that the babysitter acted with Eamon's permission? Does it follow that in acting as he did the babysitter did not infringe Eamon's right to the chocolates? It does not.[34]

33 This line of reasoning, extraordinary as it might seem, is suggested by some recent thinking in practical ethics about the right to life.

34 In *Reasons And Persons*, p. 364, Parfit appears, puzzlingly, to claim that an adult person's being pleased about the effect for him of his mother's

(iii) Felix is about to kill Gerald. Gerald can defend himself by using a weapon against Felix which will kill Felix and also two unoffending persons, Herbert (an innocent bystander) and Ivor (Felix's hostage). If Gerald uses this weapon and kills Herbert and Ivor in the course of self-defence against Felix, Gerald infringes both Herbert's and Ivor's right to life. If it is permissible that Gerald fire this weapon, this is in spite of the fact that in so acting Gerald violates both Herbert's and Ivor's right not to be killed. On the other hand, if Gerald's firing the weapon is impermissible, this is in spite of the fact that his firing it would not infringe Felix's right to life.

(iv) Jasper mistakenly believes that Kathleen is about to shoot him in cold blood. His belief is justified[ii]; and Jasper uses what he justifiably[ii] believes to be necessary and proportionate lethal force in self-defence against Kathleen. Jasper's act is justified[ii]; this is in spite of the fact that it violates Kathleen's right to life.

Each of these examples emphasizes that use of the degree of force necessary for defence against an actual unjust immediate threat to life does not violate its victim's right not to be killed. Examples (i) and (iv) also make clear that our having, or not having, a right not to be killed is an objective matter: it is not determined by the judgment of an agent using lethal force against us. Putative murderers need not violate the right to life of their victims, example (i); and putative self-defenders can do so, example (iv). Example (iii) restates the point that my having a right of self-defence against an unjust immediate threat is insufficient to establish the permissibility, all things considered, of using force in self-defence. Examples (i) and (ii) point to the relevance of the agent's motive to the justification[ii] of a particular agent's act of self-defence. The right of self-defence is grounded in the

having conceived (him) when she did, together with the fact that his mother's act benefited him, means that in conceiving when she did his mother did not infringe his (possible) rights in this regard because he has waived these rights. Gregory S. Kavka remarks that one can promote a person's interests, on balance, but violate his rights, e.g. to autonomy or to be told the truth, 'The Paradox of Future Generations', *Philosophy and Public Affairs*, vol. 1, no. 2, 1982, pp. 96–7.

fact that the act is defensive: it is an act of resisting, repelling, or warding off an unjust immediate threat. The permissibility of self-preference in the case of homicide in self-defence requires a particular specification of the scope of the right to life as entailing the right not to be killed. However, an agent's use of lethal force is not morally justified simply because it actually repels an unjust immediate threat and does not violate its victim's right to life. In distinguishing moral and legal justification in chapter 2, I commented that moral justification of an agent's act requires agent-perspectival justification, and also that the act be done for the right reason. An agent's use of necessary force against an unjust immediate threat can be morally wrongful on other grounds. For example, it can involve a vicious or morally offensive motive, examples (i) and (ii); it might violate other rights of the victim or of other people, examples (i)–(iii); it can inflict unjust and disproportionate harm on unoffending persons, example (iii).

To summarize the essential points of this section: In setting out the principles relevant to justified homicide in self-defence, I have maintained that the right to life is conditional. The particular specification of the scope of the right to life required by a unitary account of justified homicide in self-defence is this: someone who is an unjust immediate threat to the life or proportionate interest of another does not possess an unqualified right not to be killed. This specification of the scope of the right to life avoids circularity. The scope of the right to life is specified in terms of what is, and what is not, unjust treatment of, or interference with, individuals; this specification does not represent a view about what acts are justified or unjustified all things considered. This specification allows that violation of someone's right to life can be justified; for instance, an unoffending person might justifiably be killed in the course of self-defence or in circumstances of necessity. However, the killing of unoffending persons (those who are not unjust threats) must be justified on agent-neutral grounds as the lesser evil. This specification also allows that in some circumstances the use of

217

lethal force in self-defence is unjustified, even though it does not violate its victim's right to life.

6.3 GROUNDING AN APPROPRIATE SPECIFICATION

The above specification of the scope of the right to life is necessary to a sufficiently complex, unitary right to use lethal force *in self-defence*. Further, this specification excepts homicide in self-defence from the general prohibition of homicide *for the right reason*: namely, that the use of necessary and proportionate force in resisting, repelling, or warding off an unjust immediate threat does not inflict unjust harm on its victim. Shelly Kagan remarks that any exception to the right not to be harmed – in order to allow for the permissibility of self-defence – must be implied by the account offered of how and why persons have a right not to be harmed in the first place.[35] Kagan is right about this; and although the above specification of the scope of the right to life has considerable intuitive plausibility as excepting self-defence from the general prohibition of homicide, a complete justification of homicide in self-defence, in accordance with the principles that I have set out in this book, would need to defend the required specification of the scope of the right to life in the right terms.

A defence of the above specification, as derived from a view about why persons have a right not to be killed in the first place, is something that I cannot realistically attempt here.[36] Kagan suggests that two types of indirect moral theories, the two-level approach and the contract approach, might yield the desired argument: 'the promulgation of rules permitting self-defense might well be optimal; parties to an agreement might well insist that specific protections under the contract are to be conditional on conformity to that contract'.[37] Both

[35] *The Limits of Morality*, p. 135. Fried has commented similarly, *Right and Wrong*, p. 43.
[36] See also chapter 4, n36 and n66, and this present chapter, text immediately following n31, for closely related unfinished business.
[37] *The Limits of Morality*, p. 135.

these indirect moral theories have notable contemporary advocates; and *prima facie* both seem plausible candidates for generating the required exception to the relevant moral constraint in the case of self-defence. However, on closer examination, both these theories seem unlikely to ground the right of self-defence, and the corresponding appropriate specification of the scope of the right to life, *in the right terms*: that is to say, neither seems likely to ground the right of self-defence in what is morally distinctive about the use of force in self-defence. What I have to say below in support of this claim is not comprehensive or decisive. Rather, my discussion is intended to emphasize the argument of this and the previous chapter, that the justification of homicide in self-defence derives from what is morally distinctive about the use of force in self-defence: that it resists, repels, or wards off an unjust immediate threat, and that the use of necessary and proportionate force against an unjust immediate threat does not inflict unjust harm on its victim. A right of self-defence as *derived from* a moral contract, or from a two-level theory of optimality, would seem (perhaps necessarily) to miss this central point. In indicating why I think this is so, I draw upon standard criticisms of both these indirect moral theories.

Specification by contract

At first, a contract approach looks the more promising of the two indirect moral theories as generating an appropriate exception to the constraint against inflicting harm in the case of self-defence. However, in order to except all necessary and proportionate force used in self-defence against unjust immediate threats to life, the standard of each person's conformity with the constraints of the contract would need to be one of strict, or near-strict, liability for breaches of the contractual conditions. Conduct sufficient to put a person outside the contractual protections would need to include blameless attacks and assaults, even involuntary assaults, on unoffending persons. Furthermore, breaches would need to include some passive threats (e.g. Nozick's man thrown down the

219

well), which are not, strictly speaking, conduct on the part of the person who poses the threat.

Perhaps contracting parties would accept a standard of strict, or near-strict, liability for breaches of the relevant contractual constraint. But on what grounds would they accept it? If their acceptance of a very strong standard of conformity were to stem from their recognition that the use of force *in self-defence* against a transgressor – even a blameless, involuntary, or passive one – does not inflict unjust harm on this person, then the right of self-defence is recognized in, not generated by, the moral contract.[38] If the contracting parties were to accept a very strong standard of conformity on other grounds, (say) sophisticated self-interested ones, then the right of self-defence would not be derived from the morally distinctive feature of the use of force in self-defence, but from what is believed to be individually optimal on balance.[39]

Contracting parties could, of course, confine conduct sufficient to put someone outside the relevant contractual protection to culpable breaches of the contract. But if breaches must be culpable before the contractual protection is void, how culpable must they be? Deliberate or reckless breaches would no doubt be deemed sufficiently culpable to put someone outside the contractual protection. But what about careless breaches? There are degrees of carelessness, including cases of very minor forgetfulness or inadvertence which, due to very bad luck, could result in someone's becoming an immediate threat to an unoffending person's life. And if only culpable breaches put someone outside the relevant contractual protection, then the use of lethal force in self-defence against a temporarily insane person wielding an axe, an

---

[38] This is part of a more general criticism of the contractarian derivation of rights. A contract approach to the grounding of rights is subject to fatal objections in my view. See L. W. Sumner, *The Moral Foundation of Rights*, chapter 5.

[39] Perhaps I should note that a contractarian *derivation* of rights is distinguishable from the claim that particular permissions and constraints would be endorsed from a suitably objective or impartial moral perspective. The latter is a possible approach to grounding an appropriate specification of the right to life in my view.

unwitting assailant, or someone who reasonably but mistakenly believes that in using force against me he is defending himself, is either an impermissible assault on the transgressor, or else a permissible *violation* of the transgressor's moral protection under the contract. If these transgressors' rights are equal to those of an unoffending person, then in the absence of wider danger, within a contract theory it is difficult to see how self-preferential killing could be a *permissible* violation of the non-culpable transgressors' contractual protections.

The claim that *culpable* breaches put a person outside the contractual protections would also make heavy weather of the problems Thomson raises for a theory of forfeiture of the right to life. It must be said that a contract theory *can* very plausibly maintain that the tank driver forfeits his right to life by attacking me. Indeed, because a forfeit is a penalty, the claim that protections under the contract are *conditional* on conformity with that contract, and the claim that by our culpable conduct we can forfeit the right to life, seem a natural part of a contract theory. However, the problem for a theory of forfeiture which is derived from culpable transgression is that when, for instance, Thomson's unrepentant tank driver breaks both ankles, he completely *fortuitously* comes once again within the relevant contractual protection. Within a contract theory, how can this be? (If it is not so, then I do not directly wrong the tank driver by killing him in order to obtain his organs for other people.) Contracting parties might agree (again on the basis of sophisticated self-interest) to the restoration of contractual protection on account of fortuitous conformity by culpable transgressors (e.g. the tank driver). But again, the morally distinctive feature of the use of force in self-defence seems to be missing. My using lethal force against a transgressor ceases to be permissible self-preferential homicide once he is disabled, because I am no longer resisting, repelling, or warding off an unjust immediate threat: I am no longer acting *in self-defence*. The claim that it is ultimately in the interests of individual contracting parties to agree that a culpable transgressor re-aquires protection once

221

he is disabled, does not capture the morally distinctive feature of the use of force in self-defence.

A related contractarian approach to excepting self-defence from the prohibition of homicide regards the private right of self-defence as a right against the state. Here it is claimed that the state permits self-help in situations of unjust immediate threat because the state is itself powerless to perform one of its central functions, namely, the protection of the individual's right to life. Parties to a social contract may well agree to a right of self-help that lapses at the point at which a transgressor ceases to be an immediate threat and can be dealt with by the state. And in so far as the right of self-help is a civil right, this would mean that, for instance, it is impermissible to use force on the tank driver once he is disabled. The characterization of the right of self-defence as a right of self-help against the state has notable advocates.[40] It seems an unobjectionable view in so far as the right of self-defence is a civil right. But the right of self-defence is not *merely* a civil right.

Specification on a two-level theory of optimality

Can a two-level theory of optimality generate an appropriate specification of the scope of the right to life which would endorse the corresponding right of self-defence? Would promulgation of these corresponding rights be optimal?

The use of force in self-defence is not always optimal. Further, the self-defending agent can know this in the particular circumstances. For example, it might be clear that my using force in self-defence will kill one or more unoffending persons and be of very little benefit to me; it might be apparent that my using force in self-defence will inflict harm on bystanders which, if I am morally bound to achieve optimal results, is not justified by the benefit to me and to others of my survival; I might know that my using force in self-defence will cause indirect harm which won't be outweighed by the good effects of my survival. Given that in some circumstances a

[40] Locke, for instance, and recently Kadish, 'Respect for Life and Regard for Rights in the Criminal Law', pp. 884–5.

person can know that it is not optimal to use force in self-defence, why would promulgation of rules permitting self-defence nevertheless be optimal?[41]

The claim that promulgation of rules permitting self-defence would be optimal needs to address the familiar dilemma of indirect utilitarianism. A two-level moral theorist can either promulgate an exceptionless rule permitting self-defence (effective even on occasions when it is apparent that self-defence is not actually optimal), or the rule permitting self-defence can be said to admit of exceptions where self-defence is clearly not optimal. If the rule does not permit self-defence on occasions when self-defence is clearly not optimal, the background moral theory is a complex form of direct consequentialism. And in this case, the permissibility of self-defence derives from the contingent fact that the use of force in self-defence is optimal, and not from what is morally distinctive about the use of force in self-defence. On this view, there is no intrinsic moral difference between my foreseeably using lethal force in self-defence against an unjust immediate threat, and my deflecting an unjust threat to myself to a bystander, foreseeably killing her.

The alternative view is that the rule permitting self-defence is exceptionless. Can an exceptionless rule permitting self-defence be promulgated *as optimal*, and yet it be conceded (as it surely must) that in some circumstances self-defence is not in fact optimal? With recent two-level defences of the optimality of particular moral *constraints* in mind, we can anticipate that a two-level defence of an exceptionless permission of self-defence would argue along the following lines. Promulgation of a rule permitting the use of force in self-defence deters unjust aggression; the consequences of promulgation of this rule, although undoubtedly mixed, are optimal on balance.

---

[41] In the following discussion I simply assume that these would be rules permitting *necessary and proportionate* self-defence against an unjust threat, although these important qualifications might not in fact always be optimal.

223

An important strength of this argument is that it meets Kagan's requirement that the exemption of self-defence from the general prohibition of homicide be implied by the account offered of how and why persons have a right not to be harmed in the first place. The reasons now frequently invoked by two-level consequentialists in defending a constraint on killing unoffending persons in order to benefit oneself or others, are reversed in the case of self-defence. In maintaining that killing unoffending persons as a means of benefiting oneself or others is not optimal, two-level consequentialists usually concede that in some circumstances it might seem optimal that an unoffending person be killed for the good of oneself or others. For example, a crude utilitarian doctor might decide that he should secretly withdraw treatment from a derelict after a traffic accident, and then use this person's organs to save five vastly more worthwhile lives. However, it is argued, such acts are morally precluded by their *indirect* effects; compliance with constraints on such behaviour is, most likely, optimal.

This type of consequentialist reasoning in defence of a constraint against killing unoffending persons as a means to benefiting others is now reasonably familiar in practical ethics. Preference utilitarians stress the direct wrongness of killing a person who wants to go on living; and in maintaining that this wrongness will not be outweighed by the benefit to others of this person's death, two-level consequentialists invoke the general insecurity, fear, lack of trust, which would exist amongst people (especially in their dealings with the medical profession, the police force, the judiciary, etc.) were constraints against killing the unoffending as a means of benefiting others not promulgated. Consequentialist reasoning also predicts the undermining of the agent's moral character, the hardening of his or her moral sensibilities, which will be brought about by certain sorts of acts; the agent is then more likely to flout the relevant constraint in circumstances in which this is not reasonably believed optimal. Further, our imperfect knowledge about some of the effects of our actions makes it best to comply with rules which generally yield optimal results.[42]

I am unimpressed by the latter two reasons as grounds for adopting exceptionless moral constraints. As very *general* precepts, exceptionless constraints imply the sort of unreasonable moral rigidity of which J. J. C. Smart rightly accused rule-utilitarianism decades ago.[43] This criticism carries over to appeal to such considerations as justifying as optimal the promulgation of exceptionless general *rules* permitting certain acts such as the use of force in self-defence. The first reason, which appeals to the adverse effects of insecurity, fear, lack of trust, and so on, has been prominent in the responses of two-level consequentialists to examples like that of the crude utilitarian doctor. In rejecting the extension of this reasoning as *grounding* an appropriate rule permitting self-defence, I cannot here improve on J. S. Mill's aphorism that there is no parity between the desire of a thief to take a purse, and the desire of the right owner to keep it.[44] Lack of parity between these two desires does not derive from their relative *strengths*: it stems from the fact that one party's desire for the purse is for what is legitimately his, and the other's is not. There is no parity between the owner's legitimate, and a thief's illegitimate, desire for the purse, (I would add) no matter how strong the thief's desire for the purse, no matter how many thieves want the purse. Mill's principle distinguishes in kind between desires (feelings, preferences) that stem from a person's legitimate claims, and those that do not. Certainly, feelings of fear, anxiety, and resentment, and also unfulfilled desires and frustrated preferences, do not make for contented lives. But the fact that people will be offended,

---

42 If this two-level view about constraints is to allow that, e.g. Foot's tram-driver acts permissibly in killing the one unoffending man to save five, the promulgated rule against killing the unoffending may need to incorporate *as optimal* something like the Double Effect distinction.

43 J. J. C. Smart, 'An Outline of a System of Utilitarian Ethics', in J. J. C. Smart and Bernard Williams, *Utilitarianism: For and Against* (Cambridge University Press, 1973), p. 10.

44 John Stuart Mill, 'On Liberty', reprinted in John Stuart Mill, *Three Essays* (Oxford University Press, 1975), p. 103.

frustrated, made fearful by an act is not itself a morally compelling reason for protecting them from such offence, frustration, fear. However, the fact that their feelings and frustrations derive from their legitimate claims is a morally compelling reason. The claim that promulgation of a rule permitting self-defence would be optimal, because in the absence of this rule people would be insecure, fearful, anxious, resentful, and so on, is morally significant in so far as these insecurities, fears, resentments, etc., reflect the possible thwarting of people's legitimate claims by those who have no right to thwart them. And I doubt that the legitimacy of these claims, and the injustice involved in their being thwarted, can satisfactorily be explained in terms of a purely aggregative account of optimality, no matter how many-levelled this theory.[45]

What an appropriate foundation requires

Undoubtedly, normative considerations are relevant to the characterization of the use of force as defensive, as resisting, repelling, or warding off an immediate *threat*. Further, an appropriate specification of the scope of the right to life, for the purposes of excepting the use of lethal force in self-defence from the general prohibition of homicide, needs to invoke a normative *status quo* against which an immediate threat can be characterized as *unjust*. The positive *right* to use force in self-defence is not appropriately derived from the claim that an exception to the prohibition of homicide in the case of self-defence is optimal on balance, either for individual persons acting on the basis of enlightened self-interest, or in general. First, the use of force in self-defence is not always optimal, and it is sometimes unjustified all things considered. On the other hand, killing an unoffending person

---

[45] On this and the above points I have benefited especially from J. L. Mackie, 'Can There Be a Right-Based Moral Theory?', reprinted in Mackie, *Persons and Values*, Selected Papers, Vol. II (Oxford: Clarendon Press, 1985), and also from Thomas Nagel, *The View From Nowhere*, pp. 166–75.

in the act of saving others can be optimal, and is sometimes justified all things considered. Secondly, the contingent fact (if it is a fact) that a permission to use force in self-defence is optimal on balance, would not except homicide in self-defence from the general prohibition of homicide for the right reason. The morally distinctive feature of the use of force in self-defence is that it is defensive. Defensive force used against an unjust threat does not inflict unjust harm on its victim, even when such force is unjustified all things considered; force used against an unoffending person in the act of saving another or others inflicts unjust harm on its victim, even when a fair selection procedure is used and this force is justified all things considered.

In order to except the use of force in self-defence from the general prohibition of homicide, the appropriate specification of the scope of the right to life needs to reflect what is, and what is not, unjust treatment of, and interference with, individual persons. And this aspect of the specification of the right to life needs to be defended not simply in terms of the protection or promotion of the interests of the individual persons who possess this right, but in terms of the legitimate claims of these persons to non-interference in respect of their interests. (The fact that it is in the hijacker's interests that the police sharp-shooter not fire does not entail that the hijacker has a legitimate claim that the sharp-shooter not fire. And suppose it is in your interests, and also optimal, that you now have one of my kidneys. This does not give you a legitimate claim to one of my kidneys such that I would wrong you in not agreeing to a kidney donation.)

6.4 CONCLUDING REMARKS

The central point of this chapter and the last has been that the justification of homicide in self-defence derives from what is morally distinctive about the use of force in self-defence against an unjust immediate threat: it resists, repels, or wards off the infliction of otherwise irreparable unjust harm and does not inflict unjust harm on its victim. The more fundamental task of grounding the appropriate specification of the scope of the right to life within a more general derivation and theory of rights remains important, unfinished business. Such an account will be shaped in very important respects by the principles of justified homicide in self-defence that I have set out in this book.

My primary aim in this book has been to set out and discuss the principles relevant to self-defence as a justification of homicide. Self-defence is widely regarded not simply as a moral and legal justification of homicide, but more strongly, as a positive right: an exception to, rather than a justified infringement of, the general prohibition of homicide. The characterization of self-defence in these terms has made it necessary to discuss in detail a number of matters which are important in their own right. These include the complex nature of justification and the relationship between justification and excuse, the similarities and differences between moral and legal justification, the moral and legal requirements of necessary and proportionate force, the conditions under which we can be said to possess unconditional human rights, and an appropriate specification of the scope of the right to life in so far as this right is a right not to be killed.

I do not endorse the Double Effect justification of homicide in self-defence, because the intentional use of necessary force in self-defence is sometimes an intention to kill. However, my positive account of the right of self-defence is sympathetic to the natural law insight that justification of the use of force in self-defence against an unjust immediate threat arises from the fact that the act is defensive. The right of self-defence is grounded in the morally distinctive feature of the use of defensive force against an unjust immediate threat – the act directly blocks the infliction of unjust harm. Self-defence is not essentially a punitive act, nor is it essentially an attempt to bring about optimal results. It is the act of resisting, repelling, or warding off an immediate threat. Where the immediate threat is unjust, the use of force in self-defence directly blocks the infliction of imminent, irreparable unjust harm. And within moral limits, a private person has a positive right, and sometimes a duty, directly to block the infliction of unjust harm to him- or herself or others.

The conditions of necessary and proportionate force are moral limits of the right of self-defence. The fulfilment of these conditions does not establish a positive right to inflict harm on someone in the act of protecting oneself or someone else. Nor does lack of intention to kill, even where plausibly invoked, give one such a right. Justified homicide in self-defence, like other cases of foreseen self-preferential killing, requires that self-preference be justified. Where the use of lethal force is not defensive, the conditions of necessary and proportionate force, together with lack of intention to kill, are insufficient to permit self-preference. Further, self-preferential killing of unoffending persons must be justified as the lesser evil.

However, in the case of justified self-defence, the person against whom force is used him- or herself constitutes an unjust immediate threat. The justification of self-preference in the case of self-defence is based on the moral asymmetry between the parties. This asymmetry requires the specification of the scope of the unqualified right to life as a right which ceases when we become an unjust immediate threat to the life or proportionate interest of another. There are many uncontentious cases in which the threat one person poses another is unjust. An unjust immediate threat need not be culpable, nor even voluntary, conduct. Putative self-defenders, very young children, deranged persons, and sleepwalkers can constitute unjust threats to the lives of others. There are also contentious cases about which reasonable people will disagree, the most likely examples being those involving passive threats. The view I have defended in this book is that force can be used in self-defence against someone who poses a passive threat provided the threat sufficiently resembles an assault, a clear case being Nozick's man thrown down the well. Further, I accept that passive threats can be unjust threats provided they sufficiently resemble assaults on unoffending persons.

The positive right of self-defence is part of a broader permission directly to block the imminent infliction of irreparable unjust harm. The positive right of necessary and proportionate self-defence against an unjust immediate threat is exceptionless. To say that this right is exceptionless means that the use of necessary and proportionate force in self-defence against an unjust immediate threat does not inflict unjust harm on its victim. It does not follow from this, however, that the use of force in self-defence is always morally justified all things considered. Sometimes it can be wrong to protect, to insist upon, to exercise, one's rights. In some circumstances this can be true even of very weighty rights such as the right to life. Broader moral considerations which are relevant to the justification of homicide in self-defence include benevolence, and the equal rights of unoffending persons who will be adversely affected. The use of force in self-defence can be impermissible where, for example, it is of very limited benefit to me, or will directly harm unoffending persons. No doubt some people will claim that it is unrealistic, and for this reason morally unreasonable, to expect someone faced with an unjust immediate threat to life to take these sorts of broader moral considerations into account. I do not accept this claim. Certainly, someone whose life is in immediate danger will usually be very affected by fear and by the desire not to die; and he or she will probably have to make a snap decision about what to do. The urgency of the situation must bear on what standard of judgment we can reasonably expect of ordinary people on matters such as necessary and proportionate force. But the fact that someone is very affected by fear, or by the need to make a snap decision, does not justify his (say) foreseeably killing an unoffending person in the course of self-defence or for other reasons of self-preservation. Considerations like extreme fear might make self-preferential homicide excusable in some cases in which it is not justified.

My focus has been on self-defence as a justification of homicide, given the prominence self-defence is accorded as a paradigm of justified private homicide. However, the positive right of self-defence is not absolute. Appeal to rights in the moral evaluation of human conduct reflects considerations of just and unjust treatment of, and interference with, individual persons – it does not necessarily represent those acts which are justified all things considered.

Bibliography

Books and official reports

Aquinas, St Thomas, *Summa Theologiæ*, vol. 38, Blackfriars edition, London: Eyre and Spottiswood Ltd, 1966.

Anscombe, G. E. M., *Intention*, Oxford: Basil Blackwell, 1958.

Aristotle, *Nicomachean Ethics*, translated by Sir David Ross, London: Oxford University Press, 1969.

Bailey, F. Lee, and Henry B. Rothblatt, *Crimes of Violence*: (vol. 1) *Homicide and Assault*, New York: The Lawyers Cooperative Publishing Co., 1973.

Bates, A. P., T. L. Buddin and D. J. Meure, *The System of Criminal Law*, Sydney: Butterworths, 1979.

Blackstone, William, *Commentaries on the Laws of England*, vol. IV, New York: Garland Publishing, Inc., 1978.

Campbell, Robert, and Diané Collinson, *Ending Lives*, Oxford: Basil Blackwell, 1988.

D'Arcy, Eric, *Human Acts*, Oxford: Clarendon Press, 1963.

Davis, Henry, *Moral and Pastoral Theology*, 5th edition, London, 1946.

Devine, Philip, *The Ethics of Homicide*, London: Cornell University Press, 1978.

Donagan, Alan, *The Theory of Morality*, Chicago: University of Chicago Press, 1977.

Duff, R. A., *Intention, Agency and Criminal Liability: Philosophy of Action and the Criminal Law*, Oxford: Basil Blackwell, 1990.

Dworkin, R. M., *Taking Rights Seriously*, London: Duckworth, 1977.

Feinberg, Joel, *Harm to Others*, New York: Oxford University Press, 1984.

Finnis, John, *Natural Law and Natural Rights*, Oxford: Clarendon Press, 1980.
   Fundamentals of Ethics, Oxford: Clarendon Press, 1983.

Fletcher, George, *Rethinking Criminal Law*, Boston: Little, Brown, 1978.

Frey, R. G., *Rights, Killing and Suffering*, Oxford: Basil Blackwell, 1983.

Fried, Charles, *Right and Wrong*, Harvard University Press, 1978.

Gauthier, David, *The Logic of the Leviathan*, Oxford University Press, 1969.

Glover, Jonathan, *Causing Death and Saving Lives*, Harmondsworth: Penguin Books, 1977.

Green, T. A., *Verdict According to Conscience*, Chicago: Chicago University Press, 1985.

Bibliography

Greenawalt, Kent, *Conflicts of Law and Morality*, Oxford University Press, 1989.

Griffin, James, *Well Being*, Oxford University Press, 1986.

Grotius, Hugo, *The Rights of War and Peace*, an abridged translation by William Whewell, Cambridge University Press, 1853.

Hare, R. M., *Moral Thinking*, Oxford University Press, 1981.

Harris, John, *The Value of Life: An Introduction to Medical Ethics*, London, Routledge and Kegan Paul, 1985.

Hobbes, Thomas, *Leviathan*, edited by C. B. Macpherson, Harmondsworth: Penguin Books, 1974.

Kadish, Sanford, Stephen J. Schulhofer, and Monrad G. Paulson, *Criminal Law and Its Processes: Cases and Materials*, 4th edition, Boston and Toronto: Little Brown & Co., 1983.

Kagan, Shelly, *The Limits of Morality*, Oxford University Press, 1989.

Kant, Immanuel, *The Metaphysics of Morals*, translated by Mary Gregor, Cambridge University Press, 1991.

Kenny, C. S., *Outlines of Criminal Law*, 12th edition, Cambridge University Press, 1926.

Kuhse, Helga, *The Sanctity-of-Life Doctrine in Medicine*, Oxford University Press, 1987.

LaFave, Wayne R., and Austin W. Scott, Jr, *Criminal Law*, St Paul, Minn.: West Publishing Co., 1986.

Law Commission (Law Com. No. 177), *Criminal Law: A Criminal Code for England and Wales*, London: HMSO, 1989, vols. 1 and 2.

Law Reform Commission of Victoria, Discussion Paper No. 13, *Homicide*, 1988.

Law Reform Commission of Victoria, Report No. 40, *Homicide*, 1991.

Locke, John, *The Second Treatise of Government*, revised edition, edited by Peter Laslett, Mentor Books, 1963.

Low, Peter W., *Criminal Law*, revised 1st edition, St Paul, Minn.: West Publishing Co., 1990.

Maritain, Jacques, *Man and the State*, London: Hollis and Carter, 1954.

Melden, A. I., *Rights and Persons*, Oxford: Basil Blackwell, 1977.

Morris, Norval, and Colin Howard, *Studies in Criminal Law*, Oxford: Clarendon Press, 1964.

Nagel, Thomas, *The View From Nowhere*, New York: Oxford University Press, 1986.

New Catholic Encyclopedia, vol. 4, New York: McGraw-Hill, 1967.

Nozick, Robert, *Anarchy, State and Utopia*, Oxford: Basil Blackwell, 1974.

Parfit, Derek, *Reasons and Persons*, Oxford University Press, 1984.

Pufendorf, Samuel von, *De Officio Hominis et Civis Juxta Legem Naturalem Libri Duo*, vol. 2, the translation by Frank Gardner Moore, Oxford University Press, 1927.

Rickaby, Joseph, *Moral Philosophy*, London: Longman's Green & Co. Ltd, 1929.

Ritchie, David G., *Natural Rights*, 4th edition, London: George Allen and Unwin Ltd, 1924.

Robinson, Paul H., *Criminal Law Defenses*, vols. 1 & 2, St Paul, Minn.: West Publishing Co., 1984.

BIBLIOGRAPHY

Simpson, A. W. B., *Cannibalism in the Common Law*, Chicago: Chicago University Press, 1984.

Singer, Peter, *Practical Ethics*, Cambridge University Press, 1979.

Smith, J. C., *Justification and Excuse in the Criminal Law*, London: Stevens and Co., 1989.

Stephen, Sir James Fitzjames, *A History of the Criminal Law of England*, vol. 3, London: Macmillan and Co., 1883.

Sumner, L. W., *The Moral Foundation of Rights*, Oxford: Clarendon Press, 1987.

Teichman, Jenny, *Pacifism and the Just War*, Oxford: Basil Blackwell, 1986.

Thomson, Judith Jarvis, *The Realm of Rights*, Camb. Mass.: Harvard University Press, 1990.

Tooley, Michael, *Abortion and Infanticide*, Oxford: Clarendon Press, 1983.

White, Alan, *Rights*, Oxford: Clarendon Press, 1984.

Yeo, Stanley, *Compulsion in the Criminal Law*, Sydney: The Law Book Company, 1990.

Essays and articles

Alexander, Lawrence A., 'Self-Defense and the Killing of Noncombatants: A Reply to Fullinwinder', *Philosophy and Public Affairs*, vol. 5, no. 4, 1976, pp. 408–15.

Anscombe, G. E. M., 'Who is Wronged?', *The Oxford Review* 5, 1967, pp. 16–17.
'Mr Truman's Degree', reprinted in Anscombe, *Collected Philosophical Papers*, vol. III, Oxford: Basil Blackwell, 1981.
'Modern Moral Philosophy', reprinted in Anscombe, *Collected Philosophical Papers*, vol. III, Oxford: Basil Blackwell, 1981.
'War and Murder', reprinted in Anscombe, *Collected Philosophical Papers*, vol. III, Oxford: Basil Blackwell, 1981.

Ashworth, A., 'Self-Defence and the Right to Life', *Cambridge Law Journal* 34 (2), 1975, pp. 282–307.

Austin, J. L., 'A Plea for Excuses', reprinted in *Philosophy of Action*, edited by Alan White, Oxford University Press, 1968.

Barden, Garrett, 'Defending Self-Defence', *Irish Philosophical Journal*, vol. 1, no. 2, 1984, pp. 25–35.

Bedau, Hugo, 'The Right to Life', *The Monist*, vol. 52, no. 4, 1968, pp. 550–72.

Bennett, Jonathan, 'Whatever the Consequences', reprinted in *Killing and Letting Die*, edited by Bonnie Steinbock, Englewood Cliffs, New Jersey: Prentice-Hall, 1980.

Boorse, Christopher, and Roy A. Sorensen, 'Ducking Harm', *Journal of Philosophy*, vol. 85, no. 3, 1988, pp. 115–34.

Bradley, F. H., 'The Vulgar Notion of Responsibility' and Notes to Essay 1, in *Ethical Studies*, 2nd edition, Oxford: Oxford University Press, 1962.

Brandt, Richard, 'Utilitarianism and the Rules of War', reprinted in *War and Moral Responsibility*, edited by Marshall Cohen, Thomas Nagel and Thomas Scanlon, Princeton: Princeton University Press, 1974.

Chandler, John, 'Killing and Letting Die: Putting the Debate in Context', *Australasian Journal of Philosophy*, vol. 68, no. 4, 1990, pp. 420–31.

Clarke, R. F., 'The "Mignonette" Case as a Question of Moral Theology', *The Month*, 1885, pp. 17–28.

Bibliography

Colvin, Eric, 'Causation in Criminal Law', *Bond Law Review*, vol. 1, 1989, pp. 253–71.

Davis, Michael, 'The Right to Continued Aid', *Philosophical Quarterly*, vol. 33, 1983, pp. 259–78.

Davis, Nancy, 'On the Priority of Avoiding Harm', in *Killing and Letting Die*, edited by Bonnie Steinbock, Englewood Cliffs, New Jersey: Prentice-Hall, 1980.

'The Doctrine of Double Effect: Problems of Interpretation', *Pacific Philosophical Quarterly*, vol. 65, 1984, pp. 107–23.

'Abortion and Self-Defense', *Philosophy and Public Affairs*, 1984, pp. 175–207.

Devine, Philip E., 'The Principle of Double Effect', *The American Journal of Jurisprudence*, vol. 19, 1974, pp. 44–60.

Dressler, Joshua, 'New Thoughts About the Concept of Justification in Criminal Law: A Critique of Fletcher's Thinking and *Rethinking*', *UCLA Law Review*, vol. 32, pp. 61–99.

'Provocation: Partial Justification or Partial Excuse?', *Modern Law Review*, vol. 51, 1988, pp. 467–80.

Duff, R. A., 'Intentionally Killing the Innocent', *Analysis*, vol. 34, 1973, pp. 16–19.

'Intention, Responsibility and Double Effect', *Philosophical Quarterly*, vol. 32, no. 126, 1982, pp. 1–16.

Feinberg, Joel, 'Voluntary Euthanasia and the Inalienable Right to Life', *Philosophy and Public Affairs*, vol. 7, no. 2, 1978, pp. 93–123.

Finnis, John, 'The Rights and Wrongs of Abortion', reprinted in *The Philosophy of Law*, edited by R. M. Dworkin, Oxford University Press, 1977.

'Intention and Side-Effects', in *Liability and Responsibility*, edited by R. G. Frey and Christopher W. Morris, Cambridge: Cambridge University Press, 1991.

Fletcher, George, 'Proportionality and the Psychotic Aggressor: A Vignette in Comparative Criminal Theory', *Israel Law Review*, vol. 8, 1973, pp. 367–90.

'The Right Deed for the Wrong Reason', *UCLA Law Review*, vol. 23, 1975, pp. 293–321.

'Rights and Excuses', *Criminal Justice Ethics*, vol. 3, no. 2, 1984, pp. 17–27.

'The Right to Life', *The Monist*, vol. 63, 1980, pp. 135–55.

'Punishment and Self-Defense', *Law and Philosophy*, vol. 8, 1989, pp. 201–15.

'Defensive Force as an Act of Rescue', *Social Philosophy and Policy*, vol. 7, no. 2, 1990, pp. 170–9.

'Passion and Reason in Self-Defense', in *The Philosophy of Law*, edited by Conrad Johnson, New York: Macmillan Publishing Co., 1993.

Foot, Philippa, 'The Problem of Abortion and the Doctrine of Double Effect', reprinted in Foot, *Virtues and Vices*, Oxford: Basil Blackwell, 1978.

'Euthanasia', reprinted in Foot, *Virtues and Vices*, Oxford: Basil Blackwell, 1978.

'Morality, Action and Outcome', in *Morality and Objectivity: Essays in Honour of J. L. Mackie*, edited by Ted Honderich, London: Routledge and Kegan Paul, 1985.

BIBLIOGRAPHY

Frey, R. G., 'Some Aspects to the Doctrine of Double Effect', *Canadian Journal of Philosophy*, vol. 5, no. 2, 1975, pp. 259–83.

Gewirth, Alan, 'The Epistemology of Human Rights', *Social Philosophy and Policy*, vol. 1, no. 2, 1984, pp. 1–24.

Gray, John, 'Indirect Utility and Fundamental Rights', *Social Philosophy and Policy*, vol. 1, no. 2, 1984, pp. 73–91.

Greenawalt, Kent, 'The Perplexing Borders of Justification and Excuse', *Columbia Law Review*, vol. 84, no. 8, 1984, pp. 1897–927.

Grisez, Germain, 'Toward a Consistent Natural Law Ethics of Killing', *The American Journal of Jurisprudence*, vol. 15, 1970, pp. 64–96.

Hart, H. L. A., 'Are There Any Natural Rights?', reprinted in *Political Philosophy*, edited by Anthony Quinton, Oxford University Press, 1967.

  'Intention and Responsibility', reprinted in Hart, *Punishment and Responsibility*, Oxford University Press, 1968.

Held, Virginia, 'Justification: Legal and Political', *Ethics*, vol. 86, 1975–6, pp. 1–16.

Hogan, Brian, 'The Dadson Principle', *Criminal Law Review*, 1989, pp. 679–86.

Jackson, Frank, 'Decision-theoretic Consequentialism and the Nearest and Dearest Objection', *Ethics*, vol. 101, 1991, pp. 461–82.

Kadish, Sanford H., 'Respect for Life and Regard for Rights in the Criminal Law', *California Law Review*, vol. 64, no. 4, 1976, pp. 871–901.

Kamm, Frances Myrna, 'The Insanity Defense, Innocent Threats, and Limited Alternatives', *Criminal Justice Ethics*, vol. 6, no. 1, 1987, pp. 61–79.

  'Non-consequentialism, the Person as an End-in-Itself, and the Significance of Status', *Philosophy and Public Affairs*, vol. 21, no. 4, 1992, pp. 334–89.

Kavka, Gregory S., 'The Paradox of Future Generations', *Philosophy and Public Affairs*, vol. 1, no. 2, 1982, pp. 93–112.

Kenny, Anthony, 'Duress *Per Minas* as a Defence to Crime II', *Law and Philosophy*, vol. 1, 1982, pp. 197–205.

Kleinig, John, 'Human Rights, Legal Rights and Social Change', in *Human Rights*, edited by Eugene Kamenka and Alice Erh-Soon Tay, Australia: Edward Arnold, 1978.

Levine, Susan, 'The Moral Permissibility of Killing a "Material Aggressor" in Self-Defense', *Philosophical Studies*, vol. 45, 1984, pp. 69–78.

Locke, Don, 'The Choice Between Lives', *Philosophy*, vol. 57, no. 222, October 1982, pp. 453–75.

Lomasky, Loren, 'Personal Projects as the Foundation for Basic Rights', *Social Philosophy and Policy*, vol. 1, no. 2, 1984, pp. 35–55.

Mackie, J. L., 'Can There Be a Right-Based Moral Theory?', reprinted in Mackie, *Persons and Values*, Selected Papers, Vol. II, Oxford: Clarendon Press, 1985.

Mill, John Stuart, 'On Liberty', reprinted in John Stuart Mill, *Three Essays*, Oxford University Press, 1975.

Montague, Phillip, 'Self Defense and Choosing Between Lives', *Philosophical Studies*, vol. 40, 1981, pp. 207–19.

  'The Morality of Self-Defense: A Reply to Wasserman', *Philosophy and Public Affairs*, vol. 18, no. 1, 1989, pp. 80–9.

Bibliography

Nagel, Thomas, 'War and Massacre', reprinted in *War and Moral Responsibility*, edited by Marshall Cohen, Thomas Nagel and Thomas Scanlon, Princeton: Princeton University Press, 1974.

Nell (O'Neill), Onora, 'Lifeboat Earth', *Philosophy and Public Affairs*, vol. 4, no. 3, 1975, pp. 273–92.

Nickel, James W., 'Are Human Rights Utopian?', *Philosophy and Public Affairs*, vol. 11, no. 3, 1982, pp. 246–64.

Nozick, Robert, 'Coercion', reprinted in *Philosophy, Science and Method: Essays in Honor of Ernest Nagel*, edited by S. Morgenbesser, P. Suppes and M. White, New York: St Martin's Press, 1969.

Parent, W. A., 'Judith Thomson and the Logic of Rights', *Philosophical Studies*, vol. 37, 1980, pp. 405–18.

Parfit, Derek, 'Innumerate Ethics', *Philosophy and Public Affairs*, vol. 7, no. 4, 1978, pp. 285–301.

Pringle, Helen, and Robert Lawton, 'A Life Well Lost? Hobbes and Self Preservation', (unpublished paper) read to Hobbes 1588–1988 Symposium, University of New South Wales, July 9–10, 1988.

Quinn, Warren S., 'Actions, Intentions, and Consequences: The Doctrine of Double Effect', *Philosophy and Public Affairs*, vol. 18, no. 4, 1989, pp. 334–51.

Robinson, Paul H., 'Causing the Conditions of One's Own Defense: A Study in the Limits of Theory in Criminal Law', *Virginia Law Review*, vol. 71, no. 1, 1985, pp. 1–63.

Ryan, Cheyney C., 'The Normative Concept of Coercion', *Mind*, 1980, pp. 481–98.

'Self-Defense, Pacifism, and the Possibility of Killing', *Ethics*, vol. 93, no. 3, 1983, pp. 508–24.

Sen, Amartya, 'Rights and Agency', *Philosophy and Public Affairs*, vol. 11, no. 1, 1982, pp. 3–39.

Snare, Frank, 'Dissolving the Moral Contract', *Philosophy*, vol. 52, 1977, pp. 301–12.

Taurek, John M., 'Should the Numbers Count?', *Philosophy and Public Affairs*, vol. 6, no. 4, 1977, pp. 293–316.

Thomson, Judith Jarvis, 'A Defense of Abortion', reprinted in *Philosophy of Law*, edited by R. M. Dworkin, Oxford University Press, 1977.

'Self-Defense and Rights', reprinted in Thomson, *Rights, Restitution and Risk*, edited by William Parent, Camb. Mass.: Harvard University Press, 1986.

'Rights and Compensation', reprinted in Thomson, *Rights, Restitution and Risk*, edited by William Parent, Camb. Mass.: Harvard University Press, 1986.

'Self-Defense', *Philosophy and Public Affairs*, vol. 20, no. 4, 1991, pp. 283–310.

Uniacke, Suzanne, 'The Doctrine of Double Effect', *The Thomist*, vol. 48, no. 2, 1984, pp. 188–218.

'Killing Under Duress', *Journal of Applied Philosophy*, vol. 6, no. 1, 1989, pp. 53–69.

'What are Partial Excuses to Murder?', in *Partial Excuses to Murder*, edited by Stanley Yeo, Sydney: Federation Press, 1991.

BIBLIOGRAPHY

'Self-Defense and Natural Law', *The American Journal of Jurisprudence*, vol. 36, 1991, pp. 73–101.

Wasserman, David, 'Justifying Self-Defense', *Philosophy and Public Affairs*, vol. 16, no. 4, 1987, pp. 356–78.

Williams, Glanville, 'The Theory of Excuses', 1982, *Criminal Law Review*, pp. 732–42.

Index

Index